OXFORD STUDIES IN THEOLOGICAL ETHICS

General Editor
Oliver O'Donovan

OXFORD STUDIES IN THEOLOGICAL ETHICS

The series presents discussions on topics of general concern to Christian Ethics, as it is currently taught in universities and colleges, at the level demanded by a serious student. The volumes will not be specialized monographs nor general introductions or surveys. They aim to make a contribution worthy of notice in its own right but also focussed in such a way as to provide a suitable starting point for orientation.

The titles include studies in important contributors to the Christian tradition of moral thought; explorations of current moral and social questions; and discussions of central concepts in Christian moral and political thought. Authors treat their topics in a way that will show the relevance of the Christian tradition, but with openness to neighbouring traditions of thought which have entered into dialogue with it.

The Moral Gap

■ ■ ■

Kantian Ethics, Human Limits, and God's Assistance

JOHN E. HARE

CLARENDON PRESS · OXFORD
1996

Oxford University Press, Walton Street, Oxford OX2 6DP

Oxford New York
Athens Auckland Bangkok Bombay
Calcutta Cape Town Dar es Salaam Delhi
Florence Hong Kong Istanbul Karachi
Kuala Lumpur Madras Madrid Melbourne
Mexico City Nairobi Paris Singapore
Taipei Tokyo Toronto
and associated companies in
Berlin Ibadan

Oxford is a trade mark of Oxford University Press

Published in the United States
by Oxford University Press Inc., New York

© John E. Hare 1996

British Library Cataloguing in Publication Data
Data available

Library of Congress Cataloging in Publication Data
The moral gap: Kantian ethics, human limits, and God's assistance
John E. Hare.
(Oxford studies in theological ethics)
Includes bibliographical references and index.
1. Christian ethics. 2. Kant, Immanuel, 1724–1804—Ethics.
3. Ethics, Modern. 4. Man. 5. Grace (Theology) 6. Man (Christian
theology) 7. Apologetics. I. Title. II. Series.
BJ1275.H24 1996 241—dc20 95–41862
ISBN 0–19–826381–3

1 3 5 7 9 10 8 6 4 2

Typeset by Cambrian Typesetters, Frimley, Surrey
Printed in Great Britain on acid-free paper by
Bookcraft (Bath) Ltd., Midsomer Norton

ACKNOWLEDGEMENTS

I would like to express my thanks to the many people who have helped me with this book. First, there are my colleagues at Calvin, who discussed much of the manuscript in our weekly colloquia. Some earlier drafts were the object of similarly generous examination by my colleagues at Lehigh. R. M. Hare, Philip Quinn, Stephen Evans, and Oliver O'Donovan read the whole book. The list of those who have read individual chapters is too long to give, but I thank especially Tom Carson, Ron Feenstra, A. C. Genova, Allan Gibbard, Jean Hampton, Shelly Kagan, Julie McDonald, Jan Narveson, Robert Perkins, Robert Roberts, Nancy Snow, Richard Swinburne, Ray van Leeuwen, Marian Weekly, and Alan Woods. I am very grateful to the Pew Charitable Trusts for a grant which, together with support from Calvin, enabled me to take a year off teaching. Donna Kruithof and Mark Cullison have been of great assistance in preparing the manuscript. I am also very grateful to my family and especially to my wife, who has repeatedly put up with my absence because of my work on this book. She has been a model for me of how God's love comes to us through each other.

CONTENTS

ABBREVIATIONS AND EDITIONS

Works by Immanuel Kant:

CF	*The Conflict of the Faculties*, trans. Mary J. Gregor (New York, Abaris Books, 1979)
EA ·	*The End of All Things*, trans. Robert E. Anchor in *Kant on History*, ed. Lewis White Beck (Indianapolis, Bobbs Merrill, 1963)
Ed.	*Education*, trans. Annette Churton (Ann Arbor: University of Michigan Press, 1952)
Gl	*Groundwork of the Metaphysics of Morals*, trans. H. J. Paton (New York: Harper & Row, 1964).
KpV	*Critique of Practical Reason*, trans. Lewis White Beck (New York: Macmillan, 1956)
KrV	*Critique of Pure Reason*, trans. Norman Kemp Smith (New York: St. Martin's Press, 1956)
KU	*Critique of Judgement*, trans. Werner S. Pluhar (Indianapolis: Hackett, 1987)
L	*Logic*, trans. Robert S. Hartman and Wolfgang Schwarz (Indianapolis: Bobbs Merrill, 1974)
LE	*Lectures on Ethics*, trans. Louis Infield (Indianapolis: Hackett, 1930)
LPT	*Lectures on Philosophical Theology*, trans. Allen W. Wood and Gertrude M. Clark (Ithaca: Cornell University Press, 1944)
MM	*The Metaphysics of Morals*, ed. and trans. Mary Gregor (Cambridge: Cambridge University Press, 1991)
OT	*What is Orientation in Thinking*, trans. Lewis White Beck in *Immanuel Kant: Critique of Practical Reason and Other Writings in Moral Philosophy* (Chicago: Chicago University Press, 1949)
PP	*Perpetual Peace*, trans. Lewis White Beck in *Kant on History*
Rel.	*Religion within the Limits of Reason Alone*, trans. Theodore M. Greene and Hoyt H. Hudson (New York: Harper & Row, 1960)
WE	*What is Enlightenment*, trans. Lewis White Beck in *Kant on History*

Works by Søren Kierkegaard:

CA	*The Concept of Anxiety*, ed. and trans. Reidar Thomte and Albert B. Anderson (Princeton: Princeton University Press, 1980)
CD	*Christian Discourses*, trans. Walter Lowrie (Princeton: Princeton University Press, 1971)
EO	*Either/Or*, ed. and trans. Howard H. Hong and Edna H. Hong, 2 vols. (Princeton: Princeton University Press, 1983)
FSE	*For Self-Examination* and *Judge for Yourselves!*, trans. Walter Lowrie (Princeton: Princeton University Press, 1944)
JP	*Søren Kierkegaard's Journals and Papers*, ed. and trans. Howard V. Hong and Edna H. Hong, 7 vols. (Bloomington: Indiana University Press, 1978)
PC	*Practice in Christianity*, ed. and trans. Howard V. Hong and Edna H. Hong (Princeton: Princeton University Press, 1991)
PF	*Philosophical Fragments*, ed. and trans. Howard V. Hong and Edna H. Hong (Princeton: Princeton University Press, 1980)
R	*Fear and Trembling* and *Repetition*, ed. and trans. Howard V. Hong and Edna H. Hong (Princeton: Princeton University Press, 1983)
SUD	*Sickness unto Death*, ed. and trans. Howard V. Hong and Edna H. Hong (Princeton: Princeton University Press, 1980)

Other editions:

Grotius (1889)	Hugo Grotius, *A Defence of the Catholic Faith concerning Satisfaction of Christ, against Faustus Socinus*, trans. Frank Hugh Foster (Andover: Warren F. Draper)
Heidegger (1962)	Martin Heidegger, *Being and Time*, trans. John MacQuarrie and Edward Robinson (San Francisco: Harper and Row)
James (1961)	William James, *Psychology: The Briefer Course*, ed. Gordon Alport (New York: Harper Torchbooks)
Luther (1957)	Martin Luther, *The Bondage of the Will* trans. J. J. Packer and O. R. Johnston (Fleming H. Revell Co.)
Nietzsche (1967)	Friedrich Nietzsche, *On the Genealogy of Morals* and *Ecce Homo*, trans. Walter Kaufman (New York: Vintage Books)

Biblical quotations are from the King James Version except where the New International Version (NIV) is indicated.

INTRODUCTION

THIS book is about the gap between the moral demand on us and our natural capacities to live by it. The book belongs in a series on Christian ethics, because I focus on what the Christian tradition contributes to the discussion of this gap. I start with Kant, because of the influence of his ethical theory on contemporary moral philosophy and because he is still close enough to the Christian tradition to make use of its resources when he thinks he can. Starting with Kant has the advantage of making conspicuous the places where moral philosophers influenced by him no longer use these resources and the effect of their self-denial on the coherence of their theories. The book has three divisions, corresponding to the parts of the subtitle. The first is about Kant. Chapter 1 treats of his ethical theory and Chapters 2 and 3 his moral theology. The second division of the book, Chapters 4 to 7, is about various unsuccessful strategies proposed in the contemporary philosophical literature for dealing with the gap between the moral demand and the limits of human natural capacity. The first strategy is to keep the moral demand as high as Kant said it was and to exaggerate our natural capacities to live by it. The second strategy is to agree that there is a gap, on the Kantian understanding of the moral demand, and therefore to reduce the moral demand. The third strategy is to concede the gap and find a naturalistic substitute for God's assistance in bridging it. The final division of the book, Chapters 8 to 10, discusses the traditional Christian doctrines about God's assistance. In Chapter 8 I describe Kierkegaard's attack on the self-sufficiency of the ethical life. In Chapters 9 and 10 I give an account of human and divine forgiveness and the Christian doctrines of atonement, justification, and sanctification.

The book is written from the perspective of belief in what I will call 'traditional Christianity'. I will not try to define this phrase. One way to proceed would be to take the content of traditional Christianity to be given in the creeds and confessions that Kant would have learnt as he grew up in Königsberg, for example Luther's Small Catechism, which came at the end of the Prussian Catechism. I do not want, however, to imply that traditional

Christianity is Lutheran as opposed to Calvinist, or Protestant as opposed to Catholic, or Catholic as opposed to Orthodox. I will not, therefore, consciously rely on any doctrines or practices peculiar to, say, Calvinism, unless I make it explicit that I am doing so.

Writing from the perspective of traditional Christianity will already make the project suspect to much of the audience I would like to reach. I intend the book for two groups and their intersection: both for those who call themselves Christians, or at least take the claims of Christianity seriously, and for those interested in the academic study of ethics. This makes the project problematic, since many of those who fall into the second group find the attitudes and commitments of the first group incomprehensible or, if comprehensible, entirely unattractive. From the perspective of the academic study of ethics, it can seem that belief in traditional Christianity is possible for the uneducated, perhaps even desirable; but that for those who are fully alive to the movement of thought over the last two hundred years, it is no longer a serious option.

I believe, however, that a strong case can be made that this attitude within academic philosophy has led to a bad misreading of the great philosophical texts on which academic philosophy depends. I have an advantage here from an accident of my education. I did Greats at Oxford, in which the syllabus took a leap from Aristotle to Frege; and then a Ph.D. in the Classical Philosophy programme at Princeton, in which I read nothing between Aristotle's medieval commentators and Bradley. 'Modern' philosophy is therefore something I have read on my own, directly from the primary sources. I have been constantly struck by how often the Christian content of these sources has been ignored by the standard interpretations in the secondary literature. This is notably true of Kant, as I shall try to show. His system does not work unless he is seen as genuinely trying to 'make room for faith'. Failure to see this has led to heroic measures, either excising portions of text as not properly 'critical', or attributing his views to a desire to appease the pious sentiments of his faithful manservant. What is true of Kant is also true of Descartes, Hobbes, Locke, Leibniz, and even Hume. We are given a reading of modern philosophy that leads from its birth in the new science of the sixteenth century to its maturation in the death of God and the death of metaphysics. Descartes is seen as an incipient atheist, bringing in God not because of personal faith but to appease the Church. Large sections of *Leviathan*, where

Hobbes talks about the will of God, are ignored as though they were inessential to the project of the whole. In Bertrand Russell's critical exposition of the philosophy of Leibniz, God appears in none of the five original axioms. Hume is seen at the end of the *Dialogues* as insincere in portraying Philo's change of heart. It is no doubt tempting, if you cannot take Christianity seriously yourself, to interpret your favourite philosophers as sharing this distaste; but it leads to a distortion of the texts. Those engaged in the academic study of ethics ought to try the experiment of seeing what the world looks like from the perspective of traditional Christianity, even if merely to understand their own tradition. This book can be seen as such an experiment.

The second reason for attempting this is that there are problems in understanding the moral life on which traditional Christianity can shed some light. This should not be surprising, because our conception of the moral life has been deeply influenced by Christianity. We should expect to have difficulty understanding morality if we narrow the scope of considerations that can respectably be entertained so as to exclude these theological sources. 'Kantian' moral philosophies inherit, just as Kant did, concepts and problems from the Protestant Reformation and before. I try to justify this claim in this book, but it has an initial plausibility independently of the book. In the history of Western art, it would be foolish to try to understand our present situation by ignoring the contributions of the tradition of Christian theory and practice. It would be foolish even though artists in the modern period have repeatedly thought of themselves as starting afresh. The same is true of morals and moral philosophy.

The first part of the intended audience of this book consists of those who call themselves Christians or at least take the claims of Christianity seriously. The overwhelming majority of those in this group will not want to read a book of technical philosophy. They may, indeed, be as suspicious of academic philosophers as academic philosophers are of them. Paul tells us in his letter to the Colossians (2: 8) to beware of those who would spoil us through philosophy and vain deceit. It is probable that Paul has in mind here a particular philosophy, rather than philosophy in general. He allows himself, for example in his address in Athens, to use what philosophers of the past have said. But the warning has merit, even if it is taken generally. Educated Christians have got used to philosophy telling them that their beliefs are no longer possible for a responsible thinker in the twentieth century. They are now discovering that philosophy is less assured than it used to be of the grounds of its objections. It would be sad if they took this as a reason for paying less attention to philosophy. It should be, rather, the reverse. Academic ethics and traditional Christianity are now in a better position for 'constructive engagement' than they have been for a long time. But this requires the Christians to read philosophy as well as requiring the philosophers to try the experiment I referred to earlier of seeing what the world looks like from the perspective of traditional Christianity.

Christians need to think about moral philosophy because their understanding of the moral life will already have been influenced by moral philosophy, just as moral philosophy has been influenced by Christianity. It is possible to take different attitudes to this influence. Some may want to find out where the influence is in order to remove the contamination, just as some philosophers may want to find out the traces of Christianity so as to root them out. But the influence is there both ways round.

I will try to make this book accessible to those without extensive formal education in philosophy. This will be hard, because I am trying to cover such a large number of difficult topics. Kant alone is hard enough. It is discouraging to see how those who write about him, unless they are very skilful, end up writing in the same convoluted way that he does. I am also attempting to talk about Kierkegaard, who is formidably obscure in his own idiosyncratic way. Finally, I am trying to engage in contemporary discussions in ethical theory, and these discussions have reached a level of technical sophistication which makes them all but inaccessible to the general reader. It will not, therefore, always be possible to write in a non-technical way. I have found in preliminary field tests that the educated but non-academic Christians to whom I have shown the typescript have indeed found some of it too technical. I have also found that the academics have found the book too Christian. There is one group whose concerns and training fit the whole book well, and that is the group of academics who have specialized in Christian Ethics. For academic ethicists with a low tolerance for theology, I recommend excluding Chapters 8 and 10. For Christians with a low tolerance for technical philosophy, I recommend omitting Chapters 2, 4, and 7. I have tried to write the book in such a way that leaving out either group of chapters will leave a coherent remainder.

PART I

KANTIAN ETHICS

I

KANT AND THE MORAL DEMAND

I AM going to start this book with three chapters about Kant. He raises the problem of the moral gap vividly, because he both places the moral demand on us very high and recognizes that we are born with what he calls a natural propensity not to follow it. In Chapters 2 and 3 I will discuss his solution to the problem, which is to invoke divine assistance. In the present chapter I will start with Kant's account of what morality demands. I will discuss what he calls 'the categorical imperative', which he thinks to be the supreme principle of morality. This might seem easy to do, since it is done so often in elementary textbooks on ethics. But in fact the interpretation of many of the key terms is in dispute. In this way Kant is like other great philosophers; the basic components of his theory are in dispute between interpreters, and so all the parts of the theory relying on these components become controversial.[1] I will relate Kant's theory to a Kantian theory in the contemporary literature, and I will discuss how this theory deals with the gap between moral demand and natural human capacity. I will end by describing the role that Kant is going to play in the rest of the book.

a. KANT'S ETHICAL THEORY

Kant formulates the categorical imperative in various ways. In this chapter I will discuss two of these formulations, the Formula of Universal Law and the Formula of the End in Itself. In Chapter 6 I will suggest that the two formulas diverge, on one natural interpretation, but in the present chapter I am not concerned with this divergence.

---

[1] I will take a position on some of these disputes; but it would be a different project to defend an interpretation of Kant's ethical theory, given the enormous secondary literature. I will, in Chs. 2 and 3, be concerned to defend the attribution to him of certain views, which are less well known, in the philosophy of religion.

The Formula of Universal Law

The Formula of Universal Law requires that I act only on maxims that I can will as universal law.[2] What is a maxim? Kant says that a maxim is the 'subjective principle of an action'. The principle of an action is the prescription from which the action follows. If I tell myself to shut the door, and then do so, 'Shut the door' is the prescription from which my action follows. To say that this principle is subjective is to say that it is the prescription made by the subject (or prescriber) from which the action follows.

This does not mean, however, that the prescription is explicitly endorsed. A maxim is not the same as a conscious intention. According to Kant, an agent can be mistaken about the maxim of her action. There are multiple layers of self-deceit that may conceal this. I may give to Oxfam with the conscious intention of relieving hunger in the developing world, but the real motive governing my action may be to show off my virtue. This example illustrates how difficult it is to say what the maxim of an action is. Kant talks as though each action has one maxim from which it follows. There is a question, then, about what level of generality or specificity he is talking about, for there is in principle an infinite number of different maxims of different degrees on this continuum from which the same action can be said to follow. For example, my repaying a debt might follow from the maxim 'Repay debts', or 'Repay debts unless you were coerced into undertaking the loan', or 'Repay debts unless you were coerced into undertaking the loan and you would not have agreed to it voluntarily.' I think there is no determinate answer to this question from the texts. Kant says in *Religion within the Limits of Reason Alone* that there are in the end only two maxims, the good maxim and the evil maxim, and that all actions come from one or the other. The good maxim subordinates all desires to duty, while the evil maxim subordinates duty to the desires.[3] This text takes the

---

[2] I will, in referring to Kant's texts, cite first the page of the Eng. trans. I am using and then (in parenthesis) the page of the Prussian Academy edn. The English translations, and the abbreviations I have used, are listed at the front of the book. Kant's statement of the Formula of Universal Law is, 'Act only on that maxim through which you can at the same time will that it should become a universal law' (*Gl* 88 (421)).

[3] See *Rel.* 16–17 (20–1). I will in this chapter and subsequently use the term 'desires' generically, to cover all mental states of wanting something. This does not fit

level of the maxim of an action to the highest degree of generality. Another possibility (though Kant does not in fact suggest this) is to say that the maxim is the principle that prescribes exactly that action in exactly those circumstances. Such a maxim, if fully spelt out, might take a very long time to utter, since it would be completely specific to the full detail of the situation. Perhaps only an omniscient being could give such a maxim.

Kant's practice, at least in his examples, is between these two extremes, but further towards the pole of generality than towards the pole of specificity. He gives the example of the maxim of a suicide, who says to himself, 'From self-love I make it my principle to shorten my life if its continuance threatens more evil than it promises pleasure.' Or again, the maxim of a man making a false promise, 'Whenever I believe myself short of money, I will borrow money and promise to pay it back, though I know that this will never be done.'[4] We cannot always use Kant's examples, however, as the best indication of his theory, for sometimes his theory is better than his examples. He seems to hold that morally good maxims meet three conditions together: first, they are specific enough to prescribe one good action rather than another; second, they are general enough to be taught explicitly to children; and third, they are exceptionless, so that it is never the case that they should be broken. These three conditions together make it hard to give a plausible example, though it is much easier if any one of the three is removed. If, for example, we removed the first, we could give the 'good' maxim as an example, or the command to love one's neighbour as oneself. If we removed the second, we could give one of the completely specific prescriptions I have described (which perhaps only an omniscient being could give completely).

In any case, the categorical imperative is supposed to give us a test for maxims.[5] If a maxim meets the test, the action that follows from

ordinary use well, but is very convenient. In the present context, 'desires' include what Kant calls 'inclinations'.

[4] *Gl* 89 (422).

[5] It is not my purpose to discuss the secondary literature on Kant's ethical theory, but I will refer to MacIntyre (1981) because of his influence on recent theological ethics. MacIntyre has an interpretation which connects Kant, Kierkegaard, and contemporary analytic moral philosophy in a way different from mine. Following Hegel, he makes the charge against Kant of 'empty formalism'. He complains that 'Persecute all those who hold false religious beliefs' and 'Always eat mussels on

it has moral worth; if the maxim does not meet it, the action does not have moral worth. What, then, is this test? Kant states it in different ways at different times, and the number of different ways is counted differently by different interpreters. The clearest account of the Formula of Universal Law is that it requires willingness to continue subscription to the maxim of an action even if all individual or singular reference is excluded from it. Kant does not put his point this way himself, since this way of putting it relies on developments in logical theory that came after his death. It clarifies, however, at least part of what Kant means by calling his formula 'The Formula of Universal Law'. Suppose I prescribe that I should take my holiday this Christmas in the Bahamas. (Suppose also that it is December, I am starved for the sun, fed up with marking papers, and able at least barely to afford the trip.) Eliminating individual or singular reference would require eliminating reference to this Christmas, to the Bahamas, and most importantly, to *me*. We could think, then, of replacing these individual references with purely universal terms. What would guide us in this replacement is the same as what would guide us if we were moving from a singular instance of a natural phenomenon to the universal law which it instantiates. Suppose I throw a particular stone at a particular window at a particular time, and the window breaks. Assuming the regularity of nature, I can move to the law that whenever anybody throws a stone of this mass (specified in purely universal terms) at this kind of sheet of glass (specified in purely universal terms) the glass will break, other things being equal. This is what the scientist is after. In the same way, I should be able to move, according to the Formula of

Mondays in March' will count as moral maxims by Kant's version of the first formula. But Kant's use of the formula needs to be understood not only from *Gl*, but from *MM*. It is not until this work that Kant gives us an account of both the form of practical reasoning and the ends (or the matter) which practical reason sets for us; these are *one's own perfection* (moral and natural) *and the happiness of others*: see *MM* 190–2 (385–8). No free action is possible, Kant says, unless the agent also intends an end, and agents who will the happiness of others are conforming to the end which practical reason prescribes. As H. J. Paton says in his foreword to Mary Gregor's trans. of *MM* pt. 2: 'The most serious misunderstanding of all is the view that Kant's argument is based on purely logical, as opposed to teleological, consistency: he is supposed to deduce all particular moral duties from the mere form of morality (or the mere form of law) without any regard to its matter, that is, to the ends of moral action. The flat contradiction of all this in the *Metaphysic of Morals* will come to many as a complete surprise.' For a detailed rebuttal of the objection, see O'Neill (1989) 145–62. See also Auxter (1982) 103–27 and P. C. Lo (1981) and (1987) 39–75.

Universal Law, from my individual maxim about my holidays to the maxim that anyone in this kind of situation (bored with marking papers, weary of the cold and damp, moderately well off, etc.) should spend this sort of time (universally specified) in this sort of place (universally specified), other things being equal. What will guide the replacement in both cases is that I will want to preserve in the new principle what made me accept the old principle. In the case of the stone and the window, I will want to preserve reference to a certain weight and velocity and a certain degree of fragility. In the case of my holidays, I have already suggested some candidates for inclusion (boredom, sun-starvation, etc.). Unfortunately, the answer to *which* universal terms will go into the transformed principle is dependent on the answer to *which* degree of generality/specificity is required or allowed in the resultant maxim. If I am allowed unlimited specificity, I can include any universal property that distinguishes my situation from any other.[6] I may not, however, prescribe for the situation under any description which gives me one role in it rather than another.

The Formula of the End in Itself

The second famous statement of the categorical imperative, the Formula of the End in Itself, is, 'Act in such a way that you always treat humanity, whether in your own person or in the person of any other, never simply as a means, but always at the same time as an end.' When Kant says that we are to treat humanity as an end in itself, he does not mean that humanity is the goal or proper end-product of our action, but rather that humanity is a limit or constraint on our action. The kind of constraint in question can be seen most clearly by tracing the connection with the first formula, the Formula of Universal Law. According to the first formula, as I put it before, the agent must be willing to eliminate all individual reference from the maxim of her action. The most significant exclusion here is that of herself. She must, if she is to pass the test of the categorical imperative in this formulation, be prepared to go on

[6] Note that there is not yet any requirement that the universal terms that replace the individual reference in my new principle should be themselves evaluatively neutral. For example, I may not be able to describe in an evaluatively neutral way what I mean by 'anyone who is *bored*', or '*starving* for the sun'. It would require further investigation to determine whether I can do this or not, and whether there is a requirement that I do so.

willing the maxim even if it contains no reference to herself.[7] The effect of the exclusion of self-reference can be seen by going back to the example of my holiday in the Bahamas. I am fed up with marking papers, and I am proposing to leave them behind and flee; as long as I do not take much trouble with them, there will be just enough time to finish them when I get back after Christmas. But now suppose I try to see whether the maxim of my action can survive the test of the categorical imperative. Am I prepared to go on willing this maxim when all individual reference, and especially self-reference, has been eliminated?

If we take the maxim of the action (purged of individual reference) to be maximally specific, it will now be very long, perhaps unstatably long, since it will mention (in universal terms) all the features that distinguish my situation from any other. It will still be *universal*, in that it will be prescribing for *anyone* in just this sort of situation. It is natural to object that no one else is going to be in just this sort of situation, so that the principle is not going to have application to anyone besides myself. But this misses the point that in its universal (and maximally specific) form the maxim applies to the hypothetical situation in which the roles of the parties in the actual situation are exactly reversed. Suppose I were in exactly the sort of situation of my student Jeremy, who is ambitious to go to medical school, and he were in exactly mine, would I still be prepared to will the maxim that the person in the teacher's position go on holiday and neglect the marking?

Now we can draw the connection with the second formula of the categorical imperative. The constraint that this formula imposes is that the maxim of an action must be such that any other free and rational agent can adopt it. Treating humanity as an end in itself is, for Kant, respecting our capacity for free and rational choice; in his term, it is respecting our *autonomy*. I am constrained, according to this formula, by the consideration that it is wrong, other things

---

[7] She might try to disguise reference to herself by stating the revised maxim in universal terms that as a matter of fact point uniquely to herself. J. L. Mackie has an analogous case. An Italian patriot might revise a maxim giving precedence to Italy by substituting the universal term 'any boot-shaped country'. He could then be discomfited by being shown that a reunited Korea would have the shape of a boot. The point is that the categorical imperative requires the *sincere* elimination of individual reference. See Mackie (1977) 85.

being equal, to impede the agency of others.[8] To treat another human being as merely a means is to ignore the other as a centre of agency. The clearest cases here are those of coercion and deception. To take an unproblematic case of coercion, if I take the hand of one of the students in my class and with it I strike the neighbouring student's face, I have bypassed the first student's agency. I have treated her merely as a means, as though she were merely an organic hitting implement. The same is true when I deceive somebody, because if I conceal the nature of the situation, I impede her ability to make a free and rational choice for that situation.[9]

Kant goes further. He says that this second formula of the categorical imperative requires me to endeavour to further the ends of others, 'for the ends of a subject who is an end in himself must, if this conception is to have its *full* effect in me, be also, as far as possible, *my* ends'.[10] I am required, that is, to share as far as possible the ends of others. How far does Kant think this is possible? At least the requirement is limited by the need for the ends of the other person to conform also to the categorical imperative. I am not required, that is, to share immoral ends. To return to the example of my holiday in the Bahamas, I have to consider Jeremy's end of getting his papers carefully marked. Suppose he has done exceptionally well, and is hoping to go to medical school. I can ask whether his end is consistent with the categorical imperative. If it is (as seems most likely), then I am required to make his end my end.[11] To put this in the terms used earlier, I have to prescribe for the hypothetical situation in which I have his ends as well as for the actual situation in which I have my own.

Kant claims that Reason requires adherence to the categorical

---

[8] Kant seems to think there is an absolute prohibition here, but I do not want to defend that claim.

[9] It does not follow from the requirement to respect autonomy as an end that there is a requirement to respect humanity as an end, unless the premiss is added that humanity always brings autonomy with it. This makes it important to know what Kant means by 'humanity'. He is vulnerable to the criticism that he did not, for example, treat women as full centres of moral autonomy. We also need to know about humans with impaired rationality.   [10] *Gl* 98 (430).

[11] Kant does not tell us here what to do when ends which pass the test of the categorical imperative conflict. The utilitarians have an answer to this sort of question, and Mill thought of himself as working out how to apply Kant's test, not as providing an alternative account of moral worth. But it is not the purpose of this chapter to work out this connection between Kant and Mill. See Auxter (1982) Ch. 7.

imperative. One way he explains this is that self-contradiction is involved in the failure to adhere. He mentions two types of self-contradiction, contradictions in the conception and contradictions in the will.

There is an example of the first kind of self-contradiction in the maxim of making a false promise. Suppose, for example, that I am in financial straits and in order to get a loan I promise to repay it, knowing full well that I will not be able to do so. The categorical imperative gives me a test: Can I will this maxim as a universal law? In the terms introduced earlier, can I eliminate individual reference from the maxim of this action, and continue to will it? I would then be prescribing that anyone thus embarrassed by his or her circumstances may make a false promise of this kind. Kant's idea is that the institution of promising would fail if this prescription were adopted by all those to whom it applies (because 'no one would believe what was promised to him, but would laugh at any such assertion as vain pretense'). Kant thinks it is self-contradictory to will some end and not the means to that end, when the means is within our power. But if so, there is a self-contradiction in willing the maxim of the false promise as a universal law. For I would be willing some end (e.g. getting the money) and at the same time willing to make it impossible to achieve that end (because I would be willing the demise of the institution of promising as we know it).[12]

There are examples of the second kind of self-contradiction in the maxim of systematically denying assistance to others and the maxim of neglecting one's talents. Suppose, again, that I eliminate individual reference; I will be prescribing that anyone may fail systematically to give help to others and neglect her talents. Kant's idea is that it is not conceptually or logically impossible that no one help others, and that all our talents are left uncultivated, but it involves none the less a contradiction in the will. For we humans are not self-sufficient, and there are things we need which require assistance from the developed abilities of others. We get the contradiction in the will when we add to this empirical fact about humans the same logical point as before about the will, namely that it is self-contradictory to will the end and not the means to that end. Because we are not self-sufficient, we will inevitably at some time in

---

[12] *Gl* 89 (422). I am indebted to the analysis of Christine Korsgaard (1985) and (1989) 212.

our lives have some end which requires assistance from the developed abilities of others; and there is therefore a contradiction in willing that anyone may neglect to develop her abilities and deny such assistance (which is the means to this end).

We are, in Kant's conception, linked together by our needs and abilities into a single unit or kingdom, which we must be prepared to will into existence as a whole. It contains our needs and other people with the developed abilities to meet our needs; but it also contains the needs of others, and our developed abilities to meet their needs. We have to will what is consistent with the operation of this kingdom as a whole, since the categorical imperative does not allow us to make reference to our particular positions within it. Kant says that we are to act as though we were through our maxims lawmaking members of a kingdom of ends. He characterizes this kingdom as 'a systematic union of rational beings under common objective laws'.[13] All rational agents are subject to the universal laws which they themselves make, and these laws require them to treat each other as ends in themselves. They thus together comprise a kingdom constituted by these laws. This kingdom, Kant says, has members and a head. The head is also a member, being a rational agent himself; but he (unlike the others) is an infinite rational agent, being a maker of laws but not himself 'subject' to the will of any other.[14]

b. A CONTEMPORARY KANTIAN

In this section I will be examining the ethical theory of R. M. Hare. His views are conspicuously Kantian, as I will try to show, and this has the advantage of making his differences from Kant also conspicuous. His view is also typical of ethical theories in the twentieth century, which by and large hold the conviction that traditional Christianity is no longer tenable. This is the 'death of God' heralded by Nietzsche at the end of the nineteenth century. To say that traditional Christianity is no longer tenable is not yet to deny oneself the name Christian. There are all sorts of revisions that have enabled twentieth-century thinkers to retain the name. What is characteristic of them, however, is the sense of a radical departure from the tradition.

[13] *Gl* 100 (433).
[14] God, the head of the kingdom, is superior to all his creatures. He has a holy will, but they are required to submit themselves to discipline. See *KpV* 82 (80).

The prime mover in this cultural development has been the prestige of science. Thus R. M. Hare holds that it is now impossible to hold together three things: superstition (for example, belief in a supernatural God), science (or openness to the best-informed view of the empirical facts), and philosophy (or logic). Any two of these three, he says, can be held together and have been; but not all three together.[15] It is striking, though, having said this, that the ways in which the sciences are supposed to have forced this cultural development are not well formulated. Traditional Christianity is seen as having become gradually more exposed, from the Enlightenment to the end of the nineteenth century. But the cultural historian should look hard at the question of whether there was a fit between the actual advances in the sciences and the arguments (used by some of the systematizers and popularizers of these advances) against the core of traditional Christianity. The question I am asking is whether the gradually increasing sense of the vulnerability of this core was validly derived from empirically verified discoveries in the science of this period. To ask this question is not to assume the correctness of this model of scientific progress as based hard-headedly on empirical discovery. But it is nevertheless this model that lay behind the *prestige* of science in the period. It is therefore appropriate to ask whether the science that actually conformed to this model in fact contradicted anything in the core of traditional Christianity. Two alternatives, and their combination, need to be considered: that the 'science' that was used to undermine the tradition was not the solidly based discovery that was claimed, and that in any case what was undermined was not the traditional core, but material added to it for (sometimes recent) apologetic purposes.

This is a question for a different study. Given the belief that it was the sciences that were putting pressure on traditional Christianity, there are different attitudes that can be taken to this belief. For example, it is possible for one person with this belief to rejoice in the liberation of humankind from superstition, and for another person with the same belief to grieve that the tradition is no longer an available option. One response is the optimistic attitude that mankind is now free to use its own resources of intellect and will; free, so to speak, for an eighth day of creation. Another response is the pessimistic attitude that there is no satisfactory replacement for

[15] R. M. Hare (1973) 416.

the tradition, and that we are bound to live in an ever-increasing wasteland, as the various parts of our culture wither away. R. M. Hare belongs with the more optimistic attitude. He takes the view that if only we could get our thinking (and especially our ethical thinking) straight, we could go a long way towards solving our most serious problems. He thinks that we have learnt from philosophy and science that we cannot look for supernatural assistance with these problems. I want to talk in particular about his view of the relation between traditional Christianity and Kantian ethics. I will need to start, however, with a brief account of his general ethical theory, because it is only within the structure of that theory that I can make clear the debt to Kant and the place given to Christianity.

The Necessary Conditions for Moral Judgement

I think the most economical way to outline the theory is to give an account of what R. M. Hare takes to be the necessary conditions for a judgement to be a *moral* judgement. This is the place in his system which is analogous to Kant's account of the various formulas of the categorical imperative. This place in both systems is reached 'analytically'. For Kant, it is reached by proceeding 'from common knowledge to the formulation of its supreme principle'.[16] He takes himself to be giving an account of ordinary moral experience, and hence to be accountable to it. R. M. Hare takes himself to be starting from linguistic intuition, that is, from intuitions about what words (in this case, moral words) mean in ordinary use. His view is that if we examine this use, we will find that there are three logical properties which distinguish moral language from any other.

First, a moral judgement must be universalizable. His account of this condition is the same as the account I gave of Kant's first formula, the Formula of Universal Law. We can put the point this way, that if we make different moral judgements about situations which we admit to be identical in their universal descriptive properties, we contradict ourselves.[17] A moral judgement is a judgement about a *kind* of situation, a situation as described in universal terms, just as a scientific law is about a *kind* of situation. It is not supposed to matter to the validity of the scientific law *who* did the confirming experiment, or *where*, except to the degree that the person and the place are specified in universal terms (a researcher

---

[16] *Gl* 60 (xiv).
[17] R. M. Hare (1981) 21. See also, for his account of Kant, R. M. Hare (1993).

with a certain training, a laboratory at a certain altitude). In morals, the most important consequence of this requirement is that the agent is not allowed to make special exemption for her own case, for this exemption would require individual reference to herself.

Second, a moral judgement must be prescriptive. This requirement is present in Kant's description of the fundamental principle of morality as a categorical *imperative*. To make a moral judgement is to tell oneself, or someone else, what to do. If the first condition requires consistency between what we say for ourselves and what we say for others, this condition requires consistency between what we say and what we do. The idea is that a person is insincere who says he ought to do something in some sort of situation, and then repeatedly fails to do it when the situation arises and nothing prevents him.

So far, according to R. M. Hare, we do not have any condition that distinguishes moral evaluations from other kinds of evaluations. All evaluative language, he thinks, contains these logical features of universalizability and prescriptivity. What distinguishes moral evaluations from others is the feature that he calls 'overridingness'. This requirement is present in Kant's description of the fundamental principle of morality as a *categorical* imperative. The idea is, roughly, that to treat a universal prescriptive principle as a moral principle is to refuse to let it be overridden by any other kind of principle. But this statement requires clarification in the light of R. M. Hare's account of different levels of moral thinking. I will describe this account briefly, and then return to overridingness.

R. M. Hare's view is that we should distinguish between what he calls the 'intuitive' and 'critical' levels of moral thinking. The intuitive level is the application in ordinary life of moral principles which we 'know' to be right by intuition. These will very often be principles that we have grown up with, such as 'Always keep your promises.' The trouble is that these principles will not always be sufficient. They may be incomplete, or in conflict with each other, or they may be (when we come to reflect on them) plain wrong. We use, according to this theory, the *critical* level of moral thinking to evaluate the principles we use at the *intuitive* level. The method we should use is, he thinks, a form of act-utilitarianism, judging each principle by its general acceptance utility; that is, we ask about each principle whether its adoption by everyone would contribute to the satisfaction of the largest number of preferences (weighted for the intensity of preference) of all the affected parties. We can go back to the example of my holiday in the Bahamas, and suppose that the principle (or maxim) we are evaluating at the critical level is completely specific; that is, it mentions all the details of my situation in universal terms, without making individual reference to me. What I have to do, according to the theory, is to determine what are the preferences of all the parties affected by my decision, most notably all my students. I then form hypothetical preferences for what should be done to me, were I in their situations including having their preferences, and these hypothetical preferences will correspond (if I have determined *their* preferences accurately) to the actual preferences of the students for their own situations. Finally, I weigh all these preferences (which are now my preferences for all these hypothetical situations as well as for the actual situation), giving no special weight to my preferences for my own actual situation, and whatever decision satisfies most preferences is the decision I ought to take. On R. M. Hare's interpretation of Kant, this feature of moral thinking is also Kantian; or at least it can be found in embryo in Kantian texts. For Kant also requires that as a moral agent I share as far as possible the ends of all the parties affected by my decision, and to share an end is to make it my own.

To carry out moral thinking properly at the critical level requires two noteworthy achievements. It requires complete information and complete impartiality. I have to know how my decision will affect what actually happens to myself and to the other people involved, and how all those affected will evaluate what happens. I also have to be completely impartial between my own preferences and those of the others affected. It is because of the extraordinary character of these requirements that R. M. Hare calls the type of the critical thinker 'the archangel'. He calls the type of the merely intuitive thinker 'the prole'. His view is that none of us are likely to be exclusively archangels or proles, but rather that we operate on both levels to different degrees at different times.

To return, finally, to overridingness, the third characterizing feature of moral judgements. On R. M. Hare's view, to treat a principle as a moral principle is to refuse to allow it to be overridden by any other principle; but this applies only to moral principles endorsed at the critical level of moral thinking. A moral agent can, and probably should, allow her moral principles at the intuitive level to be overridden in the course of critical reflection.

As with my treatment of Kant, I am not aiming at discussing the secondary literature, but I need to refer to Alasdair MacIntyre because of his influence within theological ethics. He holds that R. M. Hare's moral philosophy reduces morality to personal choice or personal preference, and that hence morality becomes arbitrary or a disguise for power.[18] This, he thinks, is the final result of the failure of the Enlightenment project undertaken by Kant. The half-way point in this supposed breakdown is Kierkegaard's *Either/Or*, which I will discuss in Chapter 8. The result is to give us now the choice of accepting (with Nietzsche) that morality is merely a manifestation of the will to Power or returning (with Aristotle) to a pre-Enlightenment morality based on teleology. As MacIntyre puts it, Nietzsche or Aristotle. Here the meaning of the term 'arbitrary' is important. R. M. Hare is concerned to deny that moral decisions, even ultimate decisions of principle, are arbitrary in the pejorative sense. If we are asked to justify a moral decision, on his view, we should give a complete account of its effects, together with a complete account of the principles which it observed, and the effects of observing those principles. This is the critical level of moral thinking. A complete justification will end up specifying the way of life of which the particular decision is a part. But suppose we are asked now to justify that way of life. Here there will be no more for us to say, because anything that could be used in justification has already been used in specifying the way of life; we will have reached an ultimate decision of principle. It is tempting to say that such a decision is arbitrary. But Hare replies, 'To describe such ultimate decisions as arbitrary, because *ex hypothesi* everything which could be used to justify them has already been included in the decision, would be like saying that a complete description of the universe was utterly unfounded, because no further fact could be called upon in corroboration of it. This is not how we use the words "arbitrary" and "unfounded".'[19]

MacIntyre's own way of justifying ways of life is to index them to traditions, and then to ask which of the rival traditions does the best job of accounting for the competition. But any success that can be

---

[18] MacIntyre (1981) 19, 33, 240; and (1988) 396 f.

[19] R. M. Hare (1952) 69. Strictly, the analogy is with the *choice between* complete descriptions of the universe. See Piety (1993) for a rebuttal of MacIntyre's ascription to Kierkegaard of the view that moral choice is finally arbitrary.

reached in this way has *already* been included in R. M. Hare's account of ultimate decisions of principle. I do not mean that Hare took note of this type of justification, but that his account of ultimate decisions of principle requires that *everything* which could be used to justify them has already been included in the decision. If there are indeed no more reasons to be given, then there are no more reasons from MacIntyre's type of historical narrative to be given. The agent cannot at such a point proceed by giving reasons at all.

MacIntyre holds that R. M. Hare's theory means that we *create* our own values by choosing them, and therefore cannot be under their authority. We should ask, however, whether a prescriptivist can distinguish responses like equal respect for persons from responses like nausea in such a way that agents can hold their own preferences and those of others under the authority of the first kind of response and not the second.[20] Hare does in fact make this distinction in terms of objectivity. Thus, after separating a number of different senses of 'objectivity', he says that moral judgements have to be impartial, 'i.e. who is in which role in the situation being judged is not treated as relevant. Objectivity in this sense is preserved by any system of reasoning which, like my own, insists on the universalizability of moral judgements.'[21] Here is a standard to which responses can be held accountable, and it is a standard which, according to R. M. Hare, is to be found in the logic of our moral language itself; it is required by the way we use the words 'ought' and 'right' and so on. But suppose we go on to ask what it is that we value that *lies behind* this use of the words? The prescriptivist reply is that equal respect means valuing the choices people make; we acknowledge that others are sources of value by treating their chosen ends as good, and pursuing their happiness as they see it, as long as this is consistent with universalizability. Here there is a subtle distinction to be made. The above reply does not say that humans are valuable because they are capable of rational choice; it says that treating them as valuable is treating their chosen ends as good. It is true that to be a creature deserving equal respect, on this reply, requires the capacity for rational choice. But the equal respect is not

---

[20] Taylor (1989) 6, who gives this example, follows MacIntyre in the account of Kant and Kierkegaard, and he also dislikes contemporary analytic moral philosophy. But unlike MacIntyre he wants to recapture the moral sources of the *modern* identity.

[21] R. M. Hare (1981) 211.

merely a recognition of this capacity but a valuing of the ends chosen by a being with this capacity. This capacity for rational choice 'lies behind' the equal respect, in the sense that it is a necessary condition for it. But the equal respect is not merely the recognition that a being has such a capacity; it is the valuing (in as far as one can) of what the other person values. As long as this subtle distinction is made, prescriptivism is consistent with, indeed is one way to formulate, equal respect for persons.

The Three-Part Structure of Morality

I am going to comment on two features of the relation, within R. M. Hare's theory, between the moral demand and traditional Christianity. It may seem odd to think of traditional Christianity at all within the context of the account as I have presented it. I hope to make it plausible, though, that more of the tradition has survived than at first meets the eye.

The first point to note is that the position of the archangel is also taken to be the position of God. It is God who has the unlimited impartiality and unlimited information necessary to carry out critical thinking successfully. (Archangels in the tradition, at least sometimes, do not; it was Lucifer's giving precedence to himself that constituted his Fall.) The second important point here derives from the claim about overridingness. It is only judgements at the critical level, and hence judgements at God's level, that are overriding. Since overridingness is a defining characteristic of moral judgements, it is only judgements at God's level that are moral in an unqualified way.[22] We humans are limited in our impartiality and in our information, and can therefore only approximate to full-fledged moral judgement. R. M. Hare says,

The critical thinking of a perfect moral thinker manifests this full representation and identification. Archangels can do it, and of course God. We human beings are not gifted with so much sensitivity or sympathy, and for that reason have to do for the most part with intuitive thinking; but we have to try, if we are to do the critical thinking which would validate our intuitions.[23]

But if we really have not been gifted with the sensitivity and sympathy to do critical thinking, then we cannot validate our

---

[22] This point is made by Brill (1992) 544.
[23] R. M. Hare (1981) 99, 34.

intuitions in the way proposed. We can *try*, but only in the sense of trying in which this is consistent with knowing that we will never achieve what we are trying for. I will discuss the different kinds of trying in Chapter 4.

This gap between divine and human capacities is also a feature of Kant's theory. He says that 'when we pay attention to our experience of human conduct, we meet frequent and—as we ourselves admit—justified complaints that we can adduce no certain examples of the spirit which acts out of pure duty'.[24] The trouble is that as we think about the motivation of our own actions and the actions of others, we constantly come across the 'dear self'. What Kant thinks we can do, as he goes on to say, is to give examples of acts done *in accordance* with duty; though we cannot know whether they are done *for the sake of* duty, and therefore whether they have moral worth. The way for us to proceed, in this predicament, is to act *as if* our maxims were God's maxims, even though we cannot know this to be so.[25] R. M. Hare is sure that we have to *try* to do critical thinking, just as Kant is sure that we ought to try to follow practical reason; but in both cases there is the recognition of an apparent gap for us (though not for the God postulated by morality) between the 'ought' and the 'can'.

The effect of these two points is to bring it about that morality, in its full critical form, is, first, something I ought to be practising; second, something for which my natural capacities are inadequate (except by approximation); and, third, something that I should treat as the command of some other at least possible being who is practising it.[26] Morality has on this picture a structure with three parts to it: the moral demand, our defective natural capacities, and the possible being (the authoritative source of the demand). This three-part structure should strike us as peculiar. Why is not morality seen as a paradigmatically *human* institution?[27] We should wonder

---

[24] *Gl* 74 (406).   [25] *KpV* 134 (130).

[26] This possible being can be arrived at by addition or by subtraction. R. M. Hare reaches the archangel by adding complete information and complete impartiality. Brandt (1959) reached an impartial spectator by the same device. Rawls (1971) achieved the same function by subtracting behind the veil of ignorance the agent's knowledge of his identity.

[27] Thus Scheffler (1992) proposes an alternative construal by which morality 'is addressed from the outset to human beings as they are'. But on the cover of his book is a picture of Jeremiah, who knew, more than any other prophet, that we can only be pleasing to God by God's initiative (Jer. 24: 7). The moral law is for a Kantian very demanding. But demandingness is not the same as what Scheffler calls stringency,

about the genealogy of morals. I mean to suggest Nietzsche by this phrase. But looking at Nietzsche is instructive in a way he probably did not intend. For even he, I think, has his three-part structure. His positive doctrine, though hard to discern, seems to prescribe a way of life which is too hard for us, but which an at least possible being, the overman, can live. The genealogy of the three-part structure must surely include the strong influence of Christian doctrine. If we had not had the history of traditional Christianity behind us, it would have been more natural to propose a theory in which full-fledged morality was what *humans* are capable of by their own devices. This is a tentative judgement, because it is hard for me, perhaps impossible, to imagine what it would be like not to have grown up in a culture deeply influenced by Christianity. But it seems plausible to say that we have in this three-part structure a survival of the belief in a perfect and infinite moral being, whom we imperfectly resemble, and who created us to resemble him more than we do.[28]

Note that the three-part structure is not presented by either author as a proof of the existence of God. There is, however, a subsequent postulation of the existence of Providence by both authors. This is the topic of the third chapter of this book.

This three-part structure has an effect on the actual motivation of human moral life. It produces a constant and inevitable sense of failure. R. M. Hare says, 'I have myself during the course of my life been much more successful in doing good for myself than in trying, with the same or greater expenditure of effort, to do good for other people, because often they do not have the same notion of their good as I have.'[29] This kind of failure sometimes occurs, no doubt,

which is a property he wants to say morality does not have. Morality would be stringent in his sense if it were always or usually hostile to conduct that promotes the agent's well-being. It is significant, I think, that Scheffler does not even consider Kant's position on this question, even though he likes Kant elsewhere. Kant's position is that God will bring it about that happiness is proportional to virtue. He has an argument that because morality is demanding and not stringent, we have to have moral faith. It is significant that Scheffler does not even consider this possibility because it shows how far out of academic favour the notion of divine assistance has fallen.

[28] The structure is not, however, unique to Christianity. See Aristotle, *NE* 10. 7, 1177^{b}26–34, where he tells us that the best life would be superior to the human level, but we ought not to follow the proverb-writers, and 'think human, since you are human', or 'think mortal, since you are mortal'. Rather, as far as we can, we ought to be immortal.   [29] R. M. Hare (1981) 202.

because the other people were wrong about their own good; more often, it is due to a failure by the agent to understand the good of others. But this kind of failure is only the beginning. There are failures of self-deception. For example, I may magnify the intensity of my own preferences, so that they outweigh the preferences of others in the moral calculus; or I may cloak self-interest in the disguise of normative principles with the appearance of objectivity. There are failures of patience, where I am so convinced of the merit of my cause that I cannot even listen to the claims of another person. There are, above all, failures of impartiality, in which I do understand the preferences of another, and I do adopt them as hypothetical preferences of my own for the situation in which I would be that person, but I then refuse to give those hypothetical preferences equal weight with my preferences for the actual situation in which I occupy my actual role.

The effect of the three-part structure is that it makes the feeling of guilt and the desire to avoid its pain into a primary motivator of the moral life; for guilt becomes pervasive, affecting my memory of what I have done already, my perception of what I am now doing, and my expectation of what I will do.[30] In traditional Christianity, however, the three-part structure of morality is accompanied by a set of doctrines about God's initiative on our behalf to make it possible for us to live in a way pleasing to him. These doctrines take the third part of the structure as intervening to change the second part so that it is adequate to the first. Without these doctrines, or some functional equivalent, we are left in the moral gap, with the attendant sense of failure and the conceptual difficulty that we seem to be under a demand that is far beyond our capacities.[31] For purposes of clarity, I will call 'subjective guilt' the feeling of failure, and 'objective guilt' the actual failure to do what is morally good. I will return shortly to the defects of subjective guilt as the prime motivator for the moral life.

Exaggerating our Capacities and Diminishing the Demand

There are three main strategies for dealing with subjective guilt without appealing to God's supernatural work on our behalf. One is

---

[30] Aristotle says this is why non-virtuous people avoid solitude, so that they do not have to think about themselves: *NE* 9. 4, 1166ª23, 1166ᵇ15.

[31] I will describe Kierkegaard's picture of this condition in Ch. 8 below.

to produce a naturalistic substitute for God's assistance. Another is to exaggerate our sense of what we can accomplish, so as to fit the demand. The third main strategy is to reduce the demand so as to fit our capacities. I could, for example, hold myself accountable to a lower standard, if I could be content with regarding the moral demand described above as an unreachable ideal, and holding some lesser approximation as my 'realistic' goal. This is what the pastor in the sermon at the end of Kierkegaard's *Either/Or*, volume 2, categorizes as 'the easy, cozy conclusion: One does what one can'.[32]

The difficulty is in knowing what we *can* do. Kierkegaard's pastor continues,

Was not the real reason for your unrest that you did not know for sure how much one can do, that it seems to you to be so infinitely much at one moment, and at the next moment so very little, . . . that you might not have done what you could, or that you might actually have done what you could but no one came to your assistance?

He has a penetrating point in the final phrase here. He is responding to someone who argues from 'ought implies can' backwards; faced with the severity of the moral demand, she argues that because she cannot, it is not the case that she ought. The pastor responds that our sense of what we can do is variable, and it depends crucially on what kind of assistance we think is available. The transition into the religious life, as we shall see in Chapter 8, starts with a sense for a life we could lead that would not be discrepant in the way our life currently is; but this life does not seem attainable by our own resources. Kierkegaard is here in the tradition of Luther, and behind Luther of Augustine. Augustine says, 'God bids us do what we cannot, that we may know what we ought to seek from him.'[33] Luther compares us to children learning to walk, when their parent tells them to come, 'or do this or that, only in order that it may appear how impotent they are, and that they may be compelled to call for the help of the parent's hand'.[34]

It looks at first reading as though Augustine is denying the principle that 'ought implies can', for God is said to bid us do what we cannot do. But the principle is in fact preserved; for what is impossible is not our *doing* what God bids, but our doing it *without*

[32] *EO* ii. 345.   [33] *On Grace and Free Will*, 16. 32.
[34] Luther (1957) 152.

his help. Here the objection might be made that God is omnipotent; so that in this expanded sense of 'can' (where it encompasses what I can do with his assistance) I can jump to the moon. Surely this is expanding 'can' too far? But in Christian doctrine God offers us the assistance to do what he asks us to do, and he does not ask us to jump to the moon. Kant uses the term 'real possibility' for what is not merely logically possible, but grounded in some other fact whose reality is given.[35] We have, in this sense, a real possibility of living the kind of life God wants us to live, not merely because he *can* help us to live it but because he *offers* to help us to live it. If we are going to reduce the moral demand on us by indexing it to our capacity, we need to know what we are capable of if assisted in ways that are offered to us. Kant, aware of the effect of the three-part structure, is willing to talk about divine assistance; this is the topic of Chapter 2 of this book. He does not think we can *know* (in his restricted sense) whether divine assistance could help us here or not, because we can only claim to know (in his sense) what we could possibly experience with the senses. He also does not think we can *do* anything about this assistance (since the initiative, if there is such assistance, is God's). We should, none the less, make room for such assistance in our *belief*.[36]

R. M. Hare does not here duplicate Kant's structure.[37] Rather he splits up the moral domain between the specially holy people and the rest of us, and leaves the higher reaches of morality to the former. This strategy does not reduce the demand for all, but retains the higher demand just for a specialized few. This is what the Reformers objected to in medieval practice, where monks but not the rest of us were held under the so-called 'evangelical counsels', such as the demand to give up worldly goods, to turn the other cheek, and to love one's enemies.[38]

Could I not justify this thought at the critical level of moral thinking? I might say, 'If I try to apply too high a moral standard, I

---

[35] *KrV* A218 = B586. See Beck (1960) 272–3. Kant thinks the 'fact of reason' grounds the real possibility of God's assistance.

[36] I am here paraphrasing *Rel.* 49 (53).

[37] In making use of the Christian doctrine of the atonement, R. M. Hare has a difficulty different from Kant's, which is mostly with transmissible liability. He does not believe, unlike Kant, in the retributive theory of punishment. See Ch. 10 (for a discussion of penal substitution) and Michael S. Moore (1987).

[38] Calvin, *Institutes*, II. viii. 56.

will end up frustrated, and will be likely to give up the project of being moral altogether; then I will not help all those people whom I could have helped even with a lower standard.' But this strategy does not work, because it is incoherent. It requires me to use, in justification of lowering my standards, the very standards I am proposing to lower. I can indeed justify at the critical level lowering my moral standards at the intuitive level. I can perhaps use this strategy to get me through a rough patch. If I know myself well enough, I may be able to see that if I try to be terribly brave on this visit to the dentist, and refuse the anaesthetic, I will end up caving in completely to my fears, and be unable to get through the appointment. I can do this not merely for a particular occasion, but for my life as a whole. What is not coherent, however, is to use critical moral thinking to diminish the demand of critical moral thinking.

To illustrate the way in which I can coherently reduce standards at the intuitive level for my life as a whole, take the case of generosity.[39] It is useful, first, to make the distinction between external result standards (e.g. giving away a certain proportion of my income) and internal challenge standards (e.g. overcoming a certain intensity of desire to keep what I have). For me to be generous, let us say, is for me to like giving to other people things which I like; it is not generous to give to other people things I am *not* attached to myself. I can thus be prevented from generosity both by loving things too little (this is Aristotle's criticism of Plato's ascetic prescription for the ruling class in the *Republic*), and by a retentiveness which overcomes the desire to give them away. If I am the sort of person who cannot bear to give away what I am fond of, can I say to myself 'You are just not a generous sort of person', and then stop worrying about it? Perhaps I can give a causal account of my retentiveness; I grew up in the Great Depression, and I have had a sense of insecurity about my possessions ever since. Am I allowed at the critical level to argue that because I am like this, I should not make the demands on myself of generosity?

I think there are differences here between the different virtues. With generosity, it is reasonable to demand a lower external result, given my characteristic weakness. But I am still a less generous person because of this weakness, even though it may not be my fault.

---

[39] For a discussion of the nature of generosity, see J. E. Hare (1988).

It is different, I think, with bravery. We tend to admire an agoraphobic person, for example, who overcomes her fears and goes to the shopping centre, as much as a fearless person who does not have the initial panic to overcome. Aristotle would no doubt find the agoraphobic person who overcomes her fears not excellent but marred by a vice of defect. In contrast, we tend to find such a person brave. Generosity seems to fit the Aristotelian picture better than bravery. Take the example of an insecure and retentive person who none the less gives something she loves to someone else. There is likely to be a greater internal challenge for such a person to produce a given external result than for other people who find generosity easier and more natural. The first impulse of these other people, when finding something they like, is to share it with others. So which is the more generous person, the one who gives away what she likes after an internal battle, or the one who has no battle to fight? In this case I think the second person is more generous, but the first person is also admirable (though not for her generosity, but for her self-control).

The virtues are complicated mixes of internal challenge and external result standards. In the case of generosity, it is possible to argue at the critical level that I should lower my external result standards, given my characteristic weakness. This argument will be most convincing in cases where I will actually achieve a lower external result, because I despair or rebel, if I keep the internal challenge standard the same as it is for the people normally admired for the virtue. It does not seem right, on the other hand, to argue at the critical level that I should lower my internal challenge standard and worry less about overcoming my contrary desires, just because I have more of these or stronger ones to overcome than most people do.[40]

In any case, suppose we grant that there is a coherent argument at the critical level for lowering the moral demand at the intuitive level in the case of some particular virtue. It does not follow that there is a coherent argument at the critical level for lowering the moral

---

[40] The virtues have a tendency to increase external result standards as they get easier to meet. Those who have started to find it easy to give a pound a week to famine relief will start to find themselves challenged to give ten. There is not, therefore, a symmetrical argument that I can lower the internal challenge standard if I am achieving the same external result as people who are normally admired, but with less internal struggle.

demand of the critical level itself. I cannot argue at the critical level, for example, that I should not apply too high a standard of impartiality on myself because of my tendency to give more weight to my own interests than impartiality allows. What position would I be occupying in making such an argument? If I can occupy the critical level, to make the argument, I do not need to make it. If I need to make it, then I cannot occupy the position to make it. The person who makes this argument is trying to be both at the critical level and not at the critical level at the same time. Remember that the issue here is not some particular episode, where I can at a calm moment think forward to the stress I know is coming. The issue is not even the intuitions I should have over my life as a whole. Rather, the issue is how high a standard of caring about the interests of others I should apply at the critical level. If we are not 'gifted with so much sensitivity or sympathy' as to allow full impartiality, then we cannot use this deficiency to excuse us at the critical level from being fully impartial. Moreover, our deficiency will impair our ability to answer the question of what our capacities in fact are. Our estimates of our own abilities and the assistance available are suspect for the very reason the lowering of the demand was undertaken in the first place; the pervasive influence of what Kant calls 'the dear self'.

Subjective Guilt

What is wrong with the position that subjective guilt is indeed unavoidable, and unpleasant, but it serves as the best available motivator for the moral life? Why should one not say, with a wry smile, 'It's guilt that makes the world go round'? Kant already has the point that a life motivated by subjective guilt is demeaning; it is not the moral life at all. He says, 'They take all their sins and lay them at God's feet, and sigh, and think thereby they honour God; they fail to see that such mean and petty eulogy from worms such as we are is but a reproach to God.'[41] Kant is aware that there has to be something like desire to motivate humans even to do their duty; it is not subjective guilt, however, but respect or reverence for the moral law, which inspires him more even than the starry heavens above. What is admirable, and presumably pleasing to God, is a life in which the inclinations have been so trained that love of the moral law prompts action in accordance with it. In the language of Paul's

---

[41] *LE* 41. Kierkegaard says, 'Anxiety about sin produces sin' *CA* 73.

letters in the New Testament, to make guilt the primary motivator is to live under the curse of the law, rather than under grace.[42]

Second, our self-respect is necessary for the best kind of relations with others, and especially with the people we care about.[43] If I despise myself, because of my continual moral failures, I am likely either to despise other people or to idealize them. Either, that is, I will tend to think other people resemble me morally and so deserve the interpersonal version of the reproach I direct to myself, or I will think them fundamentally different from me, and I will not be able to relate to them as people with the same flesh-and-blood needs and desires as I have myself.

There is a third reply, which is equally serious. Both Kant and R. M. Hare say that if we are to persevere in the moral life, we have to believe in Providence; in the latter's words, we have to believe 'that people like Hitler come to a bad end'.[44] It is this thought that leads Kant to his moral argument for the existence of God, and I will discuss it in Chapter 3. The question in the present context is what we are to think about our own reward, if we concede that we are continuously guilty of moral failure. We could not, by this argument, continue a life of duty if we believed both in a just Providence and in our own inevitable and continual objective guilt. Leaving aside the question of whether there are rewards in the next life to compensate virtuous people for their sufferings in this life, we can ask whether virtue brings happiness in *this* life. R. M. Hare thinks he has to show that people brought up to be virtuous will usually be happy.[45] But if the end result of a good will is a life of continual and unremovable subjective guilt, then a parent who had the best interests of a child at heart would *not* bring up the child to be virtuous. Perhaps parents would choose for their children a guilt-ridden life of trying to be good rather than a relaxed life of evil. But suppose the choice were between a contented life of moral sloth (but not downright evil) and the guilt-ridden life of devotion to duty?

---

[42] e.g. *Gal.* 3: 1of.

[43] Aristotle argues that the quality of a friendship derives from the quality of an agent's relation to himself (*NE* 9.4). A person who finds it pleasant to spend time with himself, because 'his memories of what he has done are agreeable, and his expectations for the future are good', will also find it pleasant to spend time with others who share his vision of the good.

[44] R. M. Hare (1955) 101. Presumably the assumption is also that people unlike Hitler do not come to a bad end.   [45] R. M. Hare (1981) 205.

To say all this is not to deny the necessity of subjective guilt in the moral life. It is necessary, however, as a symptom not as a primary motivator. A person who does not feel subjective guilt after moral failure is either not perceiving it as a failure because she is morally blind, or else acknowledging it as a failure but not caring about it because she is amoral. But in Kant's view it is love of the moral law, not fear of subjective guilt, that is the driving force in a moral life.

Do we Know How God Thinks?

So far, I have not said anything hostile about the assumption that the critical level *is* God's level of moral thinking. I have claimed, merely, that R. M. Hare and Kant are replicating a three-part structure within traditional Christianity. In fact, however, traditional Christianity is less sanguine than either of them that we know what God's 'method' of 'moral thinking' is like. Kant's view is that 'each individual can know of himself, through his own reason, the will of God which lies at the basis of his religion'.[46] The first sentence of the *Groundwork* is that it is impossible to conceive anything at all in the world, *or even out of it*, which can be taken as good without qualification, except a good will. Kant is clear that God, the head of the kingdom of ends, is, no less than the other members of this kingdom, *rational*. God has a holy will, and is thus not constrained by duty because he has no contrary inclinations that have to be disciplined. He none the less wills, according to Kant, exclusively what reason requires. Thus he acts only on maxims through which he can at the same time will that they should become universal laws. He acts in such a way that he always treats humanity (or, better, personality), whether in his own person or in the person of any other, never simply as a means, but always at the same time as an end. Finally, he acts as if he were (because in his case, he is already fully) a lawmaking member of a kingdom of ends. Kant recognizes that God is, in the tradition, Love. This doctrine is accommodated by insisting that 'Love' here is 'Practical Love'.[47] Kant views the love which God has for us as the same in kind as the love which we are commanded to have for God, and for each other. These loves are different in that we love him because he first loved us, and not vice

[46] *Rel.* 95 (104).
[47] *Gl* 67 (399). This claim is misread by R. M. Hare (1973) 409. Practical love for Kant is a state of mind or attitude and not just a kind of behaviour.

versa; but the character of the love is the same. Now, Kant argues, we are *commanded* to love; but the inclinations or sentiments cannot be commanded, and therefore the love in question here is not a question of inclination or sentiment. Love out of inclination, he thinks, cannot be commanded because we are passive with respect to it (it either happens to us, or it does not); commanding someone to love out of inclination would be like commanding someone to be *in* love. The love of God is thus 'practical' and not 'pathological', 'residing in the will and not in the propensions of feeling, in principles of action and not of melting compassion'. The effect of this reading is to make God's love the same as his practical reason.

This means that, for Kant, some of the actions ascribed to God in the tradition are unintelligible, for example the choosing of a special people (which is, says Kant, arbitrary). In Chapter 2, I will discuss Kant's method with some parts of the tradition, which he does not reject, but also does not accept within the domain of reason. In the case of the belief in God's special election of the Jews, he says that Judaism failed, because of this belief, to be suitable for the requirements of the church universal.[48] He does the same with God's instructions in the Ten Commandments (which deal, says Kant, merely with outward observance) and God's promises to future generations (for God's favour is only appropriately shown, says Kant, to those who *themselves* try to lead the life of virtue). Thus the Abrahamic, Mosaic, and Davidic covenants are not the acts of the God of Christianity, to the extent that we understand his acts within what Kant calls 'the pure religion of reason'. If I am right about the core of traditional Christianity, the new covenant is also unintelligible for Kant within these limits. God chooses by his sovereign will to 'graft onto the vine' those whom he chooses to redeem; the church does not replace Israel, on this picture, but is made the recipient along with Israel of God's promises. But this choice by God must be just as arbitrary, for Kant, as the original selection of a chosen people.

R. M. Hare is as clear as Kant that we know the method of God's moral thinking. It is, as for Kant, rational, and conforms to the method prescribed at the level of critical thinking.[49] For R. M. Hare, utilitarianism (of the type he favours) is the best way to understand what is meant in traditional Christianity by God's love

---

[48] *Rel.* 117 (127).   [49] R. M. Hare (1981) 34.

(agape), and the love we are commanded to have towards each other. He quotes Joseph Butler with approval:

From hence it is manifest that the common virtues, and the common vices of mankind, may be traced up to benevolence, or the want of it; and this entitles the precept, *Thou shalt love thy neighbour as thyself*, to the pre-eminence given to it; and is a justification of the Apostle's assertion, that all other commandments are comprehended in it (Sermon 12).[50]

R. M. Hare is not saying that the content of the tradition on this topic is *exhausted* by this form of utilitarianism, but that the main part of what is *salvageable* from the tradition is preserved in this form. There are parts of the tradition that have to be discarded, he thinks. 'Once people realize that they can have a rational morality without the orthodox God, and cannot have one with him, one of his chief props (indeed, perhaps, his only surviving prop with any strength) will have disappeared. And it is this situation for which Christians ought to be preparing.'[51] Both he and Kant are concerned to frame a religion that can survive within the constraints of what can be used by reason. There is much of traditional Christianity that has to be left out in this project: for example, any doctrine of special providence, any belief in sacramental efficacy, any belief in a historical atonement. So far they agree. But R. M. Hare goes further than Kant, because he wants to put the constraints on what we can meaningfully assert which Kant puts only on what we can know in his sense of 'know', namely the limits of possible sense experience.[52] Kant, I shall argue in Chapter 2, wants to make room for belief in God's action on our behalf, even though we cannot *know* that such action occurs. For example, he thinks we should believe, and hence should assert, that a 'divine supplement' is available for bridging the moral gap. On R. M. Hare's more restrictive view of meaning, we cannot make a meaningful factual assertion beyond the limits of possible sense-experience. Many of the beliefs I shall attribute to Kant will fail this test for assertability.

c. THE CHRISTIAN SERIOUSNESS OF KANT

In this concluding section of the chapter, I want to tie what I have said about Kant and R. M. Hare into the project of the book as a

---

[50] See R. M. Hare (1992) 62.   [51] R. M. Hare (1973) 422.
[52] Ibid. 416; see Kant, *Rel.* 48–9 (53).

whole. In particular, I want to defend the claim that Christians should find Kant both compelling and helpful. I have observed the opposite; especially in America, Christians who know about Kant tend to think of him as the major philosophical source of the rot which has led to the decline of Christianity in the West in the last two hundred years. He is seen as having taken a decisive step, perhaps the decisive step, away from the traditional faith. He is lumped into 'the Enlightenment' without remainder, and the Enlightenment is charged with casting off tradition and community and narrative and the virtues.[53] This book will take the opposite approach of seeing how close Kant is to the Christian tradition he grew up in. Christians should find the three-part account of morality entirely familiar. Kant holds that humans have an original predisposition to the good, overlaid with an innate but imputable propensity to evil, which can be overcome only by a revolution of the will which itself requires what he calls a 'divine supplement'. Kant is here replicating the structure of creation, fall, and redemption. It is true that he attempts to translate these doctrines within the limits of the pure religion of reason. This can seem scandalous to those who believe in the doctrines in their traditional form. But I shall try to show in Chapter 2 that Kant does not mean us to conclude that we should believe in the doctrines only in their translated form. Without this addition, there should be nothing scandalous in the project of seeing how much of the gospel is intelligible in terms of general revelation.[54] It is entirely consistent with this to argue (as I shall) that Kant's project fails at certain key points. He is not able to make the translated doctrines do the work in his theory which he needs them to do.

There is great profit, I think, from looking at Kant this way. The gap between the moral demand and our natural capacity is made tolerable, in the tradition, by belief in God's work on our behalf. 'Ought', as Kant says, 'implies can'. If it is not the case that we can live by the moral demand, it is not the case that we ought to live by it. But he concedes that our initial condition is one of bondage to

---

[53] Hauerwas and Willimon (1989) 79: 'Growing up, becoming a mature, functioning adult is thus defined as becoming someone who has no communal, traditionalist, familial impediments. This heroic, radically individual and subjective ethic was best articulated by Kant.'

[54] But see ibid. 21: 'By the very act of our modern theological attempts at translation, we have unconsciously distorted the gospel.'

radical evil, in which the fundamental maxim of our lives subordinates duty to inclination. In order to persevere in the moral life we have to have what he calls 'moral faith', which has two components: faith in the actuality of virtue and in the consistency of happiness and virtue. I will discuss the details of his argument in Chapters 2 and 3. The moral person has to believe that the revolution in her will has actually been accomplished, and she has to believe that it is not necessary for her to do evil in order to be happy. Kant thought that both components of moral faith required belief in God's work on our behalf. But this belief has entirely dropped out of the professional literature in ethical theory. Looking at Kant's arguments has the merit of exposing the vulnerability of the attempt to do Kantian ethical theory without the Kantian postulates.

In the second division of the book I will discuss three contemporary groups of failures to deal with the moral gap without invoking God's assistance. One group proceeds by keeping morality as demanding as it is in Kant, but exaggerating our natural capacities to live by this demand. This is the topic of Chapters 4 and 5. I will consider in detail some recent utilitarian writing, which urges that if we only thought harder about the effects our actions would have on others, we would be inclined to do what the utilitarian principle requires. I will also look at an account of 'the natural structure of desire', which includes nice features we naturally aim at, such as deep personal relations and significant accomplishment, but does not include nasty features, such as power over other people. The second group consists of attempts to restructure the moral demand to fit our capacities. I will look at some recent feminist work which denies that morality is necessarily universal, in the sense I have attributed to Kant and R. M. Hare. I will concede the central point, that not all moral judgements are universalizable. But I will argue that this does not have the effect of diminishing the moral demand. This is the topic of Chapter 6. In Chapter 7 I will look at a third group, who propose naturalist substitutes for God's work on our behalf. The moral gap would not be threatening if we could show that there are social or biological evolutionary forces which produce both our morality and the religious 'preachments' which accompany it, or if we could show that the machinery of the rational bargain takes us from self-interest to the disposition to be moral.

Chapter 8 is the beginning of the third division of the book, which is about Christian doctrine. I will try to show that Kierkegaard already saw the threat to ethics which the moral gap presents in the absence of belief in our relation to a transcendent God. I will interpret him as presenting in *Either/Or*, volume 2, a picture, in Judge William, of a person trying to live an ethical life in the absence of such a belief. Judge William is thus a picture of what it would be like to live within the limits of Kant's pure religion of reason. Kierkegaard's narrative gives a vivid psychological portrait. It also suggests how we might retranslate Christian doctrine back out of the pure religion of reason into what Kant calls historical faith. In Chapters 9 and 10 I try to be more specific about what traditional Christianity has to say about God's assistance. I proceed by examining first what it means for one human being to forgive another. I then look at the ways in which God's forgiveness is said to be both like and unlike human forgiveness. This means looking primarily at the doctrines of atonement, justification, and sanctification.

Suppose all the arguments in the book worked, what would the book have accomplished? Would it, for example, have proved the Christian doctrines about God's work in our salvation? Not at all. All it would have shown is that *if* we keep morality as demanding as Kant says it is, *and if* we want to concede what Kant says about our natural propensity not to live by it, *and if* we want at the same time to reject these traditional Christian doctrines, then we will have to find some substitute for them. This book has no way to show that there is no successful substitute, either in some other religion or in some non-religious system of belief.

2

GOD'S SUPPLEMENT

IN chapter 1, I gave a brief introduction to Kant's ethical theory and attributed to him the picture of morality as a three-part structure containing the demand on us, our natural capacities, and the source of the demand.[1] This structure presents what I called a 'moral gap' between us and the demand on us. Kant's problem with this gap is acute, because he believes that 'ought' implies 'can'; if it is not the case that we can live by the moral demand, then it is not the case that we ought to. He also rejects the idea that being with other people enables us to live morally even though we cannot on our own. I will discuss this in Chapter 3. Like Rousseau he holds that other people make the situation worse, not better. His solution is to appeal to the possibility of assistance by God. In other words, he uses the third part of the structure to deal with the gap between the first and the second. His most detailed discussion of this is in *Religion within the Limits of Reason Alone*, but I will also make reference to a number of other late works. These texts make frequent use of traditional Christian doctrines, such as those of atonement and justification. It is hard, however, to pin down the spirit in which Kant employs them.

He usually confines his use of them within what he calls the pure religion of reason, but what is this constraint? I shall suggest that Kant is not a deist about special revelation. I am convinced that he personally continued to believe in the central doctrines he was brought up with. But this is not necessary to my argument, and Kant is anyway silent about his personal religious beliefs. What *is* important to my argument is to show that Kant is what he calls a 'pure rationalist', namely someone who 'recognizes revelation, but asserts that to know and accept it as real is not a necessary requisite to religion.' I will discuss especially Kant's treatment of the

---

[1] Some material in this chapter has appeared already in J. E. Hare (1994*b*). I want to thank my commentator at the American Philosophical Association meetings, A. C. Genova, for his comments on a previous draft.

Christian doctrines about God's work in our salvation. I will argue that his translation of these doctrines within the pure religion of reason fails; it fails to do the work for him which he needs it to do in relation to the moral gap. This does not show that his project was bound to fail. Perhaps there is a better translation of the traditional doctrine within Kant's constraints. If there is not, and if the tradition does have resources to help with the problem of the moral gap, then we have a choice between accepting his constraints and using these resources.

a. REVELATION

Kant's Two Experiments

In the preface to the second edition of *Religion* Kant says that he has to clarify the meaning of the title of his work. This is his main substantive addition.[2] He tells us that doubts had been expressed about his intention in giving the work its title. One problem must have been that some of his audience did not understand what place, if any, he retained for revelation. For the point he makes in the preface is that revelation can be held to include the pure religion of reason, but at least the historical part of revelation cannot be included in the pure religion of reason. We can understand Kant's idea here in the same way we understood his ethical theory, though again he does not put it this way. The pure religion of reason, because it is universal like the pure principles of morality, has to be shorn of all reference to individuals and particular times and places (such as Golgotha or Sinai); but there is nothing in the idea of revelation to prevent this pure religion of reason from being *revealed* by God to human beings.[3] In what follows I will call 'special

---

[2] The changes to the 2nd edn. of *Rel.* show a pattern of responsiveness to the worries of traditional Christians who wanted to accept Kant's teaching. Unfortunately this pattern cannot be followed in the standard Eng. trans., by Greene and Hudson, because they often omit the information that a passage was added in the later ed. In many of these additions Kant tells us how to translate particular biblical teachings within the pure religion of reason. For the purposes of this chapter the most important additions are those where Kant talks about the enduring utility of biblical revelation. See pp. 49 (53), 83 (88), 126 (135), 163 (175). There is a parallel here with the attitude towards metaphysics taken in the second pref. of *KrV*, as opposed to the first pref.

[3] There is within traditional Christian theology the distinction between *general* revelation (given to all people, and demonstrated especially in nature, history, and the

revelation' divine revelation to us through temporally and geograph-
ically limited vehicles such as Scripture, and this will not include
God's revelation to reason.

Kant proposes as an experiment that the relation between special
revelation and reason can be seen as the relation between two
concentric circles, with special revelation being the part of the larger
circle not included in the smaller one, and the pure religion of reason
being on the inside. This analogy means, he goes on to say, that
there will be not only logical consistency between Scripture and
reason, but unity, in the sense that if a person follows the first she
will also be following the second. The experiment here will be
defeated if it can be shown that the contents of the outer circle are in
fact inconsistent with reason or that the two fail to have this sort of
unity.[4]

He then proposes a second experiment, which is to show that
certain items in the outer circle lead back within the inner circle
when looked at in the light of, or translated in terms of moral
concepts. He says he is going to do this 'in a fragmentary manner',
that is, individual belief by belief. But in fact what he does is to take
the central claims of Christianity in the traditional order of creation,
fall, redemption, and second coming. Note that Kant is not saying
either that the experiment will be successful or that it will not; he is
proposing to take the claims one by one and *see* whether the
experiment works.[5]

There is a third experiment which could also be conducted in
terms of the two concentric circles. The second experiment is a kind
of raiding party; leaving the inner circle, we investigate the outer

moral and spiritual qualities of human beings) and *special* revelation (given to
particular persons at particular times and places, especially in the Bible). See *Rel.* 99
(108).

[4] Kant explains the title of the work at the end of *MM* 276 (488): 'We can indeed
speak of a "Religion *within the Limits* of Reason Alone", which is not, however,
derived *from* reason alone but is also based on the teachings of history and revelation,
and considers only the *harmony* of pure practical reason with these (shows that there is
no conflict between them)' (emphasis in Mary Gregor's trans.). Note that in this
passage the limits of reason alone include those parts of the outer circle which are seen
to be consistent with pure practical reason, and these limits are therefore wider than
the limits of the pure religion of reason itself. See Despland (1973) 241 for an
elaborated diagram of the concentric circles.

[5] 'One by one' is misleading, since the claims of special revelation do not come in
isolable units like that. Kant's actual practice in *Rel.* is to take the central claims of the
tradition in order, the claims about Creation, Fall, Redemption, and Second Coming.

circle to see if we can bring back any doctrines found there into the domain of pure reason by translating them under appropriate constraints. The third experiment works the other way round. We investigate the inner circle to see whether the beliefs and practices we find there require support from beliefs and practices in the territory of the outer circle. To say they require support is not to say that all people who have the first set of beliefs and practices in fact have the second; but rather that if they do not, they will be left with a certain kind of incoherence which I will try to characterize. I will return to this third experiment at the very end of this book.

Is Kant a Deist?

If we restricted our attention to the second experiment, we might reach the conclusion that Kant is a deist.[6] In Kant's terms a deist, in his understanding of God, 'understands merely a blindly working eternal nature as the root of all things, an original being or supreme cause of the world.'[7] Kant is not in this sense a deist, because he thinks our moral faith requires belief in a God who is alive, who knows and who wills. None the less, it might be claimed that in the *ordinary* sense of 'deism' Kant is a deist. Deism in this sense is 'the opinion of those that acknowledge one God, without the reception of any revealed religion.'[8] I want to argue that Kant is not a deist in this sense either.

A good text for posing the question is the opening of book 4, part 1 of *Religion*:

[6] I am responding here to a paper by Allen Wood (1991). The papers by Joseph Runzo and Denis Savage in the same volume, Rossi and Wreen (1991) (eds.), argue for the same conclusion as Wood. See also Wood (1992). I am very grateful to Wood for a detailed reply to a draft of this section. In criticizing the view that Kant is a deist in the ordinary sense, I am following the interpretation which Michel Despland (1973) gives of some of Kant's central texts; but Despland is (in my mind) too beholden to Tillich, and concedes that he has imported Tillichian terminology without much explicit warrant in Kant's writings (p. 119). For *Rel.* as 'a deistic classic', see Theodore M. Greene, Introd. to *Rel.*, p. lxxvii.

[7] *LPT* 81.

[8] The phrase is quoted by Wood from John Dryden's *Religio Laici* (1682). By 'revealed religion' here we should understand special revelation; the deist does not want to deny general revelation. There is another 'ordinary' sense of 'deist', which involves denying any divine intervention in the working of the world (once it is created), not denying special revelation in particular. This deism sees God as like a watchmaker, who leaves the watch working on its own once he has made it.

Religion is (subjectively regarded) the recognition of all duties as divine commands. That religion in which I must know in advance that something is a divine command in order to recognize it as my duty, is the *revealed* religion (or the one standing in need of a revelation); in contrast, that religion in which I must first know that something is my duty before I can accept it as a divine injunction is the *natural* religion. He who interprets the natural religion alone as morally necessary, i.e., as a duty, can be called the *rationalist* (in matters of belief); if he denies the reality of all supernatural divine revelation he is called a *naturalist*; if he recognizes revelation, but asserts that to know and accept it as real is not a necessary requisite to religion, he could be named a *pure rationalist*; but if he holds that belief in it is necessary to universal religion, he could be named the pure *supernaturalist* in matters of faith.

Kant is, in the terms of this passage, a rationalist (and is therefore committed to denying pure supernaturalism) and not a naturalist (because naturalism transcends the limits of human insight just as supernaturalism does).[9] Given the categories Kant lists in this passage, there is therefore a strong suggestion that he wants us to conclude that he is a pure rationalist. I think he does indeed want us to conclude this. But if Kant is a pure rationalist, then he is not a deist in the 'ordinary' sense, since this kind of deism is inconsistent with 'the reception of any revealed religion'. The pure rationalist, on the other hand, accepts special revelation, but holds that it is not a necessary requisite for pure religion.

The claim needs to be defended, therefore, that Kant intends us to think of him as a pure rationalist. The first question to ask is why Kant should have introduced the category of pure rationalist at all, as the alternative rationalist position to naturalism, if he did not intend us to opt in favour of this position.[10] One possibility is that Kant is tailoring his rhetoric so as to make his view sound more palatable to certain audiences than it actually is. There is a long history of interpretations of Kant which suppose that he is making

---

[9] Despland (1973) 220 regards the passage as endorsing pure rationalism, but eliminating rationalism, on the grounds that (like naturalism) it denies the interest of reason in supernatural conceptions. On my view, pure rationalism is consistent (as a species) with rationalism (the genus).

[10] Wood (1991) 11 says, 'But "pure rationalism" seems scarcely deserving of its name, and it is hard to imagine anyone who would hold it. For it apparently takes the position that God has given us certain commands supernaturally while denying that we are morally bound to carry them out. This surely cannot be a position Kant intends to embrace. Kant's only purpose in mentioning pure rationalism at all seems to be the rhetorical one of cushioning his evident denial of pure supernaturalism.'

concessions to Christianity in order to appease his faithful man-servant, or to appease the Prussian censors, or to appease his own conscience, formed as it was by a pietist upbringing.[11] But Kant is committed to presenting an account 'with the utmost conscientious-ness'.[12] The constraint of sincerity falls not merely on the views he expresses, but on the form of expression; he regards himself as soon to appear before a judge who judges these matters with the benefit of insight into men's hearts. As long as there is another interpretation which makes sense of the texts, we should not interpret Kant as 'tailoring' his rhetoric.

The second reason is that the term 'pure rationalist' is the sort of phrase we should expect Kant to use as an honorific. Thus he holds that Christ should be reverenced as the first introducer of teachings which are those of *pure reason* and as such carry their own proof within them.[13] Within *Religion* this is his usual vocabulary.[14] We should not accept, unless forced, the view that 'pure rationalism' is Kant's name for a position in the philosophy of religion which he finds he cannot embrace.

Third, Kant sees special revelation as a 'vehicle' in God's dealings with human beings. He argues that reason is entitled to believe in a supernatural supplement to fill what is lacking in man's justification,

but we need not be able to understand and state exactly what the means of this replenishment is (for in the final analysis that is transcendent and, despite all that God Himself might tell us about it, inconceivable to us); even to lay claim to this knowledge would, in fact, be presumptuous.

---

[11] One interpretation alone these lines is that of a student of Hegel, Heinrich Heine (1959) 119: 'and Old Lampe stood there, a mournful spectator, his umbrella under his arm, cold sweat and tears pouring from his face. Then Immanuel Kant relented and said, half good-naturedly and half ironically, "Old Lampe must have a God, otherwise the poor fellow can't be happy." ' See also the phrase in E. Troeltsch, 'utterances of prudence', quoted in Despland (1973) 105 f., and the phrase in Yovel (1980) 114, 215, 'cover' techniques.

[12] *CF* 19 (10). Kant pictures a judge standing at his side to keep him not only from error but from careless expression. See also *KrV* A748–50 = B776–8.

[13] *Rel.* 147 (159). See also *OT* 301 (142): 'A pure rational belief is, therefore, the signpost or compass by which the speculative thinker can orient himself in his rational excursions in the field of supersensuous objects.' Kant goes on to recommend pure rational belief for practical as well as theoretical reason.

[14] 'Pure religious faith alone can found a universal church; for only (such) rational faith can be believed in and shared by everyone' (*Rel.* 94 (102–3)). In the pref. to the 2nd edn., the pure religion of reason is what lies in the inner circle, which is the preferred territory of the philosopher.

[15] *CF* 77 (44), emphasis added.

Accordingly, scriptural texts that seem to contain such a specific revelation must be interpreted as concerning, not moral faith (for all men), but only the *vehicle* of that moral faith, designed to fit in with the creed which a certain people already held about it.

Kant goes on to say that we can consider the Christian Bible as 'the *vehicle* of religion and accept it, in this respect, as supernatural revelation', because it 'promotes moral precepts of reason by propagating them publicly and strengthening them within men's souls'.[15]

Kant's point at the end of this passage is to deny that the Christian Bible is necessary for pure religion. He is not, that is, a pure supernaturalist. But he wants to allow the usefulness of Scripture beyond those parts of it which are without qualification necessary for eternal life (and are already contained within the pure religion of reason).[16] There are, he thinks, historical parts of supernatural revelation which have introduced people to pure religion, and which can have, for certain people and certain eras, the power of replenishment and strengthening in the moral life. This is how hope can be awakened in us 'by the example of humanity as pleasing to God in His Son.'[17] This additional power is not, indeed, necessary for all rational agents, and is not in that sense universal. But Kant is also of the opinion that it is necessary for many people at his own time, and this is what justifies the government's interest in biblical preaching.

The pure rationalist accepts special revelation but nevertheless

---

[16] I say, 'without qualification' because the Bible can still be necessary, given certain limitations. It is significant that pure rationalism is defined as denying that accepting special revelation is a *necessary requisite* to religion. The italicized phrase may be mere pleonasm or reduplication, but it may be making the careful point that the pure rationalist allows that accepting special relevation may be requisite for some rational agents, though it is not a requisite for rational agents as such. See *CF* 63 (37): 'But the Scriptures contain more than what is in itself required for eternal life; part of their content is a matter of historical belief, and while this can indeed be useful to religious faith as its mere sensible vehicle (for certain people and certain eras), it is not an essential part of religious faith'. It is true that Kant also says, 'the historical element, which contributes nothing to [making men better], is something which is in itself quite indifferent, and we can do with it what we like. Historical faith "is dead being alone"; that is, of itself, regarded as a creed, it contains nothing, and leads to nothing, which could have any moral value for us' (*Rel.* 102 (111)). But this passage and others like it make the point that historical faith can have its special power *only* as the vehicle of pure religious faith.   [17] *CF* 75 (43).

does not think its acceptance is without qualification necessary to religion. This means that she believes it is not necessary for herself purely as a rational agent to accept it (even though she does accept it) in order to have pure religion. She will believe that there may be commands given supernaturally by God which not all rational agents are bound morally to carry out. Does not this mean that she has to believe that *she* is not bound to carry them out, even though she also believes they are God's commands? I think Kant's attitude is that as long as the statutes given in the Bible are consistent with practical reason, she should, if she is among those 'strengthened' by the biblical stories, treat the statutes as commands of God. She will then be treating herself, but not treating all rational agents, as bound by them. Religion, after all, is a purely moral order only in form; 'but as for the *material* aspect of religion, the sum of duties to God or the service to be rendered Him, this could contain particular duties as divine commands—duties which would not proceed merely from reason giving universal law and which would therefore be known to us only empirically, not *a priori*.'[18] We should be grateful to Providence as the origin of the statutes and stories which serve as the vehicle for the introduction of 'the purest moral doctrine of religion in its completeness', and hence as the vehicle of an enlightenment which is not yet by any means complete.[19]

I think we should conclude that Kant is a pure rationalist, and therefore is not in the ordinary sense a deist.

Kant and the Reduction of Religion to Morality

Kant is thus the ancestor of such views of the Bible as those of R. B. Braithwaite and R. M. Hare, both of whom want to *deny* that they are reducing religion to morality. The two twentieth-century authors go beyond Kant, however, by applying criteria for what we can meaningfully assert which are analogous to the criteria Kant used to determine what we can claim to know, but not what we can say or believe. I will start with the similarities, and end with the difference.

'A man is not', says Braithwaite, 'a professing Christian unless he

---

[18] *MM* 162 (486).
[19] See *Rel.* 97 (106). Philip Quinn, in response to a version of this chapter, urges that since Kant holds that all normal humans are rational agents, he ought to hold that accepting revelation is not necessary for *any* of them. My position is that for Kant no human being is purely a rational agent, and so accepting revelation may be *subjectively* necessary.

both proposes to live according to Christian moral principles, and associates his intention with thinking of Christian stories.'[20] Both Braithwaite and R. M. Hare acknowledge a power in the traditional stories, which may be confined to those brought up in the tradition but are none the less of great importance in helping those people live a moral life. The stories are the vehicle of the religion.

For all three authors, the vehicle is not merely a means for primitive peoples, to be rejected as soon as mankind has developed beyond such tutelage.[21] Kant adds in the second edition of *Religion*, 'Not that [the historical faith] is to cease (for as a vehicle it may perhaps always be useful and necessary) but that it be able to cease; whereby is indicated merely the inner stability of the pure moral faith.'[22] The historical must be eliminable in principle, in other words, just as singular terms must be eliminable in its maxim if an action is to be morally permissible. But how could the historical faith be both always necessary and yet able to cease? Perhaps the point is that those who have the belief revealed within the inner circle of reason have all that is objectively necessary, or necessary for any rational agent as such; but that if they belong to the community introduced to this faith by historical revelation, the traditional stories may continue to be subjectively necessary for them to sustain the moral life (necessary, that is, given their circumstances and limitations). It would be consistent with such a view to hold that the ideal state, symbolized by eschatological language about Christ's return, would be one in which this contingent necessity ceased.

Kant makes a similar point in *The End of All Things*. Christianity, he says, is worthy of love. He explains this by distinguishing the subjective motive for actions from the objective motive. Human nature, he says, is imperfect, in that reason's prescription is not sufficient for action. Therefore 'love as the free reception of the will of another person into one's own maxims will certainly be an indispensable complement to the imperfection of human nature'.[23] Christ, that is to say, 'brings to the hearts of his fellowmen their own

---

[20] Braithwaite (1964) 246. See also R. M. Hare (1973) 406 f.
[21] *WE* 4 (36).
[22] *Rel.* 126 n. (135 n.). But see also *Rel.* 116 (107), with the suggestion that a historical (ecclesiastical) faith might finally—however distant this future event may be—pass over into pure religious faith.   [23] *EA*, 82 (338).

well-understood wills, according to which they would act spontaneously of themselves if they proved themselves fitting'. Christianity has, Kant says, remained worthy of love in this way, and indeed the light of its worthiness is brighter 'at the time of the greatest enlightenment which ever was among men'. If Christianity remains worthy of love, and refuses the temptation to become dictatorial, Kant thinks it is destined to be the universal world religion.

Braithwaite's view is also *unlike* Kant's. Braithwaite is an empiricist about the conditions for meaningful assertability and holds that the Christian stories should not be taken as assertions of empirical fact, because they go beyond the limits of possible sense experience. In the same way R. M. Hare says that because the traditional stories can no longer be understood as assertions, the person who believes in them and tells the stories is to be construed as expressing a 'blik',[24] that is, roughly, an attitude towards the world as a whole. For Kant, by contrast, it is the test for knowability, not the test for assertability, which the stories fail to pass. Not only the stories themselves fail this test, but so too does any claim to have received them from God. 'If God actually spoke to a human being, the latter could never know that it was God who spoke to him.'[25] It is misleading to conclude from such passages that Kant is simply an agnostic about supernatural revelation. This is true only in Kant's narrow sense that the claim to have received supernatural revelation cannot be *known* to be true, in his narrow sense of 'know'. That is, as he goes on to explain, 'It is absolutely impossible for a human being to grasp the infinite *through the senses*' (emphasis added). It no more follows that we should not *believe* in supernatural revelation than that we should not *believe* in God.[26] Kant is not, in the ordinary sense, an agnostic about God. He thinks there are good moral grounds for theistic belief. Does he think there are moral grounds for believing that God has given us special or historical revelation? The answer is that a person who already understands the claims of duty will find the teachings of Christianity worthy of love, even though they are not objectively necessary. '[Christianity] is able to win to itself the hearts of men whose understanding is already illuminated by the conception of the law of their duty.'[27]

---

[24] See R. M. Hare (1955).   [25] *CF* 115 (63).
[26] *LPT* 123: 'For God's wisdom is apparent in the very fact that we do not *know* that God exists, but should *believe* that God exists.'   [27] *EA* 83 (339).

None of these philosophers, then, reduces Christianity to morality. All three want to retain the assistance of the central Christian stories in living a morally good life. Kant, unlike the other two, retains the possibility of their meaningful assertion. In the following section, I will claim that he also believed in their truth, though this claim is not essential to the argument of my book as a whole.

Kant and the Pietists

I think that Kant regarded himself as one of those people introduced to the pure religion of reason by the vehicle of special revelation. As a pure rationalist, this would mean that he could go on believing it, while still not thinking it necessary for all rational beings. I do not see any good evidence that he rejected belief in supernatural revelation, or that he did not believe in the truth of the central stories revealed in the Christian Bible. It is no doubt possible to interpret him as sceptical and silent, for prudential reasons, about his scepticism; but this is again to suppose that he is tailoring his rhetoric. It is true that he did not participate when he was Rector of the University in religious ceremonies. But that may have been because of his dislike of the pressure towards conformity imposed on the public use of reason by such ceremonies; they tend to make Christianity dictatorial.[28] The more a liberal finds the traditional beliefs of Christianity worthy of love, the more he will hate any attempt to impose Christian belief on public discussion. In other words, Kant may have refused to attend because he loved the doctrines, not because he rejected them. Under the title 'On a Pure Mysticism in Religion' he adds, in an appendix to *The Conflict of the Faculties*, the text of a letter from a young friend which describes a group who 'consider themselves religious people and indeed Christians' but who did not attend divine service. His friend adds that among them he had found Kant's teachings put into practice almost verbatim. They differed from Quakers not in their religious principles, but because they adopted no distinctive dress and paid both state and church taxes.[29] Perhaps Kant was a 'pure mystic'! In

---

[28] *WE* 5 (37). Kant did not object, however, to the state's enforcement of biblical *preaching*. See Despland (1973) 107: 'His abhorrence . . . seems to me to derive from an intense respect for the privacy of other consciences . . . and a constant desire to have his own heart protected from preying minds.'

[29] *CF* 127 (69). Kant is careful to say that he is not guaranteeing that his views coincide entirely with the author's; but his disagreements seem to have been about the nature of understanding (Ibid. 219, editor's n. 27).

any case, with Kant as with Kierkegaard we have to distinguish between their relations with the visible church and their relations to the faith. It is possible to love the faith and feel quite distant from most of the people around one who claim to share that love.

It is useful to see Kant's polemic against ecclesiastical faith against the background of the pietistic movement in which he grew up. His mother was an admirer of F. A. Schultz, who was himself a student of August Hermann Francke. Francke is credited, together with Philipp Jakob Spener, with shifting the religious emphasis of his entire age. This shift 'was from "true" doctrine to right action, from theological speculation to devotional earnestness, from ontological to psychological interest, from an intellectualized to an experiential approach to the Christian faith, from systematic theology to biblical exposition, from that which God has done in history to that which he wants to do in every human being now, from passive reliance on God's initiative to human responsibility'.[30] It is easy to trace these emphases in Kant. There is in both authors the primacy of practice over theory in the life of faith.[31] Both thinkers insist on the personal appropriation of faith, rather than doctrinal or sacramental formalism.[32] Both remove the emphasis on history, and place it instead on what God wants to do in every human heart. Both thinkers downplay the passive waiting upon God's action (even though they both admit his sovereignty) and emphasize instead the required human response.[33] Both, however, insist that human beings are

[30] Stoeffler (1973) 23.

[31] Count Zinzendorf, the pietist founder of the Herrnhut community and himself a student of Francke, insists that 'he who wishes to comprehend God with his mind, he becomes an atheist.' Zinzendorf distinguished between *Verstand* (understanding) and *Vernunft* (reason). It is *Vernunft* that has led to faithlessness, and needs to be kept in check. See Pinson (1934) 52–3.

[32] Francke has a sustained attack on those who affirm the creeds, and take the sacraments, but whose lives do not display the resurrection of Christ. 'But when we consider the lives of those who profess this truth, who received the sacramental tokens of it in their Baptism, who repeat it daily in their creeds, and meet here yearly for the solemn celebration of it, as a fundamental article of their faith: when, I say, we consider the lives of these professors, . . . where is that self-denial, that watchfulness over our own hearts and attention to the omnipresence of God, that exact justice in our dealings, that warm benevolence toward all men, and in a word, that zealous preparation against the Day of Judgement which an effectual assurance of our own resurrection would certainly oblige us to?' (Erb 1983: 128–9).

[33] Thus in 1709 Francke published a tract called 'A Short Instruction concerning the Possibility of True Conversion to God and Active Christianity, Being a Scriptural

unable to destroy by their own natural capacities the root of evil in
their souls. Both refuse to allow the existence of neutral ethical
territory; Francke holds that a line of action either serves the self and
is, therefore, sinful, or it serves God and is, therefore, acceptable in
his sight. Both have a distrust of the natural inclinations, but think
they can be trained so as to serve God either directly or indirectly.
Both have the vision of a world-wide moral and spiritual renewal.
Both think of the external church as a potential hindrance to this
renewal.[34]

Given these similarities, we should be open to the possibility that
Kant's polemic is against what he sees as a corruption of Christianity,
rather than against Christianity itself. He belongs by the strong
influence of his upbringing in a Christian movement which was
aiming at many of the same targets within Christendom that he aims
at in *Religion*. We have to avoid hearing Nietzsche in his work louder
than Luther. On the other hand Kant's position is not simply that of
a pietist. He reflects also the polemic *against* pietism found within
the Christianity of his day.[35] Francke would not object, as Kant
does, that 'the supposed favorite of heaven mounts to the point
where he fanatically imagines that he feels special works of grace
within himself (or even presumes to be confident of a fancied occult
intercourse with God').[36] The objection to 'fanaticism' and to basing

Answer to the Frequent but Meaningless Excuse that in one's own Strength one
cannot be Converted or Become more Pious.' Kant insists that we should not suppose
a guilty person can be saved merely by reaching out for supernatural assistance, while
he 'postpones resolving upon a good course of life until he is first clear of those debts'
(*Rel*. 105 (115)). Traditional Christianity has not supposed that belief in Christ as
Saviour is sufficient for salvation without belief in Christ as *Lord*. See 2 Pet. 1: 11, and
Bonhoeffer (1963) 45–7 on 'cheap grace'. Kant agrees with Francke in both admitting
the necessity for divine assistance and in refusing to use this as an excuse. Thus
Francke holds that following Christ is both necessary, and impossible by our own
powers. But he goes on to complain of those who say, 'Yes we are poor weak men who
can do nothing but sin; there is nothing in our own power able to bring forth or to
even think of good.' Francke replies, 'But listen, dear man, God the Lord will not
accept this excuse' (Erb 1983: 140–1).

[34] Francke cites Luther's picture of the visible church as a pigsty.

[35] In *CF* 99 f. (55 f), he discusses both Francke and Zinzendorf, and comments
that 'to claim that we *feel* as such the immediate influence of God is self-contradictory,
because the Idea of God lies only in reason.' He also objects to the pietists' 'fantastic
and—despite all their show of humility–proud claim to be marked out as
supernaturally favored children of heaven, even though their conduct, as far as we can
see, is not the least bit better in moral terms than that of the people they call children
of the world.'   [36] *Rel*. 189 (201).

religion on 'enthusiasm' was characteristic of orthodox Lutheran opposition to pietism throughout the eighteenth century.[37] But this opposition is also within traditional Christianity, not against it. The combination of both oppositions is distinctive of Kant, and I am not claiming that he is altogether at home within orthodoxy. We should avoid reading his polemics anachronistically, however, as evidence that he did not believe in central doctrines of Christianity, like the historical resurrection of Christ.

Kant and the Mysteries

We can now understand Kant's way of dealing with what he calls the 'mysteries' of the Christian faith against the background of his account of revelation. A mystery is, for Kant, an object of reason which can be 'known from within adequately for practical use, and yet not for theoretical use'.[38] It is an object of *reason* because it is holy, and so moral, and so an object of reason. The territory of the mysteries thus lies for him between theoretical reason and inscrutability. Theoretical reason cannot give him what he needs in order to make sense of the moral life, and the central Christian doctrines in their traditional forms are beyond his reach as a philosopher.[39] Thus the origin of the original predisposition to good is inscrutable, and so is the (subsequent) cause of the propensity to evil. Moreover, the reascent from evil to good is inscrutable, as is the divine assistance which makes this possible. Finally, it is inscrutable how the idea of an ethical commonwealth is translated into actuality. In this way, Kant concedes inscrutability at each of the four focal points of traditional Christianity: the creation, the fall, the redemption, and the second coming. He wants to try the experiment, however, of seeing whether he can use the doctrines about these focal points as *mysteries*, that is, as capable of being known from within adequately for practical use. This project is thus the second experiment, mentioned above, of translating items in the outer circle of revelation into the language of the moral concepts.

Just how he does this can be seen best in the detail of his

---

[37] See Brown (1962) 140–58. See also Stoeffler (1973) 65–6.

[38] *Rel.* 129 (137).

[39] For Kant's appeal to inscrutability, see *Rel.* 38 (43), 40–1 (45), 45 (49) and 130 (139), where his phrase is 'the abyss of a mystery'.

discussion of each mystery. The overall aim, though, is to make 'scrutable' as much as he can of the core of the traditional faith. Much of it, he thinks, cannot be rescued for *theoretical* reason at all, because of the various limitations of reason in this employment. He does, however, think it worth trying the experiment of seeing how much of this core can be put to use by *practical* reason. When he succeeds in this with some doctrine, it counts as a mystery in his terminology. He has taken one of the 'parerga' (which do not belong within the pure religion of reason, but border upon it), and found an interpretation of it which allows him to take it inside.[40]

The use of a doctrine as a mystery in this sense does not, however, exhaust the usefulness for Reason of the 'parerga'. If Kant cannot find an interpretation of the required kind, there are various different explanations. If the particular item he is examining is shown to be inconsistent with Reason (either theoretical or practical), it has to be rejected. If it is not inconsistent, we may continue to believe it (indeed we may be required to do so), even though we cannot *make use* of it with our reason in either its theoretical or its practical employment. For example, the idea of supernatural assistance (God's supplement to our moral endeavour) cannot be used, as it stands, by either theoretical or practical reason.[41] Theoretical reason is limited by the requirement that our use of the concept of cause and effect must be confined to what we can possibly *experience*, and supernatural causes do not qualify. Practical reason is limited by the requirement that it must give us maxims for actions that we can take ourselves. But it is self-contradictory to give such practical application to the idea of supernatural assistance. This is because we cannot tell ourselves to do anything which some other person (in this case a divine person) has to do. We may, however, have to believe that supernatural assistance is available, even though we cannot use this belief in theoretical or practical maxims. If we do this, we are not 'appropriating this idea as an extension of [Reason's] domain'. We are also not treating it as a mystery in Kant's sense. None the less, Reason may allow or even require the belief. 'We can admit [*einräumen*] a work of grace as something incomprehensible, but we

---

[40] *Rel.* 47 (52).
[41] I am paraphrasing here the argument at *Rel.* 48 (53). This important passage is added in the 2nd edn.

cannot adopt it into our maxims either for theoretical or for practical use.'[42]

b. KANT'S ACCOUNT OF GOD'S WORK ON OUR BEHALF

Why should we have to believe that divine assistance is available? Kant starts with what he calls 'Spener's problem' after the famous pietist. The problem is, how can we become *other* men and not merely better men (as if we were already good but only negligent about the degree of our goodness)?[43] We all of us, in Kant's view, start off with our wills subordinate to the evil maxim which tells us to put our happiness first and our duty second. We are thus corrupt in the very ground of our more specific maxims, all of which take their fundamental moral character from this one. Kant is clear that duty puts us under the good maxim, which reverses the order of incentives, telling us to follow after happiness only so long as the maxims of our actions pass the test of the categorical imperative. The revolution of the will, by which this reversal takes place, must therefore be possible. But how? How can a person, as Kant also says, become a 'new man'? He is clear that the propensity to evil is radical, and inextirpable by human powers, 'since extirpation could occur only through good maxims, and cannot take place when the ultimate subjective ground of all maxims is postulated as corrupt'.[44] What we have here is an antinomy, an apparent contradiction, which is solved by appeal to a 'higher, and for us inscrutable, assistance'.[45]

Kant gives an account of this assistance in book 2 of *Religion*, section 1. He divides the assistance into the work of God the Father, the Spirit, and the Son, and his account of the work of each person of the Trinity is motivated by trying to find an answer to a different difficulty arising within practical philosophy. There are two stages to the task of understanding Kant here. The first is to identify what version of Christian doctrine he is trying to fit within the pure religion of reason. The second is to see what the doctrine looks like after the translation, when singular reference is removed by thinking of God the Son as humanity in its moral perfection, God the Holy

---

[42] See *KU* 12 (176): 'But what cannot enter into the division of philosophy may yet enter, as a chief part, into the critique of the pure faculty of cognition in general, viz. if it contains principles which are available neither for theoretical nor for practical use.
[43] *CF* 97 (54).   [44] *Rel.* 32 (37).   [45] Ibid. 41 (45).

Spirit as the good disposition which is our comforter, and God the Father as the Idea of Holiness within us. One key to interpreting this part of *Religion* is to decide at each point whether Kant is laying out the original doctrine, or translating it, or commenting on the translation.

The account of the work of God the Father arises from the difficulty of finding a way to say together three things: first, that God is just, and not indulgent; second, that rational but finite beings never reach, at any point in their infinite progress, to holiness of the will; third, that God gives us (rational finite beings) a share in the highest good which is only justly given as a reward for holiness. Any two members of this triad can be asserted together without difficulty. For example, if God is indulgent, he can give us a reward which we do not deserve. But Kant wants to maintain all three. He accomplishes this by invoking his distinction between the world of our experience and the world of things in themselves, which we cannot experience except as they appear to us. After the birth of the new man, the heart, as it is seen by God, is 'essentially well-pleasing to him', even though all we can ever experience is gradual improvement, infinitely extended.[46] Kant is not saying here that our experience and the temporal sequence by which it is informed are illusory. He is saying, rather, that God, whose intuition is not limited by the temporal sequence or by our physical nature, can see the stable disposition of the heart.[47] He judges us as a completed whole 'through a purely intellectual intuition'. Intellectual intuition, in Kant's doctrine, is productive. God does not passively receive what he sees; he makes it. When he sees us as 'essentially well-pleasing to him', he makes us so. In Lutheran terms, justification is constitutive.[48] God is not, as it were, counting us as righteous *because of* the infinite progress towards holiness which he sees all at once. Rather, as the Lutheran Formula of Concord puts it, '[he]

---

[46] Ibid. 60–1 (67).

[47] The term 'stable' is appropriate here only negatively, in the sense of 'not susceptible to change'. Strictly, 'the subjective moral principle of the disposition, according to which alone our life must be judged, is of such a nature (being something supersensible) that its existence is not susceptible to division into periods of time, but can only be thought of as an absolute unity' (*Rel* 64 (70)). This notion of the disposition is obscure. There is a good treatment in Michalson (1990) 63–70.

[48] See Murray (1977) 207. See also Ch. 10, Sect. *b* below.

bestows and imputes to us the righteousness of the obedience of Christ; for the sake of that righteousness we are received by God into favor and accounted righteous.' When God looks at us, he sees his Son, because he is imputing to us his Son's righteousness. This doctrine would not be tolerable within the pure religion of reason, if we did not translate God the Son as humanity in its moral perfection, and God the Father as the Idea of holiness (the Idea of a morally perfect life). With these translations, we are no longer using 'God' as a term with singular reference. The doctrine becomes a way of saying that a human being comes to have a morally good disposition when the Idea of holiness counts the disposition as instantiating humanity in its moral perfection. I shall consider in the final section of this chapter what this amounts to.

The work of God the Spirit concerns primarily our present experience, while this work of God the Father concerns our fitness for future reward.[49] Kant is giving us a version of the doctrine of the assurance of salvation, a doctrine important for anyone who both wants to hope for an eternal life given to the pure in heart and holds that the condition of our own hearts is opaque to us. The difficulty that motivates Kant here is that perseverance in the life of duty requires some assurance of 'the reality and constancy of a disposition which ever progresses in goodness'. But this disposition is not something that Kant thinks I can see directly, since I do not have God's ability to see things as they are in themselves. I do have access to it, however, indirectly, by observing my actions (which are, Kant says, its appearances). I can see, if indeed I have put myself under the good maxim, a fundamental improvement in my way of life, judged by moral standards. It is true that I can only *conjecture* from this that there has been a revolution in my inner disposition; but Kant thinks it is none the less reasonable for me to hope that this is indeed the case. Kant thinks of the good disposition as a 'good spirit' presiding over us. This spirit is our Comforter, since it gives us indirectly (through our actions, which we can observe) the assurance we need of its presence within us. Kant does not want to think of this comfort as occurring through a direct communication between the disposition and our feelings. 'To trust to such feelings, supposedly of a supersensible origin, is a rather perilous undertaking; man is never more easily deceived than in what promotes his good opinion of

---

[49] The temporal distinction is emphasized in Green (1978) Ch. 4.

himself.' To rely upon this kind of direct communication from the supersensible would be, in Kant's term, fanaticism.

Kant deals with the work of God the Son in its connection primarily with the past. He describes the difficulty which motivates his account as apparently the greatest difficulty, and he deals with it at the greatest length. He starts with the premiss that the Son of God is to be understood as humanity in its complete moral perfection. This premiss means that man, so conceived, is not created but begotten (through eternity), that all things are made for him, that he is the brightness of God's glory, and that only through him can we hope for salvation. Kant ends this list, nonchalantly, with 'etc.', meaning that we are to do the same kind of translation with the rest of traditional Christian doctrine about the Son of God. The difficulty that Kant is trying to deal with in his account of the work of God the Son is that before the revolution which takes place when a person adopts the good maxim, his life has been under the evil maxim. We know this because we know that all humans are born with the propensity to evil.[50] Indeed, our guilt is infinite for what we perform under the evil maxim, because we are thereby willing to subordinate at any time the moral law to our inclinations; and it is this, rather than our particular offences, which is judged by God.[51] The problem is that when God evaluates a life, he evaluates it as a whole, by looking 'at the heart'. How, then, can we escape punishment for the state of our dispositions *before* the revolution of the will? It might be hoped that by being extra good after the revolution, we could wipe out our earlier deficiency. But Kant rules this out. We cannot accumulate a surplus of good in this way because we can at our best only do our duty. Kant here quotes from Luke 17: 10 (NIV): 'So you also, when you have done everything you were told to do, should say, "We are unworthy servants; we have only done our duty." ' We are faced, then, with another troublesome triad: First, God is just, and

---

[50] Because of the predisposition to goodness, the propensity to evil must result from a 'real and contrary determination of the will, i.e. of an opposition to the law, i.e. of an evil will (*Rel.* 18 n. (23 n.)). Kant is anxious to deny, however, that man's evil can be inferred from the *concept* of human nature. For the relation of propensity to predisposition, see Wood (1970) 214 f.

[51] *Rel.* 66 (72). Arendt (1965) says that Eichmann was not moved by monstrous intentions, ideological convictions, or insanity; rather, he had an inability to think from the point of view of others.

not indulgent; second, we humans have all lived under the evil maxim; third, God gives us a share in the highest good which is justly given only as a reward for holiness in an entire life. Kant wants to maintain all three, and he accomplishes this again by means of his distinction between the world of our experience (the phenomenal world) and the world of things in themselves (the noumenal world), which we cannot experience except as it appears to us.

In the traditional Christian account, the vicarious atonement takes place when Christ takes our sins (and God's punishment of them) upon himself on the cross. There are two objections which prevent this entering as it stands within the domain of reason. The first is the objection to historical reference, such as the place and time of the crucifixion. The second is that 'according to the justice of our human reason' there is no *transmissible liability* for evil, which could be handed over to another person like a financial indebtedness. I think Kant is wrong on this second objection, even between human beings, but I will not argue that until Chapter 10. What he does is to translate the traditional doctrine so that it refers to the Son of God as the new man, humanity in its complete moral perfection. There is, Kant points out, considerable sacrifice resulting from the revolution by which a person is reborn. There is the suffering involved in remorse, in self-discipline, and in reparation. Traditional doctrine talks of 'the death of the old man' and 'the crucifixion of the flesh'. Kant's reconstruction is as follows. The new man suffers these sacrifices *vicariously*, on behalf of the old man, who properly deserves them. It is thus, as in the traditional doctrine, the innocent who suffers.

There is a problem with understanding Kant here. He asks whether this punishment of the new man can take place after the revolution or only during the revolution itself. On the one hand, he says

after his change of heart, the penalty cannot be considered appropriate to his new quality (of a man well-pleasing to God), for he is now leading a new life and is morally another person; . . . Since the infliction of punishment can, consistently with the divine wisdom, take place *neither before nor after* the change of heart, and is yet necessary, we must think of it as carried out *during* the change of heart itself, and adapted thereto. Let us see then whether, by means of the concept of a changed moral attitude, we cannot discover in this very act of reformation such ills as the new man, whose disposition is now good, may regard as incurred by himself (in another state) and, therefore, as constituting *punishments* whereby satisfaction is rendered to divine justice.[52]

This passage might seem to settle the question, except that Kant goes on to say, 'The coming forth from the corrupted into the good disposition is, in itself, a sacrifice and an entrance upon a long train of life's ills', suggesting that the pain of the disciplining of the flesh belongs *after* the change of heart. Kant also talks about the suffering which the new man, in becoming dead to the old, must accept *throughout life*.[53] But either the new man is guilty of the wrongdoing of the old man, or he is not. If he is, then he cannot perform the vicarious sacrifice because he is no longer innocent; if he is not, then he cannot perform the sacrifice because only the guilty party can appropriately be punished, by the principle of no transmissible liability. This is why Kant suggests that the vicarious atonement cannot take place either before or after the revolution. Does the suggestion that it takes place during the change of heart help resolve this problem?

It is noteworthy that Kant says here that the ills are incurred in *this very act of reformation*. This is significant because of his distinction between revolution and reform. The distinction should be understood against the background of the theological distinction between justification and sanctification, which Kant is here translating within the pure religion of reason. What God sees (by intellectual intuition) is revolution; what we experience is reform. We cannot see by introspection into our own hearts. We experience merely the outworking of the revolution in a gradual process of reformation which, Kant thinks, we will not at any time experience as complete. The phrase 'this very act of reformation' is thus peculiar. Reformation has duration, and during the reformation what we experience is a mixture; since we are still sinners we are still capable of subordinating duty to the inclinations, even though we are moving in the direction of not being able to do so (which is holiness). There is not, strictly, an *act* of reformation at all.

This is one of several difficulties.[54] Let me start, though, by

---

[52] *Rel.* 67 (73).   [53] *Rel.* 69 (74).

[54] Kant has to explain how a noumenal self can change, if revolution is a kind of change. See Michalson (1990) 86 f and (1987) 261. See also Mulholland (1991) 86 f. One problem is to explain how the noumenal self at the time of the revolution can choose any differently from at any preceding time. Also, in what sense can the

conceding a partial success in Kant's account. There is, he sees, a problem within practical reason: how can a just God reward us for a life of virtue when we started off our lives under the dominion of the evil maxim? So Kant performs an experiment, a raiding party into the territory of the inscrutable doctrine of the atonement. He finds that there is something here that practical reason can use; there is a mystery. Suppose we understand 'Christ' to mean the 'new man', that is the person after the revolution or reascent which takes him from adherence to the evil maxim to adherence to the good maxim. We find that living the life of virtue is continually painful, partly because of the remaining pull of the old way of life and partly because of the residue of unfinished business from past failures. The new man has to suffer because of the transgressions of the old man. Kant's suggestion is that we can see these sufferings as a vicarious punishment, deserved by the old man but paid by the new.[55] Since the punishment *has* now been paid, we can (Kant suggests) solve this problem within practical reason; we can reconcile God's justice with his rewarding our endeavours at virtue. There is a kind of plausibility to this account in terms of our intuitions about our own guiltiness. It seems appropriate, and not merely arbitrary, that we should suffer the results of the flaws in our previous dispositions. To put this in more Kantian terms, it seems plausible to say that a world that contained this feature is a world that Reason might create. It also seems plausible to describe this in terms of a fundamental change within a person. A person can change from an underlying allegiance to her own interests to a recognition that she is not in herself any more valuable than anyone else. Her sufferings after this change can make some restitution for failures before the change.

---

revolution have duration (to allow for punishment) at all? One radical possibility is to suppose that Kant came in *Rel.* to accept 'the fundamental temporality of human agency' (Rossi 1991: 160) not only for individuals but for the race. But this is an interpretation of last resort, given Kant's critical thought as a whole.

[55] There is another problem about whether this punishment fits the offence, given that the offence is (in Kant's view) infinite. He says, 'the difference separating the good which we ought to effect in ourselves from the evil whence we advance is infinite' (*Rel.* 60(66)). This is the appropriateness he finds, within the limits of reason alone, of the doctrine of an immeasurable gulf between heaven and hell. But the sufferings of the repentant sinner are not easily understood as infinite. Perhaps Kant can say that there is an infinity in potential in both cases; just as the unregenerate is willing to override duty at any time (and so is infinitely guilty), so the regenerate is willing to atone at any time (and so is infinitely punished).

Kant is careful to say that this restitution is not *enough*; there must also be reparation to the people harmed, as far as this is possible. If I have cheated someone, because I gave sole or disproportionate consideration to my own interests, I must pay him back materially as far as I can.[56] But my suffering is a partial recompense. Suppose (as Kant thinks) morality requires us to believe in the existence of a system in which eternal happiness is the reward of virtue. Then we will have to deal with the problem of our *unworthiness* to be happy, and our suffering in remorse and self-discipline and awareness of loss seems a partial solution.

c. KANT'S FAILURE

The Central Problem

Overall, however, Kant's translation project, his second experiment, is a failure. It does not give him 'mysteries' which will allow him to solve the antinomy within practical reason produced by the moral gap.

In the general observation at the end of the first book of *Religion*, Kant starts from the premiss of the pure religion of reason which I will call the 'Stoic maxim', that a person herself must make or have made herself into whatever, in a moral sense, whether good or evil, she is to become.[57] A person can be morally good or evil, on this view, only if she is responsible for this character, and if it is thus imputable to her. Kant then concedes that it wholly surpasses our comprehension to understand how it is possible for a person who is not naturally good to make herself a good person.[58] This is Spener's problem, mentioned before. Kant's initial suggestion, in mitigation of this difficulty, is that the fall is just as incomprehensible as the

---

[56] How would this actually be worked out? It would help, as Cephalus remarks in Plato's *Republic* (331b), to be *rich*. I return to this question in Ch. 9.

[57] This is what Wolterstorff (1991) 48 calls 'the Stoic maxim that a person's moral worth is determined entirely by that person himself'. This is one extreme on the spectrum that has on the other extreme an insistence that humans can do nothing at all, that it is all God's work. In between are various kinds of semi-Pelagianism or synergism (in which God and humans share the work). Kant's account is odd because it starts with a notion of radical evil that leads to a Luther-like *sola gratia* at one end of the spectrum, but then *as translated* the doctrine ends up on the other end. In between, there are frequent texts which suggest that we should believe that a person must make an initial effort before meriting God's assistance; see *Rel.* 107 (117), 132 (141).   [58] *Rel.* 40 (44).

reascent; if we declare the former possible, even though we cannot understand it, we have no grounds for denying the possibility of the latter. His second suggestion is that we may have to grant that some supernatural co-operation is necessary if a person is to become good. Suppose that we grant that we *can* (because we *ought* to) live by the moral law, it does not follow that we can do this entirely by our own work. This supernatural co-operation might take a negative or a positive form, either removing obstacles to our reascent or actually giving us the strength to make it ('a positive increase of power').[59] Kant insists that there must be an initial effort by a person, in order to merit this assistance. He also insists that a seed of goodness remains in us, despite the propensity to evil, and this seed is still pure and uncorrupted, even though we are not. None the less, his view in this passage is that supernatural assistance is required for the acquisition of the morally good disposition. What, then, are we to make of the Stoic maxim? On Kant's principles it is perfectly fair for him to refuse to give an account of how supernatural assistance might work to enable a person who is not naturally good to make herself a good person. It would indeed be inconsistent for him to presume to give such an account, which would go beyond the proper limits of our understanding. But it is not legitimate, on Kant's principles, simply to say that a bad person's becoming a good person must be possible somehow or other and to leave it at that. This is not legitimate because it leaves us with an antinomy, with the apparent conclusion that the revolution of the will both is possible (because obligatory) and impossible (because the ground of our maxims is corrupt). What Kant has to do is to show that the revolution is possible, and he does this by pointing to the possibility of supernatural assistance. His failure, however, is to show how he can

---

[59] Francke illustrates this distinction between negative and positive in a key passage in his autobiography, where he describes his conversion in Lüneburg. First, 'The external hindrances were now taken away at once by the dear God. I had a room to myself in which I could not be disturbed or distracted from good thoughts by anyone, and I took my meals with Christian and godly people.' Later he knelt to pray, and '[God] immediately heard me. My doubt vanished as quickly as one turns one's hand; I was assured in my heart of the grace of God in Christ Jesus and I knew God not only as God but as my Father. All sadness and unrest of my heart were taken away at once, and I was immediately overwhelmed as with a stream of joy so that with full joy I praised and gave honor to God who had shown me such great grace. I arose a completely different person from the one who had knelt down' (Erb 1983: 105). Kant had hesitations about this kind of account; see *CF* 103 (57).

appeal to such assistance given the rest of his theory, and in particular given the Stoic maxim. He has to show, we might say, not *how* supernatural assistance is possible, but *that* he can appeal to such assistance given the rest of his theory. This is what he fails to do, as I shall try to demonstrate by presenting a dilemma.

Kant's Dilemma

The work of God the Father is said to be to see us (by intellectual intuition) already as we are not yet, and will not be completely at any time. What does this mean, however, when translated within the pure religion of reason? Here is the dilemma. Either (the first horn) Kant means to reject the notion of extra-human assistance within the pure religion of reason, or (the second horn) he means to retain it. I will pose this same dilemma in understanding Kant's treatment of the work of God the Holy Spirit and God the Son. Suppose, first, he means to reject the notion of extra-human assistance. As translated within the pure religion of reason, justification by God the Father comes to mean that our fundamental disposition (which we cannot inspect ourselves, but which is the spring of our actions) comes to be characterized by the Idea of holiness as instantiating humanity in its moral perfection; and hence we can be justly rewarded with happiness. The question that needs an answer, however, is whether this is possible given the radical evil of our nature.[60] As translated, the work of God the Father does nothing to show the possibility of the revolution of the will; it merely restates in other terms that the revolution in fact occurs. Suppose on the other hand we retain the notion of extra-human assistance. Now we have additional resources to show the possibility of the revolution of the will. But now Kant cannot continue to insist on the Stoic maxim, that becoming good people is something we have to do ourselves.

The work of God the Spirit is said to be to give us assurance of the fact that we have made this choice for the good maxim, since we cannot be sure of this by our own experience. But again there is the dilemma about extra-human assistance. Kant speaks of 'that good and pure disposition of which we are conscious (and of which we

---

[60] Francke puts the problem this way: 'In vain does the law encounter [this corruption of our nature] with her impotent discipline. In vain does she set before us her rigorous commands and prohibitions. These all serve to show us our guilt and danger, but cannot work our deliverance' (Erb 1983: 132).

may speak as a good spirit presiding over us)'. He says that this good spirit can 'create in us, though only indirectly, a confidence in its own permanence and stability, and is our Comforter (Paraclete) whenever our lapses make us apprehensive of its constancy'.[61] Again, on the first horn of the dilemma, the work of God the Spirit does nothing to show the possibility of this assurance; it merely states it in different words. The doctrine will be that the good disposition (translating 'the Holy Spirit') manifests itself indirectly in our actions. But the question which needs an answer is whether we *can* have the requisite confidence in the nature of our fundamental disposition. Suppose on the other hand we retain the notion of extra-human assistance. Now we have additional resources to see how, as Paul says and Kant quotes, 'The Spirit itself beareth witness with our spirit, that we are the children of God.'[62] But now Kant cannot object to reaching the required assurance 'fanatically, through pretended (and merely passive) inner illumination'.[63]

The work of God the Son is said to be a vicarious atonement, by which our previous unworthiness to be happy is paid for. It is clear that Kant's translation of the atonement presupposes that the revolution of the will is antecedently possible.[64] There has to be a new man in order to pay for the unworthiness of the old man. This point about the atonement is explicit in Kant's treatment of the three nested mysteries of the divine call, of atonement and of election. Suppose we admit the possibility of vicarious atonement, as this is translated within the pure religion of reason. Kant continues, '[That] already presupposes in man a disposition which is pleasing to God; yet man, by reason of his natural depravity, cannot produce this within himself through his own efforts.'[65] This is a good text for understanding the difficulty Kant is in. The work he can assign to God in three persons, as translated within the pure religion of reason, leaves still unresolved the question whether the revolution which produces a disposition pleasing to God can take place. Again we have the dilemma about extra-human assistance. Either it is just humanity that atones, in which case we are not helped to see that we

---

[61] *Rel.* 65 (71).   [62] Rom. 8: 16.   [63] *Rel.* 78 (83).
[64] See Michalson (1990) 94: 'Notice to begin with how Kant begs his own question [concerning how someone with a corrupt disposition can become good again] by simply assuming at the outset of his answer that this transformation has already occurred.'   [65] *Rel.* 134 (143).

can get into a position in which we are entitled to make vicarious atonement; or something beyond the human atones for us, in which case we cannot object to transmissible liability. The same is true with the doctrine of election. It can be understood without extra-human assistance as an expression of our ignorance of the causes why one person chooses for good and another for evil, and our need, therefore, to leave judgement to Providence. But this interpretation does not help us with our initial difficulty. To be sure, we are ignorant of the causes why some people choose for good, and others for evil. The problem, though, is to see how *any* people can choose for good, given the fact of innate (though imputable) depravity. Alternatively we can suppose that extra-human assistance is possible. Now we have additional resources to see how some humans might choose for good. But now Kant cannot continue to insist on the Stoic maxim.

The Reason for Kant's Failure

I think we should say two things about Kant's treatment of God's work in salvation. The first is that Kant several times makes reference to the need for 'heavenly influences' or 'cooperation from above', even though he denies a *use* for such thoughts in theoretical or practical reason.[66] He feels constrained to make these references because he sees the problem for morality that is caused by the bondage of the human will. The second thing to say, however, is that when Kant comes to his second experiment, the project of seeing whether the doctrines of Christianity lead back within pure rational religion, he carries this out in a way that does not make reference to extra-human assistance. This is true whether he is talking about election, call, atonement, justification, assurance, or sanctification. In his actual practice, he translates within a certain constraint, which prevents him from providing a solution to his initial problem of showing the possibility of human goodness. The constraint is that 'the calling to assistance of works of grace cannot be adopted into the maxims of reason, if she is to remain within her limits'.[67] Kant accordingly understands God the Father as the moral task presented to our practical reason, God the Son as mankind in its complete moral perfection, and God the Spirit as the moral disposition within a good person. He cannot therefore use traditional Christian

---

[66] See *Rel.* 49 (53), 83 (88), 47 (52), 108 (117).   [67] *Rel.* 48 (53).

doctrines of atonement, justification, and sanctification to present the possibility of extra-human assistance. But given the premiss about natural (though imputable) depravity, it is the possibility of extra-human assistance he needs. In our original condition before the revolution we do not have a good will, though a 'seed of goodness' survives in us. The moral task is *not* yet calling to us with sufficient power, we have *not* yet been united with our moral perfection, and the good disposition is *not* yet alive within us. If we are corrupt in the ground of our maxims, then the revolution is not possible for us on our own.

Kant shows, in the passages I have discussed, that he is aware that atonement (together with justification, and the rest of God's work in salvation) plays the role in traditional Christianity of accounting for how human beings, corrupt by nature, can become well-pleasing to God.[68] These passages also show Kant to be aware that this is a role that needs to be played. But Kant's *own* final translation of these doctrines does not allow them to play this role. His own account within the pure religion of reason assumes that we can by our own devices reach an upright disposition; but Kant is not justified, in his own terms, in supposing that we can do so. What produces this result is that Kant has subtracted from the traditional understanding of God's work in salvation any mediating role for anything that is not already human.

Kant is therefore left with an incoherence in the pure religion of reason. He is not allowed, by his own principles, to say that we are capable even of small improvements by our own efforts. This is because 'the ultimate subjective ground of all maxims is postulated as corrupt'.[69] The seed of goodness in us cannot develop (as it otherwise would) unless we can eradicate the 'foul taint in our race', which is the disposition to put our happiness first and our duty second. Kant is not saying that we adopt evil *as evil* into our maxims.[70] But he does think that we confuse the rightful order of incentives, taking the satisfaction of our inclinations as the condition of obedience to the moral law. The good seed is thus prevented from developing as it should by an innate (but imputable) tendency to get the priority of our incentives wrong. The reversal of this priority is

---

[68] He describes atonement as 'reparation for man's debt, redemption, and reconciliation with God' (*Rel.* 106 (116)).   [69] *Rel.* 32 (37).

[70] See John Silber, Intrcd. to *Rel.*, p. cxxix.

both a condition for any moral improvement, *and* something we cannot accomplish on our own.

Kant's translation within the pure religion of reason of the Christian doctrines about God's assistance fails, if I am right, to solve what he calls Spener's problem. What is Kant's own attitude to the historical faith before translation? I claimed earlier that he is a pure rationalist, and accepts the traditional doctrines about Christ's work on our behalf. He wants to insist, however, both that no particular historical faith is available for everyone, and that saving faith must be available for everyone; what follows is that saving faith must be possible without any particular historical faith.[71] Reason itself, Kant thinks, is available for all, but does not tell us anything of a man who through his holiness and merit rendered satisfaction for human sin. He is saying that historical faith is disqualified from being necessary for saving faith because of its contingent limits of influence. It can 'extend its influence no further than tidings of it can reach'.[72] If belief in the historical Christ were really necessary for saving faith, then God could not save anyone who had not heard the Christian story. This is a point accepted by one line of traditional Christianity, which promotes evangelism but does not hold God limited in his saving work by the evangelists' reach.[73] There are, however, ways for traditional Christianity to grant the point, without supposing that there is a pure religion of reason which is necessary and sufficient for saving faith. Perhaps, to give just one alternative, God confronts every individual at death with the option of believing or refusing to believe in the historical faith. Or perhaps he gives through the Holy Spirit a unique special revelation during their life on earth to those he chooses. In any case, believing that the righteous pagan can be saved does not require denying that the righteous pagan is saved through the death of Christ.

---

[71] See also *Rel.* 99 (107): 'special revelation, being historical, can never be required of everyone.'

[72] *Rel.* 94 (103). See Wood (1991) 14 f. Wood goes on to say that Kant's 'statement of his argument seems encumbered with a certain tact, or even fear, which makes him reluctant to express with perfect candor what he really thinks about this issue.' If we can avoid this sort of interpretation, we should.

[73] 'But I do say that Christ, the Second Person of the Trinity, and the Holy Spirit, the Third Person of the Trinity, in addition to the light of nature [*Rom.* 1: 20] do communicate with lost souls in ways which human intelligence cannot directly connect with the main stream of revelation in the Judeo-Christian tradition' (Buswell 1962: 353 f).

There is a distinction to be made between what is in fact necessary for salvation, and what those who are saved have to believe in order to be saved. A pure rationalist could believe that Christ's death and resurrection are necessary, but that the historical faith that God has acted in all these ways is not *itself* necessary for salvation. But *Kant's* kind of pure rationalist also believes that there is a kind of faith which is without qualification necessary for salvation, and which would be sufficient for salvation if we could hold it all by itself, namely the pure rational faith that he also calls the pure religion of reason. In his actual translation of Christian doctrine within the limits of *this* religion, Kant systematically excludes any trace of extra-human assistance. He does this by translating 'God' language into talk of 'task' or 'disposition' or 'perfection', in which no singular reference to a non-human being is required. My claim has been that this translation leaves him with an incoherence in practical reason. It is not merely that he cannot explain *how* the moral gap is bridged; such an explanation, he can legitimately claim, is beyond him. The problem is that he cannot give us a reason to suppose *that* the gap is bridgeable, given the rest of his theory.

Kant's attempts to construct an answer to the difficulties of practical reason without historical faith failed. Observing this should lead us to be sceptical about whether Kant did in fact find a pure rational religion which is all that would be necessary for saving faith, if we could hold it by itself. Perhaps there is no such pure rational religion. In this case those at home within the structure of morality Kant describes will remain with the difficulties for practical reason which he acknowledges; they will have either to revise the structure or to go outside the domain of pure reason in order to find a solution. If I was right earlier, the failure is only within the inner circle, within the pure religion of reason. Kant concedes the need to make reference to 'heavenly influences' or 'co-operation from above', even though he denies a *use* for such thoughts in the maxims of theoretical or practical reason. This means that the inner circle is *not* something we can hold on its own, because we are not purely rational beings. We could put this point in terms of the two experiments in the preface to *Religion*. The second experiment fails to give him a way out of Spener's problem, but this does not mean that the first experiment, the experiment of seeing the relation between special revelation and reason as the relation between two concentric circles, fails. It might still be the case that the contents of historical faith are consistent with reason, and the two have the sort of unity that means that if a person follows the first she will also be following the second. If so, we can insist that our ordinary notion of the moral life leaves us with a problem for which the resources of the pure religion of reason are inadequate, and we can go on to explore the outer circle, the historical faith, for additional resources. This is the third experiment I mentioned at the beginning of this chapter, and I will return to it at the end of this book.

3
MORAL FAITH

KANT uses God to bridge the moral gap in two different ways. He recognizes accordingly two kinds of moral faith, by which we believe in these works of God. I discussed the first in Chapter 2. To have moral faith of this kind is to believe that 'Heaven will find the means to make up our deficiency'. This faith is necessary because although we have a seed of goodness in us, this seed is insufficient for a morally good life, given our propensity to evil.[1] There is another kind of moral faith, which is the topic of the present chapter. It is a person's faith that her future happiness does not require her to give up the attempt to lead a morally good life. This faith bridges the moral gap also, because it makes it possible for her to combine her built-in desire for her own happiness with a commitment to morality. If she has this second kind of moral faith, does she still need the first? She does, because morality requires its followers not only to pursue both duty and happiness, but to give duty priority over their other commitments. The first kind of moral faith allows her to believe that she can give morality this kind of priority, and that this revolution of the will has actually been accomplished in her.

Kant argues that the second kind of moral faith requires us to postulate the existence of a being 'who assigns not only the proper outcome to our good conduct, but also to our good dispositions whatever reward seems adequate to His good pleasure'.[2] There are two parts to this idea. First, we believe that this being orders the world in such a way that we are often enough successful in our attempts to do good to make it worth while persevering in the attempt. Second, we believe that this being rewards our fundamental

---

[1] *LE* 91–3: 'Moral belief is belief in the actuality of virtue.'

[2] *LE* 92, where Kant distinguishes what he means by 'the proper outcome of our good conduct' from reward. For 'moral faith' see also *CF* 77 (44) and *Rel.* 126 n. (135n.). Kant has various other phrases to describe the condition of the moral person who goes beyond the empirical evidence of evil, e.g. 'a faith of pure practical reason', (*KpV* 151 (146)). For a list see Beck (1960) 255.

orientation to the good with happiness, so that we do not have to do evil in order to be happy. This is not what the protestant reformers labelled 'works righteousness', the belief that if we do good works we will go to heaven. Kant is clear that what is rewarded is the disposition of the heart, which has chosen to put obedience to God (or doing our duty as his command) above every other commitment. In the present chapter I will try to defend the argument for the postulate, though in a more modest version than Kant's own. I will try to defend the view that we need to believe in a moral order, though not Kant's view that we need to believe in a moral orderer.

Kant argued that we are required to postulate the existence of God in order to solve what he called 'the antinomy of practical reason'. An antinomy consists of the conjunction of two apparently contradictory but both plausible assertions, which I will call 'the thesis' and 'the antithesis'. In Chapter 2 I discussed a different antinomy within practical reason, where the thesis was that the moral law is binding on us and the antithesis was that this demand is too high for our natural capacities. I will take it that the thesis of our present antinomy is that the highest good is possible, and the antithesis is that it is not.[3] Roughly, the highest good is happiness proportional to virtue; the more virtue, the more happiness, and the less virtue, the less happiness.[4] For Kant, the apparent contradiction between

---

[3] This version of the antinomy is the third of the three alternatives Beck considers, adapting it from August Messer. See Beck (1960) 245–8. The first is to take the two assertions as given in Kant's statement, 'The desire for happiness must be the motive to maxims of virtue or the maxim of virtue must be the efficient cause of happiness.' The second alternative is to take the initial assertion as 'The maxim of virtue must be the efficient cause of happiness', and the second as 'The maxim of virtue is not the efficient cause of happiness.' The first alternative does not give a proper antinomy. The difference between the second and third alternatives is not very great. The most significant divergence is that the initial assertion states that the highest good is actual, on the second alternative, and merely possible, on the third alternative. My suggestion, to be argued shortly, is that Kant believes that the highest good in the less ambitious sense is actual and in the more ambitious sense is possible. It is this doctrine that is threatened by the antinomy on both second and third alternative readings. On both alternatives, the work done by the resolution is to show that the highest good is *possible*. The choice between the alternatives comes down to whether we prefer closeness to the text or appropriateness to the context. Which we choose is not going to make a significant difference to the doctrine of the passage.

[4] Kant often adds 'exactly' to proportional, e.g. *KpV* 115 (110), *KrV* A814 = B843. I will not try to defend the 'exactly', even though it is important for Kant in showing that it has to be God who does the proportioning. Reason might be prepared to grant that human life in the phenomenal world does not allow for the kind of precision that would be needed even by an omniscient and omnipotent agent who was trying to proportion happiness to virtue exactly. See Aristotle, *NE* I. 3, 1094^{b}11–12.

the thesis and the antithesis can be resolved only if we think of there being a God who does the proportioning between happiness and virtue.

I will start by discussing in more detail what the highest good is. I will distinguish a less ambitious sense, in which the highest good is the existence of a system in which virtue is rewarded by happiness, and a more ambitious sense, in which the highest good is when everyone is virtuous and everyone is happy. I will then defend the coherence of the highest good in both senses against an objection; is not morality corrupted by the proposed connection with happiness? I will argue that living morally does require believing in the possibility of the highest good in the more ambitious sense, and the actuality of the highest good in the less ambitious sense.[5] But if this is right, we have to deal with the antithesis of the antinomy, namely that the highest good is impossible. I will describe two different interpretations of what this antithesis means. Kant's solution of the antinomy is that we should believe in a causation which is in principle outside our experience, namely the action of a God who knows our hearts, supplies our deficiencies, and then rewards our virtuous dispositions with happiness. I will end by giving more detail about the version of moral faith I want to defend, namely a person's belief that her continued well-being is consistent with her trying to live a life that seems to her morally good.

a. WHAT IS THE HIGHEST GOOD?

A prior question, however, is what Kant means by 'the highest good'. If it is happiness proportional to virtue, what is virtue and what is happiness? For Kant, virtue is 'the firmly grounded disposition strictly to fulfil our duty'.[6] I described in Chapter 2 his notion of the revolution of the will by which this disposition is created. Happiness is, in Kant's technical sense, an 'idea', not the sort of thing of which we can have experience. This is because,

---

[5] It is a hard question what Kant means by saying that the highest good is *possible*. I will assume that he means real possibility, and not logical possibility. See Beck (1960) 272–3: 'To be really possible in the sense meant in the second Critique is to be (*a*) logically possible and (*b*) related necessarily to some other fact (viz. the moral) whose reality is given. Thus the fact of pure reason is the practical corrolary of intuition in converting mere concepts of the logically possible into cognitions that the logically possible is really possible.' [6] *Rel.* 19 (22).

although the elements which belong to the concept of happiness (like friendship) can be experienced, happiness itself has to encompass the whole of experience. 'For the idea of happiness an absolute whole, a maximum, of well-being is needed in my present and in every future condition.'[7] It is lives as wholes that are happy or unhappy, on this view, and not afternoons or holidays or marriages.[8] Kant wants to insist, on the other hand, that the elements which belong in the concept of happiness *can* be experienced. He does not want to confine these elements too narrowly, as he thinks the Stoics do when they say that happiness is consciousness of one's virtue.[9] The Stoic sage may be conscious of his virtue even on the rack, but such consciousness 'is the effect of a respect for something entirely different from life, in comparison and contrast with which life and its enjoyment have absolutely no worth. He yet lives only because it is his duty, not because he has the least taste for living.' Happiness, then, for Kant, is the maximum satisfaction as a whole of our needs and desires as rational but *finite* beings, creatures of need and not merely rational or moral agents.[10]

Given these definitions, I want to distinguish two interpretations of what the highest good might be. Both have justification from Kant's texts. The first is that the highest good is a world with a system in place in which virtue results (not necessarily directly) in happiness. Kant says, 'In the highest good . . . virtue and happiness are thought of as necessarily combined, so that the one cannot be assumed by a practical reason without the other belonging to it.'[11] I

---

[7] *Gl* 85 (418).

[8] See Bittner (1989) 123. Following an idea of Wittgenstein, he says, 'Happiness eludes our grasp not like something especially fleeting but like the horizon of our field of vision.' See also Aristotle, *NE* 1.10, 1100^{b}1–5.

[9] *KpV* 115 (111), and 91 (88). Kant talks about 'moral happiness' which does consist of a consciousness of progress in goodness (*Rel.* 69 n. (75 n.)), but he wants to deny that all happiness is moral happiness.

[10] There are two ways to take this account of happiness; one of them is Kant's, and the other I shall use in my notion of moral faith. For Kant, happiness is an idea of the imagination according to which everything goes according to my wish and will. But the second idea, that of a *maximum* satisfaction of my needs and desires, is consistent with most of my needs and desires being frustrated, as long as there are more of them satisfied than would be satisfied in the other ways of life open to me. I will use the notion of 'my continued well-being' to mark the limit of possible frustration foreseen by moral faith, though I do not claim to know where this limit is. In other words, moral faith requires believing that enough of my needs and desires will be satisfied to enable my continued well-being.   [11] *KpV* 117 (113).

will call this the 'less ambitious' sense. It is the predominant sense of 'highest good' in Kant's *Critique of Pure Reason*.[12]

The second thing the highest good might be is a world in which everyone is virtuous and everyone is happy. 'This highest good in the world consists in the combination of universal happiness, i.e., the greatest welfare of the rational beings in the world, with the supreme condition of their being good, namely, that they be moral in maximal conformity with the [moral] law.'[13] This adds to the less ambitious sense merely that everyone is virtuous; for if the system is in place by which virtue is rewarded, everyone's virtue will result in everyone's happiness. I will call this the 'more ambitious' sense. It is this second sense that is predominant in Kant's *Critique of Practical Reason*.

It might be the case that the highest good in the more ambitious sense is possible and the highest good in the less ambitious sense is actually in place. I think Kant thinks this is what we should believe. He is giving a reading of Romans 8: 28: 'All things work together for good to them that love God, to them who are the called according to his purpose.' What is actually in place, on this view, is the system in which virtue is rewarded; but not all actual persons engage the system to their advantage by being virtuous. I will try to show that morality requires us to believe in the possibility of the highest good in the more ambitious sense and the actuality of the highest good in the less ambitious sense.

A second question about the highest good is about when and where the rewarding of virtue is supposed to take place. I will assume that the rewards start now on earth, but continue in an afterlife.[14] This, I think, is the predominant view of the *Critique of*

---

[12] *KrV* A812 = B840.   [13] *KU* 343 (453).

[14] See R. Z. Friedman (1984). There are two other possibilities that have justification in Kant's texts. One is that the rewarding takes place in the future on earth, as in the traditional notion of a millennium, a thousand years in which Christ is fully king on earth. Luther was not in favour of this version of eschatology (see *Augsburg Confession*, art. 17). For Kant's view of the millennium, see *Rel.* 30 (34): 'a wild fantasy'. But see Reath (1988), who discusses a secular conception as the best expression of Kant's view. See also Anderson-Gold (1991) and Rossi (1991). My own view is that Kant does think we should hope for a juridico-civil commonwealth on earth, a peaceful federation of republics, though even this requires the assistance of Providence (see *PP* 100 (356)); but Kant does not think we should hope for an ethico-civil commonwealth on earth. Despland (1973) argues that Kant changed his mind on this after 1793. A second possibility is that the rewards are in the future in

Practical Reason.[15] Kant says, 'It is not impossible that the morality of intention should have a necessary relation as cause to happiness as an effect in the sensuous world; but this relation is indirect, mediated by an intelligible Author of nature.'[16] This view of the kingdom of God locates us already inside it, although we do not yet see it in its fullness. In this kingdom, all things *already* work together for good, here as well as in heaven, to those who love God; but not all those with whom we live now and here do love God and his kingdom, and so this world does not *yet* manifest the kingdom completely. The fact that this world is inhabited by many people who are not committed to moral goodness is what causes much of its misery. On this view, the highest good in the less ambitious sense starts in this life. The highest good in the more ambitious sense should be an ideal for us, something we should strive for and whose prospect should inspire us. We should expect to see partial glimpses of it, as we see cases of apparent goodness and apparent happiness allied. But its full realization on earth, though we should regard it as possible, we should not expect.

b. IS THE HIGHEST GOOD COHERENT?

The highest good in the less ambitious sense is, Kant says, a world morality would create.[17] If we were omnipotent and omniscient and

---

heaven. This is the view at e.g. *KrV* A811 = B839. Beck (1960) suggests this passage belongs in a separate remark about self-rewarding morality. Wike (1994) 155–9 gives an excellent list of the texts and concludes, 'While the texts (and reason) allow that the highest good may be possible in the world, there is evidence to suggest that the texts (and reason) generally think of it outside the world.' Auxter (1979), arguing against Silber (1962–3), distinguishes 'the otherworldly condition for which a virtuous person might hope', claims that this is the dominant conception in the dialectic of *KpV*, and concludes that it is an 'extra-moral' theological intrusion into Kant's analysis of morality.

[15] Kant talks about the bliss which is attainable only in eternity (*KpV* 133 (129)); but this is the completely proportionate well-being, which may not be attained on earth even though the *rewarding* starts on earth. I say '*starts* now on the earth' because, as Kant says, 'the purposive destination assigned to my existence by the [moral] law [is] a destination which is not restricted to the conditions and limits of this life but reaches into the infinite' (*KpV* 166 (162)). Strictly, a listing of possible meanings of the highest good should distinguish between the many different possible views that locate the rewarding not completely in one 'world' or another, but have it shared between both.   [16] *KpV* 119 (115).

[17] *KpV* 116–17 (112); see also *Rel.* 5 (5).

morally good, we would, when creating a world, create one in which morality (including our own) was rewarded by happiness (including our own, if we were the sort of beings who could be happy). But how can this be if, as Kant also says, the good will is motivated solely by respect for the moral law?[18] Why should happiness come in at all? If our end is not just virtue, but virtue conjoined with happiness, is not the purity of our respect for the moral law corrupted?

There is a standard and parallel embarrassment faced by those who want to combine Christianity with the belief (we can call it 'psychological eudaimonism') that humans always act with their own happiness in mind. This belief does not yet condemn humanity, for perhaps humans were created to pursue happiness. We are, Kant says, creatures of need, and this is not a fault in us unless we put the desire to satisfy our needs above our duty. By Christian doctrine those who follow Christ will win eternal happiness, and there is nothing wrong with desiring this happiness. But those who follow Christ merely in order to win eternal happiness will not succeed.[19] The Christian who is a psychological eudaimonist has to say that the following is a coherent frame of mind: to desire my own happiness in everything I desire, to know that following Christ will lead to my happiness, but nevertheless to follow Christ for his own sake and not merely as a means to my happiness. Certainly there are great opportunities for self-deception in such a frame of mind. I can pretend to myself that I am following him for his own sake, while actually following him merely as a means to my own happiness. But does it have to be this way? One way out of the difficulty would be to adopt a parallel doctrine to the one Kant attributes to the Stoics, to say that the Christian's happiness lies in knowing that she is following Christ. But suppose the Christian who is a psychological eudaimonist resists this doctrine, perhaps on grounds parallel to Kant's rejection of the Stoics. In that case the coherence of the position will depend on what is meant by the clause 'to desire my own happiness in everything I desire'. If this means that I desire

[18] There is a good discussion of this difficulty in R. Z. Friedman (1984).

[19] See Job 13:15: 'Though he slay me, yet will I trust in him.' Thomas à Kempis, in *The Imitation of Christ*, is severe on the desire for eternal bliss. He imagines Christ speaking to the disciple, 'For that is not pure and perfect, which is tinctured with self-seeking. Ask not for that which is delightful and profitable to thee, but for that which is acceptable to Me' (iii. ch. 49).

everything else simply as a means to my happiness, the position is incoherent; for it rules out following Christ or doing anything else for that matter for its own sake. Suppose we grant, however, that some things can be pursued (as Socrates argued for the case of justice in the *Republic*) both for their own sakes and for their beneficial consequences. Can the Christian who is a psychological eudaimonist say that following Christ is her purpose both for its own sake and for its reward? She will not, in this case, be following Christ *merely* in order to win eternal happiness.

But surely following Christ is a higher end for me if I *never* pursue it for the sake of anything else than if I *both* pursue it for itself and for something else beside it?[20] And surely following Christ ought to be the highest kind of end? Perhaps, though, this talk of ends and means is not the only way to classify how I can pursue things. Perhaps the psychological eudaimonist wants to say that I have to be able to foresee my own happiness as consistent with everything I desire, but not that I have to desire everything else at least partly as a means to my own happiness. In this case the Christian who is a psychological eudaimonist has a coherent frame of mind. She can follow Christ for his own sake and foresee her own happiness as consistent with following him.

Kant can say the same thing about following the call of duty. The maxim of every human action, he might say, will contain reference to the ingredients of the agent's own happiness (at least implicitly; perhaps the explicit reference to 'happiness' itself is very rare in practical reasoning). What is all-important to Kantian morality, however, is whether the incentive provided by the agent's happiness is subordinate to the incentive provided by the moral law, or vice versa.[21] If the agent's happiness is the sole end, or even if everything else in the maxim is partly desired as a means to the agent's happiness, then the agent has reversed the proper (the moral) order of incentives. But it does not follow that an agent has reversed the proper order if she feels the call of duty for its own sake, and also feels the need to be able to foresee her own happiness as consistent with following that call. As before, there is a good opportunity here

---

[20] I am following here Aristotle's language about the most complete good, at *NE* i. 7, 1097^{a}30f.
[21] *Rel.* 31 (36). See also above, Ch. 1 n. 27. Morality can be demanding, in Samuel Scheffler's sense, without being stringent in his sense.

for self-deception. Kant indeed holds that the fundamental maxims of our actions are opaque to us. We may often think that we are merely foreseeing happiness as consistent with the pursuit of virtue, when in fact we are pursuing virtue at least partly as a means to happiness. This is why, on Kant's terms, we should be more ready to believe in the moral worth of an action if we can detect no inclination towards it. But the fact that we are often deceived does not show that the frame of mind of a person pursuing both virtue and happiness is incoherent. Such a person will pursue only virtue as good without qualification, but will not therefore be required to be blind to the good she foresees as consistent with that virtue.

The difficulty is not yet solved, however. For if the agent is *constrained* by the need to be able to foresee her own happiness as consistent with following the call of duty, then surely she is making her happiness the *condition* of her following the moral law? If so, she is again reversing the proper order of incentives. But what kind of constraint will this be? Here, I think, we can appeal to Kant's notion that the inclinations can be trained so as to be progressively consistent with the moral law.[22] This is not the doctrine, which he attributes to the Stoics, that our happiness comes to consist solely in knowing that we are doing our duty, for we will continue to have desires for other things (chocolate éclairs, good reviews for the books we write) and it is quite proper that we should. But once a person starts on the endless progress towards holiness of the will, she can expect fewer of these desires to be constrained by her respect for the moral law, and her urge to follow this law to be less constrained by her other desires. This does not necessarily mean she will feel less *sense* of constraint. Kant is aware of the sense of battle which accompanies sanctification; the greatest saints feel the battle most keenly. But there is none the less progress, in that what was once a temptation, and hence a cause of battle, is so no longer. Gradually the whole package of what she wants for herself and for others becomes more unified, though she may be increasingly aware of some stubborn inclinations which resist the process. But now if we take someone fairly advanced in this discipline, she can say that she is still a person who looks forward to her own happiness, but that fewer and fewer of the elements which belong to the concept of that happiness are in tension with her duty, as she sees it.

---

[22] See *Ed.* 2–4 (441–2), 86–7 (482).

For this kind of training to take place, however, at least two things have to happen. The first is that she come to desire overwhelmingly to lead a morally good life.[23] I have discussed some of the difficulties in seeing how this can happen in Chapter 2. When this happens, there will still be two principles at war in her, though in Kant's doctrine the good will finally win. She will still feel the tug of the way of life which puts her happiness first and her duty second; but now she will have the fundamental commitment to a goal which, by its very nature, excludes partiality towards herself. In order for this to happen, she has to come to believe something else, that if she organizes her life around the moral goal, this is consistent with her happiness. This belief is the second kind of moral faith which I distinguished at the beginning of this chapter. The function of this belief is to give the victory in the internal battle to her moral commitment, though this will not be the end of the war. The victory is, so to speak, prospective, looking forward to a unification of the package of what she wants for herself and for others which is not yet in place. Is the victory Pyrrhic? Does this moral faith concede so much to the need to be able to foresee her own happiness that she cannot any longer be wholeheartedly committed to the moral goal? I think this would be so only if she viewed this moral faith as the justification for her commitment to morality, or if she saw her commitment even partly as a means towards her happiness. But neither of these is the case. It is true that if she had what Kant calls a 'holy will', she would not need this moral faith. To this extent her commitment to morality is less pure than that of a rational being who is not also, as Kant says, a 'dependent being' or a 'creature of need'. But this limitation need not prevent her from being genuinely committed to the moral life.

c. THE IDEA OF SELF-REWARDING MORALITY

I will start with the first part of the thesis of the antinomy, namely the assumption that the highest good in the more ambitious sense is possible. I will argue that this is implied by other assumptions about

---

[23] I am using the term 'desire' as a convenient generic term, but this ignores various ways in which the term is in ordinary use more specific. For a good summary of the ways in which desiring something is, in ordinary use, different from merely wanting it, see Bittner (1989) 100.

the moral good (i.e. what the moral law permits) which an agent
must make if she is to persevere in the moral life. I am not claiming
here that these other assumptions are true, but that moral agents, in
as far as they are moral, have to make them. I am also not saying that
these assumptions have to be explicit. They are required, rather, for
anyone who has thought through the conditions that make the moral
life possible.[24] Finally, I am not claiming to give a complete list of
such assumptions. My argument is that these assumptions, taken
together, imply that the highest good in the more ambitious sense is
possible. I think that they are indeed assumptions necessary for a
fully reflective living of the moral life, and therefore that a fully
reflective living of the moral life requires believing in the possibility
of the highest good in the more ambitious sense.

The first of these assumptions (1) is that the moral good aimed at
by action is possible.[25] If, for example, the good at which I am
aiming is the happiness of others, I must assume that the happiness
of others is possible. This was Mill's concession to Carlyle in the
second chapter of *Utilitarianism*: 'If [we know] no happiness is to be
had at all by human beings, the attainment of it cannot be the end of
morality or of any rational conduct.' There might be, for instance,
the equivalent for our moral life of the evil genius which Descartes
imagines in order to make vivid the predicament of our knowledge.[26]
If the world (under the ministrations of this genius) were such that
whenever I tried to do good, it resulted in harm, I would stop trying
to do good.

The second assumption (2) adds to the first that the moral good I
am aiming at is a possible result of my attempt to produce it.[27] What
is necessary is not merely that good happen in a non-random way
after my efforts, but that it result *from* my efforts. Suppose that
whenever I tried to do good, good happened, but from causes totally
unrelated to my efforts. Suppose, for example, that the good would

[24] See *L* 76: 'If we merely look to action, we do not need this belief. If, however,
we want to expand ourselves through action to the possession of the end thereby
possible, we must adopt this end as being possible throughout.'

[25] There is a very short form of the argument which goes like this. The highest
good is the moral good aimed at by moral action. The moral good aimed at by moral
action must be believed possible by the moral agent. Therefore the moral agent must
believe the highest good is possible. I want to construct an argument, however, which
does not assume this first premiss.

[26] For a functional substitute for the evil genius, see Frankfurt (1988a) 7.

[27] There must be at least a non-random connection between my efforts and my
success (where an inverse relation would be non-random, but would not count).

have happened anyway, whether I had made the efforts or not. This would be sufficient to remove the *point* of the efforts. It is not clear how tight the connection between my efforts and my success has to be; but it must be true at least that I do not succeed just as much when I do not try as when I do.

The third assumption (3) adds to the second that it is possible for me to *know* that the moral good I am aiming at is produced, when it is produced, by the means I have planned. To see the need for this, consider the case where my efforts are non-randomly connected with the production of good, but I totally misidentify what that good is going to be. I go to the hospital to cheer up my neighbour who is recovering from an operation. I find he has checked out of the hospital, and on the way back home I run over his dog, which has just been bitten by a rabid badger. If this is the way in which my actions are usually connected with the good, I will stop planning what to do. The good has resulted from my actions; but I will conclude that there is some invisible hand guiding me into these right paths, and there is no point in thinking ahead about what those paths might be. Deliberation in a broad sense, the selecting of ends and means, is an essential part of the moral life.

The fourth assumption (4) is that I myself can will what is morally good. I have to be either naturally fitted to what morality requires, or at least trainable or changeable so that I can tolerate it. I discussed this kind of training in Section *b*. If it is not the case that I can will the good, then it is not the case that I ought to will it; willing the good would be out of my range, and I should keep to some lesser goal such as enlightened self-interest. The difficulty of making this fourth assumption, if we grant that humans start with the propensity to evil, was the topic of Chapter 2. I have to be able to will the good not just once or twice, but regularly. For Kant, the proper objects of moral evaluation are not so much actions, or even the principles that prescribe actions, but rather the fundamental choices that shape a life either around respect for the moral law or around the agent's own happiness.[28] For the purposes of the present argument, the

[28] Kant has reasons for thinking that it is the shape of a whole life that is in question. These reasons are well explored in Mulholland (1991) 91-5. For Kant, moral choice is timeless; but I will not here discuss the difficulties of this view. See also Feldman (1986) 36 f. for a defence of the view that what we should be evaluating is not just individual acts or even individual lives, but the whole worlds accessible to us at a time (where these worlds include the subsequent histories of our own lives).

claim that a whole life is shaped is unnecessarily strong.[29] But Kant is right, I think, to point to the connection between moral choice and moral character. A single action is not enough to show a character, and a character is (on a standard interpretation) a disposition settled for a long period. We assume, then, that a virtuous disposition is sustainable once it is acquired, though it would take more argument to show that we assume it sustainable for a whole lifetime.

Next, there are assumptions about (roughly) everybody else. There is the assumption (5) that the moral good they aim at is possible. This is the social analogue of (1). Added to this is the assumption (6) that the moral good they are aiming at is a possible result of their efforts to produce it. This is the social analogue of (2). There is also the assumption (7) that it is possible for them to know that the moral good they are aiming at has been produced by the means they have planned. This is the social analogue of (3). Finally there is the assumption (8) that it is possible for them to will what is morally good. This is the social analogue of (4).

There are three routes by which to get to these social analogues. The first route is that at least in the case of the first three assumptions what makes them reasonable for my own life also makes them reasonable for me to assume about (roughly) everyone else. The assumptions about myself are reasonable not because of anything idiosyncratic, but because of the way I assume the world is and the humans in it. The fifth assumption is not that all agents can get what they want, but that if what they want is morally permitted, it is not ruled out by the way the world is. Morality permits us to pursue only what all moral agents in the kingdom of ends could agree to. So it is not an objection to this assumption that people want manifestly incompatible things. If there were, contrary to the first assumption, a malicious demon, it would make not merely my efforts but any moral efforts by anybody pointless. But if I am to persevere in the moral life, I cannot believe in such a demon.

If I assume (2) that the world allows me to achieve the moral good through my efforts, this may be because I am, for example, rich. But if this is what *any* moral agent has to assume, it must be because of the way humans in general are, and the world in which they live. An

---

[29] We do not need to know for the purposes of this argument whether e.g. 'there are techniques of suspended torture and psychological persuasion capable of breaking any mind.' See Farrer (1961) 152–5.

objection here might be that the effectiveness of a moral agent (the extent to which she achieves the moral good she aims at) depends to a great extent on the virtue of other agents. There may not be any reasonable assumption about the effectiveness of (roughly) everyone else without adding information about the assistance available. But if assumption (8) is required, that it is possible for (roughly) everyone else to be virtuous, then we can say that given the realization of this possibility, the objection to assumption (6) would fail. In the case of assumption (7), if I can know that it is through my efforts that the good is achieved, this is because of what human beings in general can know.

In the case of assumption (8), however, the inference is uncertain from the possibility of my virtue to the possibility of (roughly) everyone's virtue. This is a hard question, depending on what sorts of obstacles to virtue I am supposing have to be and can be removed. If the problem is something like radical evil, as in Kant, this is something species-wide. But suppose the obstacles are social or societal, might they be removable in some social conditions and not removable in others? If so, I might make the assumption that they are removable in my situation but not in that of many other people.

This difficulty can be finessed by considering the second route. Morality requires equal respect, and equal respect requires the assumption that all other human beings are capable of willing the good.[30] This view of morality is inconsistent with Aristotle's argument for the view that there are natural slaves, because they are not capable of virtue.[31] There will be hard cases like irreversible brain damage. But I think Kant is right about equal respect. The hard cases show not that equal respect is independent of assuming the capacity for virtue, but that we are not confident that *all* humans deserve equal respect. Or perhaps there is a kind of equal respect which does not require us to believe that the person we respect has the capacity for virtue; but morality requires more than *this* kind of respect. The capacity of others for virtue requires the same assumptions for others as were required for the possibility of my virtue, namely assumptions (1) to (4).

The third route relies on the social conditions for virtue. This is not a familiar part of Kant's view; he is often construed as an individualist about virtue. But Kant argues that human morality has

---

[30] Cf. *Gl* 98–9 (431).   [31] *Politics* 1.5, 1254^{a}21–4.

particular difficulties to encounter that are specific to human beings
and not, for example, angels.[32] He says, 'Envy, the lust for power,
greed, and the malignant inclinations bound up with these, beseige
his nature, contented within itself, *as soon as he is among men*.'[33] In a
way reminiscent of Rousseau, it is what we are to each other which
brings on the evil inclinations. Again, 'Despite the good will of each
individual, yet, because they lack a principle which unites them,
they recede, through their dissensions, from the common goal of
goodness and, just as though they were instruments of evil, expose
one another to the risk of falling once again under the sovereignty of
the evil principle.'[34] In these passages, Kant is led towards the view
that because of the social obstacles to virtue, there are social
conditions for the attainment and maintenance of virtue.[35] He
translates within the domain of practical reason the theological
terminology that salvation belongs inside the church. Kant uses the
language of the invisible church (a mere idea of the union of all well-
disposed people), the visible church (the actual union into a whole
which harmonizes with that ideal), and the congregation (a separate
society under law).[36] The church is a body, the members of which
depend on each other like the members of a body. Using this
language, we might say that the possibility of individual virtue
requires the possibility of a virtue-building and virtue-sustaining
congregation. Congregations, moreover, are not isolated from each
other. Kant predicted increasing interdependence through trade and
communication. We cannot live virtuously, for example, if our
society is greedy, and causes envy and resentment to other less
wealthy societies. As the world gets more and more interconnected,
the virtues of one congregation will depend more and more on the
virtues of all the others.

---

[32] See Smith (1984) 172.   [33] *Rel*. 85 (93–4).

[34] *Rel*. 88–9 (97). This is puzzling because Kant also has a rendering of the
doctrine of the perseverance of the saints, according to which the new disposition of
the heart after the revolution of the will is unchangeable.

[35] For Kant, pointing to the social conditions for virtue does not eliminate the need
for God's assistance. For Kant does not see how we can get ourselves into 'a system of
well-disposed men, in which and through whose unity alone the highest moral good
can come about' (*Rel*. 89 (97)). There is a problem, however, with saying that there
are social conditions for individual virtue, if this means that an individual cannot be
virtuous without the conditions being met. The implication would be that individuals
who have grown up in an environment where these conditions are not met could not
be held accountable, by God or anyone else, for their moral failures.

[36] *Rel*. 92 (101).

From assumptions (1) to (8) I think it is possible to derive the assumption (9) of the possibility of what Kant calls 'the Idea of self-rewarding morality'. This is the system in which morality does its own rewarding. Kant describes it this way: 'Freedom, partly inspired and partly restricted by moral laws, would itself be the cause of general happiness, since rational beings, under the guidance of such principles, would themselves be the authors both of their own enduring well-being and that of others.'[37] Suppose it is true that there is a causal connection of the right kind (falling under assumptions (1) to (3)) between my aiming at the good of others (roughly, my virtue) and my achieving the good of the others I plan to help (roughly, their happiness). This does not yet show that there is any connection between my virtue and *my* happiness.[38] But now suppose that my virtue requires me to acknowledge the possibility of (roughly) everyone's virtue. Suppose, finally, that there is a causal connection of the right kind (falling under assumptions (5) to (7)) between peoples' virtue and their bringing about by their actions the good of the others they plan to help. Given all these suppositions, given (that is to say) that all these possibilities are actualized, would we not be justified in supposing also that in the world we have together planned and brought about roughly everyone is happy? A world in which moral evil was largely absent, given the ubiquity of virtue, might still contain natural evil (such as hurricanes); but natural evil without moral evil (such as shoddy construction) would not be sufficient in most cases to destroy happiness.

There is an apparent problem here. What Kant needs is not merely that the virtuous are happy, but that only the virtuous are happy. As I have constructed the argument so far, there is the appearance of something like a contradiction: the virtuous should surely try to make all people happy, not merely the other virtuous; but then (if they are successful), happiness will be distributed to everybody, including the wicked. The solution is that what Kant calls 'the Idea of self-rewarding morality', which is as far as we have got in this argument, 'rests on the condition that *everyone* does what he ought'.[39] This is the condition whose possibility is stated in assumption (8). Self-rewarding morality is a system in which the

---

[37] *KrV* A809 = B837.
[38] Kant is not here making the mistake that Moore (1903) 104 attributes to Mill.
[39] *KrV* A810 = B838.

morality of everybody results in everybody's happiness. As such a *system*, it is also an example of the highest good in the less ambitious sense, but it is a system put into use by (roughly) everybody. In Section *d* I shall draw a distinction between this kind of system and the kind of system whose actuality Kant thinks we should believe in.

The highest good in the more ambitious sense is not merely a possibility but an ideal, though its possibility is all this section has argued for. Those who have been inspired by the vision of the kingdom of God have been moved not merely by the desire that everyone be happy, but by the thought of a world (in the words of Psalm 85) in which righteousness and peace have kissed each other. In such a world people would not merely be happy in the sense that they would have what they wanted, but what they wanted would be consistent with the moral law. Such a world would be full of morally good people who were happy.

d. THE HIGHEST GOOD IN THE LESS AMBITIOUS SENSE

In this section, I want to move to the second part of the thesis of the antinomy, namely the assumption that the highest good in the less ambitious sense is actual. This assumption will not rely on the Idea of self-rewarding morality, which was the destination of Section *c*. The difference is that the new assumption is that the virtue of a person results in the happiness of *that person*. What we got in the previous section was an indirect connection through the virtue of others. The argument was that my virtue requires me to assume the possible virtue of (roughly) all rational agents, and the possible success of their virtuous intentions; if these possibilities were to be realized, my happiness would then result indirectly from their success. This is not yet what Kant thinks morality requires us to believe actual. Believing in the actuality of the highest good in the less ambitious sense requires me to believe that my virtue will be rewarded *whether (roughly) everyone else is virtuous or not*. It is true that Kant likewise argues for an indirect connection between virtue and happiness, one mediated not by the virtue of other humans but by the will of a being who both desires my good and is sovereign over the world. His idea is that if my desires are consistent with the holy will of the Author of Nature, who is sufficient (as I am not) to succeed in whatever he intends, then what happens under his Providence will be consistent with my desires and therefore with my happiness. But this kind of indirect connection does not require the virtue of (roughly) all the other human beings who affect my life. This is not to deny the influence that other people have over my happiness. But I will be placing my confidence not directly in them but in Providence to bring it about that in the long run what is needful for my happiness will be provided. I will return to this point at the end of this chapter.

I want to claim that we do ordinarily think that we will be happiest if we try to be moral; or that we at least think that being moral has a higher chance than any other strategy. That is why we teach our children to be moral, or at least we try to. We would not try to teach this to them if we did not believe it would make them happy, because we *care* about their happiness. Or perhaps we might choose for them unhappy virtue over happy vice, because we care even more that they not be vicious; but if we did not believe that virtue was consistent with their happiness, we would choose for them morally slothful happiness over virtuous unhappiness. On the other hand, we do not think that this connection between virtue and happiness requires mediation by the virtue of (roughly) all rational agents. This is because we are not confident that (roughly) all rational agents are virtuous in the required way. We try to teach our children to be moral even though we do not think that they will be living in a society where all or even most of their fellows will be virtuous. The Idea of self-rewarding morality cannot be, therefore, what we are assuming to be the case. We need the assumption that the agent's virtue is consistent with her happiness, whether (roughly) all other rational agents are virtuous or not.

Perhaps the system we are assuming to be actual is that enough other people around the agent are sufficiently virtuous so that the agent's virtue will be consistent with her happiness? This assumption might be expressed in terms of comparative likelihood, rather than guaranteed result: there is enough moral goodness around so that a person probably does not have to do what is morally wrong in order to be happy. The assumption would have to be conjoined with an assumption about natural evil, that its effects could usually be sufficiently mitigated by the efforts of other people. This line of thought brings the highest good in the less ambitious sense and the Idea of self-rewarding morality together, by assuming that the system by which an agent's virtue is rewarded is the presence in the world of enough other virtuous people. The highest good in the less ambitious sense does not, however, need this assumption; it needs only the existence of a system which operates so as to make an agent's virtue consistent with her happiness. My claim in the previous paragraph was that we *do* need the assumption that there exists such a system if we are going to persevere in morality, but we do *not* need to assume that the system in question is the Idea of self-rewarding morality. I think there is very widespread ambivalence about the extent to which the people who affect our lives are (and not merely could be) morally good people. There is widespread cynicism, gloom about the decline of virtue, and distrust of other people. But the belief that being morally good is consistent with long-term happiness has been held by people who lived in societies in which they were persecuted and exploited. It has also existed in societies undergoing radical change, where no one could have much sense of what sort of social conditions would prevail. The belief does not depend on a previous belief that most people who affect our lives are morally good.

One premiss in Kant's own argument is what I called earlier 'psychological eudaimonism', the view that humans always act with their own happiness in mind. He says in theorem 2 of the *Critique of Practical Reason*, 'All material practical principles are, as such, of one and the same kind and belong under the general principle of self-love or one's own happiness.'[40] This does not necessarily mean that all material practical principles are selfish. Kant sometimes allows that we have an 'instinct to benevolence'.[41] Suppose that happiness is, as he says, when everything goes according to my wish and will, this allows for some of my wishings and willings to be for the well-being of others. Their well-being will then be required for my happiness without being desired *as* necessary for my happiness. Whatever else I desire, however, as a human being I am bound to desire my own happiness, and (on the interpretation in Section *b* of this chapter) I will need to be able to foresee this happiness as consistent with my basic choices. I have to be able to believe, as R. M. Hare says, 'in my own continued well-being (in some sense of that word that I may not now fully understand) if I continue to do what is right according to my

---

[40] *KpV* 20 (22). At *Gl* 83 (415), Kant says that we can assume with certainty that all rational dependent beings have by a natural necessity the purpose of their own happiness.   [41] *LE* 194.

lights'.[42] He continues that I have to be able to believe 'in the general likelihood of people like Hitler coming to a bad end'. This adds the constraint that takes us to a Leibnizian kingdom of grace; lack of virtue is proportionate to lack of happiness. He concludes, 'Perhaps a formulation less inadequate than most is to be found in the Psalms: "The earth is weak and all the inhabiters thereof; I bear up the pillars of it." '[43]

As a human moral agent I have to believe that my continued well-being is consistent with my living a moral life as best I can. This allows me to suppose that how I conceive my well-being will change as I succeed in this attempt. But there will be limits to such change that come from my being human. Humans are, as Kant says, creatures of need. However virtuous we are, we do not have what he calls 'holy wills', and we cannot avoid the quest for happiness, or having some elements in that happiness remain good in our eyes independently of the demands of duty. If we are to endorse wholeheartedly the long-term shape of our lives, we have to see this shape as consistent with our own happiness. But the self-rewarding morality of Section *c* is insufficient. In the fully realized kingdom of God a self-rewarding morality might be enough. But in a world in which there are many rational agents who have willed not to live by the moral law, I cannot rely on the virtue of others to get me from my virtue to my happiness. The result is that I have to believe that there is in operation a system in which my virtue is rewarded without it.

e. THE ANTITHESIS

I have interpreted the thesis of the antinomy to be that the highest good in the more ambitious sense is possible, and that the highest good in the less ambitious sense is actual. The antithesis is, if I am right, that the two parts of this claim are false. Kant is not clear whether the antithesis is 'empirical' (something we are supposed to

---

[42] R. M. Hare (1955). I am quoting here from R. M. Hare's response to Antony Flew's retelling of John Wisdom's story of the Invisible Gardener.

[43] *Ps.* 75: 4. In the more extended Nathaniel Taylor lectures at Yale in 1968, R. M. Hare endorses that part of what is called Christian belief which is the belief in Providence, that our moral policies are not futile, and that it is not pointless to pursue them. See R. M. Hare (1973).

know from experience), or whether it is what he calls 'transcendental'. Transcendental knowledge is knowledge of the very preconditions of experience, and hence is not known from experience (since experience already presupposes these preconditions).[44]

To support the first interpretation, that we know the antithesis from experience, there is a passage in the *Critique of Judgement* where Kant uses Spinoza as an example of a righteous man who does not believe in God or the immortality of the soul. According to Kant, Spinoza will constantly experience the lack of fit between what virtuous people deserve in the way of happiness and what they in fact get, namely 'all the evils of want, disease, and untimely death, just like the beasts of the earth'.[45] One commentator says, 'It is discovered at once that . . . the world seems not to reflect in any way the good man's striving to bring about goodness in it.'[46] This looks like empirical evidence that the highest good in the less ambitious sense is not actual. It is also evidence that the highest good in the more ambitious sense is highly improbable.

The second interpretation is that the lack of fit between virtue and happiness is not something we *could* confirm or disconfirm by experience.[47] To put it more vividly, even if there were in experience a complete fit between virtue and happiness, and none of the wicked could be seen to prosper, this would not blunt the attack in the antithesis. This is because, on the second interpretation of the antithesis, it is an a priori claim, known on the basis of knowledge of the preconditions of experience. Belief in the highest good would require, on this interpretation, that the will knew the laws of nature and could manipulate them for its purposes (thus producing our happiness if we were virtuous); then we could talk about happiness

[44] Some philosophers have argued that no transcendental claims make sense. This is not an issue I can engage here. The theory of meaning on which this argument against Kant depends no longer commands consensus. It needs to be shown that it does not make *sense* to postulate that something is the case, namely God's rewarding of virtue, which we cannot know through experience. This is different from claiming merely that we do not need or should reject such a postulate.

[45] *KU* 342 (452). This passage is puzzling. R. Z. Friedman says, (1984) 333, 'What Kant does argue is at best inconsistent and at worst ill-conceived and contradictory.' I think Kant is claiming that the position of Spinoza, the moral man without faith, is rationally incoherent, but psychologically tenable as long as the full consequences of the position have not been displayed.   [46] Wood (1970) 158–9.

[47] See Wood (1978) 22.

necessarily correlated with virtue. According to the antithesis, however, the truth is the opposite: we know that the will does not have this power or this knowledge, and hence that the highest good is impossible.

The second interpretation fits better with Kant's solution to the antinomy, which he explicitly makes parallel to his solution of the third antinomy of pure reason in the *Critique of Pure Reason*. In both cases he solves the antinomy by showing that the antithesis claims to know that there could not be a necessary connection, whereas in fact we do not know this; given all that we know on the basis of the preconditions of human experience, God could bring about the required sort of connection. The transcendental interpretation of the antithesis in the antinomy of practical reason makes the antithesis into the claim that there could not be the required kind of connection between virtue and happiness. This is the kind of claim that the parallel with the *Critique of Pure Reason* requires.

Kant does not distinguish between these two interpretations. He ought to do so, because in his view an empirical claim cannot be a transcendental claim, or vice versa, though this might not prevent these two different kinds of claim being made in the same words. Perhaps we should say that there are two arguments to be found here, each of them plausible. The empirical version is more vivid, relying on our experience of evil in the world. The transcendental version fits more neatly with Kant's method elsewhere.

Both of these arguments have a great deal of plausibility. The world does contain many people who have clearly tried to lead good lives, but have been overwhelmed with natural and moral evil. And we know that we do not have the sort of knowledge or control of the world which would enable us to bring about the proportioning of happiness and virtue. A plausible case can be made that the ancient Greek picture of tragedy and the vulnerability of human life to fortune is closer to our actual experience of the human situation than the picture of moral faith I have been presenting. Thus it is said of Sophocles and Thucydides that they represent 'human beings as dealing sensibly, foolishly, sometimes catastrophically, sometimes nobly, with a world that is only partially intelligible to human agency and in itself is not necessarily well adjusted to ethical aspirations'.[48]

---

[48] See Williams (1994) 163–4 and Nussbaum (1986) 318 f.

f. MORAL FAITH

Kant's solution to the antinomy is to to bring in the possibility that the relation between virtue and happiness is 'mediated by an intelligible Author of nature'. The recognition of this possibility allows him to deny the claim that we know that the highest good is impossible. The antithesis goes beyond the limits of human knowledge. We can recognize this sense of human limits in Greek tragedy. It may be true that in Sophocles' tragedies Oedipus and Ajax are made to suffer by an agency which they do not understand. But it would be anachronistic to see this as a proto-Nietzschean announcement that 'God is dead.' Sophocles was notorious in Athens for his piety; he was entrusted with the sacred snake of Asclepius during the great plague. Our failures to understand what is happening to us do not license the conclusion that the impact of chance is uncontrollable. Kant's argument is for a Sophoclean humility in what we claim to know. He rejects the inference from our limitations to the denial of a moral order. He is limiting knowledge in order to make room for faith. But given the moral need to believe in the highest good, the structure of his conclusion is like the conclusion of the ontological argument, that if God's existence is possible then it is necessary.[49] In the present case, the necessity is moral. If it is possible that we are in the hands of Providence, the argument is that we are morally required to believe that we are.

Kant claims that postulating the existence of a good, just God is the *only* way to solve the antinomy. A defence of this would require looking at other possible solutions, to see if they can be rejected. I have not done this, and will not do it. What I do think I have done is, first, to defend the claim that there is an antinomy here that requires solution. If I am right, and if Kant's proposal does solve it, then (if we do not want to postulate the existence of God) we will have to show either that his postulate is unacceptable on grounds independent of the antinomy, or that there is a solution of the antinomy that does not require the postulate. Second, I think I have given an argument for the conclusion that perseverance in the moral life requires what I have called, in Kant's phrase, 'moral faith'. This moral faith can be defined as the trust that things are so ordered that my future well-being is consistent with my trying to live a life that is morally good.

[49] Malcolm (1965) 145.

To put this the other way round, it is the trust that I do not have to do what is immoral in order to enjoy future well-being. Moral faith then requires to this extent a belief in a moral order. It does not require, at least not without additional argument, belief in a moral orderer.[50] But believing in a moral orderer is one way to accomplish belief in a moral order. A moral argument for the existence of God would have to examine whether there are other ways to accomplish the same result.[51]

The definition is vague in several ways. How confident a belief is required by moral faith, and trust about how much of the future, and about how large a part of the agent's total well-being? Before coming to these questions, however, it will be useful to relate the notion of moral faith to the traditional problem of evil. This problem is usually presented as a challenge to the belief in a moral orderer of the universe; but if the challenge works, it works also against belief in a moral order. Ivan Karamazov's speech to Alyosha in Dostoevsky's *The Brothers Karamazov* sometimes appears in philosophy textbooks as a classic presentation of the problem. Evil is made there so vivid that it is hard to read the passage without agreeing with Ivan's conclusion, 'It's not that I don't accept God, Alyosha, I just most respectfully return him the ticket.'[52] But the danger of taking a passage like this out of a novel, in order to make a philosophical point, is that the context of the character's life is lost. What is Dostoevsky doing in giving these words to *Ivan*, and making *Alyosha* their recipient? We need to look at what happens to the two characters in the rest of the novel. What happens to Ivan is that the tension between the moral demand, which he goes on feeling, and his own capacity and experience of life grows so extreme that he goes mad. He imagines the devil has taken to visiting him, a devil who can be construed as part of Ivan himself. The novel ends with Alyosha repeating his creed to a group of adoring children. All this is not to deny that Ivan's initial speech is a powerful presentation of a point of view. Dostoevsky, like Shakespeare, can make one seem to

---

[50] Kant's argument is that we need to 'believe that the cause of the world operates also with *moral* wisdom toward the highest good', and has to be therefore personal. See *L* 75.

[51] There is interesting empirical evidence that conservative religious people in America tend to have a more robust belief in a moral order, by their definition of morality, than the American population at large. See Groen-Colyn (1982).

[52] Dostoevsky (1990) 245.

feel the torment of a character from inside. But, also like Shakespeare, the torment is embedded in a narrative structure which itself has point. Ivan does not have what I have called moral faith. Because he feels the force of the moral demand, he is in pain. He does not adopt the strategies either of exaggerating his capacity or of diminishing the demand. And he goes mad.

When I was writing about the problem of evil, I had the opportunity to talk with a survivor from the German concentration camps of World War II. Her name was Eva. She said that her experience had been that those who went into the camps, like her, with a strong faith in God had their faith strengthened. They came out (if they came out at all) with a stronger faith than they went in with. Elie Wiesel, just before he was awarded the Nobel Peace Prize for 1986, said that he had often questioned why God would have allowed such a catastrophe. 'I have not answered that question,' he said, 'but I have not lost faith in God. I have moments of anger and protest. Sometimes I've been closer to him for that reason.'[53]

Most of the discussion of the problem of evil has been devoted to the question Wiesel said that he had not answered. There has been a sustained discussion of whether the existence of any evil in the world, or of the amount of evil in the world there actually is, makes it hard or impossible to believe in the omnipotent, omniscient, omnibenevolent God of the Christian tradition.[54] The approach of this chapter has been different. People like Eva and like Elie Wiesel have abundant evidence for the truth of the assertion that virtue is not consistent with happiness. They qualify as experts, if we take Kant's argument empirically. It is interesting to compare them with Ivan Karamazov, who merely imagines the evil he describes (though it is clear in the novel that he also suffered grievously as he was growing up). Some writers claim that one cannot maintain a traditional belief in God if one thinks seriously about a child dying of a painful disease; but they should be troubled by the testimony of those who have gone through the experience of losing a child without seeing the reason God allowed it, and have persevered in their faith.[55] Such

---

[53] *New York Times*, 15 Oct. 1986.   [54] See J. E. Hare (1991).

[55] See Wolterstorff (1987). See also Lewis (1963), Vanauken (1977), and Tada and Estes (1978). What seems characteristic of this literature is the sufferers' experience of God's or Christ's presence with them in their suffering. There is, moreover, the sense that God has a reason, even though he may not have shared it with the sufferer.

testimony does not prove the philosophical point, because it is always possible that such people are confused or self-deceptive. Moreover the testimony of those who suffer is not one-sided, though perhaps those who despair write books less often. But the testimony of those who persevere is telling against the philosopher who merely imagines the evil which he claims makes faith untenable. In any case, the point of this chapter has not been that moral faith is philosophically or theoretically proven, but that it is necessary for perseverance in the moral life. It is some support for this to see that some people, faced with extreme evil, have been able to persevere and have had such faith. The structure of the moral argument is that as long as reason in its theoretical employment cannot rule out the legitimacy of moral faith, reason in its practical employment requires it. If moral faith is possible, then it is necessary.

I will end by trying to describe in a little more detail what moral faith is like. How confident a belief is required, and trust for how much of your future, and for how large a proportion of your total well-being? It would be foolish to think that exact answers could be given to such questions. But I think more can be said than I have so far. First, I think moral faith is consistent with some doubt about whether your continued well-being is consistent with your trying to live a morally good life. 'Lord, I believe; help thou mine unbelief' is a possible frame of mind.[56] It is possible especially when faced with the demand for a particularly daunting sacrifice of what you had thought necessary for your happiness, or when faced with a particularly glaring example of the suffering of the innocent and the triumph of the guilty. It is a hard question whether the doubt can become so strong that someone who is wholeheartedly committed to morality can then become uncommitted again. Kant thought not, though he does speak at one point about a person who has adopted the good maxim needing 'to guard against a relapse'.[57] The theological counterpart of this question is the dispute about the perseverance of the saints.

Second, moral faith does not require believing that all your

---

[56] Mark 9: 24.

[57] *Rel.* 71 (77). But the main doctrine is that after the revolution of the will, the new maxim is unchangeable; see *Rel.* 43 (47). One difficulty is that for Kant we do not know which is our fundamental disposition, and so we must approach every situation as if presented over again with the problem of rejecting the evil maxim in favour of the good. See Mulholland (1991) 84.

present preferences for the future will be secured if you try to live a good life. There are at least two reasons for this. You can foresee that your preferences will change, as the process of moral discipline or sanctification takes hold. You may foresee the need to rethink what your happiness consists in. The second reason is that you can be aware that your preferences are not coherent, since they cannot all be satisfied together. You may now want your future to contain both lots of ice-cream and a slim figure. Moreover, moral faith does not require believing that all your future preferences for your future will be secured if you try to lead a good life. The same two reasons I have just given can be given at any point in your future, even though the tension between the package of what you wish and will and the moral demand may be decreasing over time, in the manner I discussed in Section *b* of this chapter. Most important, however, is a different point. Moral faith is consistent with believing that you will not get many of the things you want, even though they are morally legitimate and coherent with the rest of what you want. At least as I have presented it, moral faith requires believing that your continued well-being is consistent with trying to lead a morally good life; it does not require believing that you will get any particular proportion of the things you want, even more than half of them. It may be that the amount of happiness available for us is rather small, at least in this life. This might be because so much of our happiness is dependent upon other people, and is therefore vulnerable to their moral failures. It is true that if you have moral faith you will believe that what happiness is available to you is consistent with trying to lead a morally good life; but this amount of happiness may be rather small. The only constraint I have put on this is that you have to believe that you are not destroying your chances of continued well-being. But it is not clear how many of the things you want you have to get before we can talk correctly of your well-being.

Moral faith, as I have described it, is consistent with a number of different views about the nature of well-being, the nature of virtue, and the kind of causation by which the two are connected. It is consistent, for example, with the views about virtue and happiness which Kant attributes to the Stoics. If the Stoic sage is truly self-sufficient, and his happiness does not depend on anything except his virtue and his being conscious of his virtue, then his moral faith will reside in the faith that if he is virtuous, he will continue to be able to know it. Within the Christian tradition, moral faith is consistent with taking the second approach mentioned earlier (in Section *a*) about when and where happiness begins. The Christian might believe that our happiness begins only in heaven. Or she might, like Thomas Aquinas, associate the concept of happiness in Aristotle's *Nicomachean Ethics* with imperfect happiness, whereas 'perfect human happiness is reserved for the life to come' and consists in the beatific vision.[58] If our happiness in heaven consists solely in seeing God, and this vision is indeed the complete satisfaction of all human aspirations, then the Christian's moral faith can be a trust that all the desires and needs that we then have would be satisfied. But it is not necessary for a Christian to believe this. Perhaps we get the beginnings of happiness here on earth, and perhaps even in heaven there is sorrow, for example, over those who have not repented.[59] In any case moral faith, as I have construed it, does not require any particular view about how much happiness is available, or what it consists in, or when and where it begins.

[58] *Summa Theologiae* Ia-IIae q. 2 a. 8 and Ia-IIae q. 3 a. 4.
[59] *Luke* 15: 7; see 12: 6. But see also Rev. 21: 4: 'And God shall wipe away all tears from their eyes.'

PART II

HUMAN LIMITS

4

PUFFING UP THE CAPACITY

THIS chapter marks the beginning of the second division of this book, which is about human limits and various attempts in contemporary moral philosophy to make sense of morality given these limits.[1] The first division was about Kant, and especially his attempts to deal with what he called Spener's problem after the Lutheran pietist: 'How can we become *other* men and not merely better men (as if we were already good but only negligent about the degree of our goodness)?' There are two strategies that Kant did *not* accept for dealing with this gap between demand and capacity: namely exaggerating our powers to fit the moral demand, and reducing the moral demand to fit our powers. On the one hand, Kant referred to 'man's self-conceit and the exaggeration of his powers'; on the other hand, 'we may imagine that the moral law is indulgent as far as we are concerned'.[2] The present chapter and Chapter 5 are about the first of these two strategies, Chapter 6 is about the second, and Chapter 7 is about a third strategy of providing a naturalistic substitute for the divine assistance which Kant invoked to bridge the moral gap.

The problem of the moral gap, which generates these strategies, is conspicuous within moral theories that are often distinguished from Kant's. In the present chapter I will look at some recent utilitarian writing in order to illustrate the first strategy, that of 'puffing up the capacity'.[3] The idea behind this strategy is to concede that if the

---

[1] Some of the material in this chapter has appeared in J. E. Hare (1994a). I want to thank my commentator at the American Philosophical Association meetings, Tom Carson, for his comments on a previous draft.

[2] *LE* 126.

[3] There are many other ways to carry out this strategy. In Ch. 8 I will look at the strategy of 'finding God inside oneself', which is Kierkegaard's characterization of Judge William's ethical life. The culture is full of examples outside technical philosophy: the therapy of Carl Rogers, school curricula that assume we need merely to clarify the values children already have, New Age books about 'the god within', self-realization manuals for coping with stress or anxiety. My project is restricted, however, to the philosophical literature in a narrower sense.

moral demand is binding upon us, we must have the capacity to live
by it; but to eliminate the gap which then threatens by puffing up to
godlike proportions our capacity to live the moral life. A conspicuous
optimist of this sort is Shelly Kagan, in his book *The Limits of
Morality*. He makes the claim that if all our beliefs were vivid,
including especially our beliefs about the interests of others, we
would tend to conform to the impartial standard that utilitarian
morality requires. In this chapter I will argue that this claim is false.
The chapter should not be construed, however, as an attack on
utilitarianism as such. It is possible, I think, to construct versions of
utilitarianism which do not exaggerate our natural capacities to live a
moral life. But there has been a tendency in utilitarianism from the
beginning to produce versions of the doctrine which do exaggerate in
this way.[4]

a. UTILITARIANISM AND THE MORAL DEMAND

For a utilitarian, the moral demand is that we are to perform those
acts which can reasonably be expected to lead to the best
consequences overall, impartially considered. I am not going to try
to give an account of what this principle means in more detail than
this. I will make do with an example, since the only point I want to
make about the moral demand, as this is seen within utilitarianism,
is that the demand is far higher than most people are comfortable
with. This does not yet show that utilitarianism puts the demand *too*
high; for it may be that we are not supposed to be comfortable with
the moral demand. Deriving an *objection* to utilitarianism at this
point requires more argument. Let me start, though, with an
example of the demand as it is construed by the utilitarian. Suppose
I am considering going to the cinema, and I realize that the money
that I am about to spend on my ticket could be used, instead, to feed

---

[4] Mill's *Utilitarianism* is full of extraordinary estimates of the power of education,
e.g. (p. 269) 'that education and opinion, which have so vast a power over human
character, should so use that power as to establish in the mind of every individual an
indissoluble association between his own happiness and the good of the whole; . . . so
that not only he may be unable to conceive the possibility of happiness to himself,
consistently with conduct opposed to the general good, but also that a direct impulse
to promote the general good may be in every individual one of the habitual motives of
action, and the sentiments connected therewith may fill a large and prominent place in
every human being's sentient existence.'

a starving Somali for a week. I am required, by the utilitarian principle, to ask which use of the money can reasonably be expected to lead to the best consequences overall, impartially considered. I am not allowed, for instance, to give my own pleasure more weight in the decision just because it is *my* pleasure. But if it seems that life for a week is a better consequence overall than two hours' pleasure, it is unlikely that the principle will allow me to buy the ticket. The application of this principle to my life makes a radical difference to it. Not only the film will be forbidden me, in all likelihood, but a great deal of the expenditure that is entailed by my current standard of living.[5]

Now it can be said that on this construal the moral demand is too great for human nature to bear. I will focus here on the utilitarian demand for impartiality between persons, though there are other features of the utilitarian principle that are demanding in themselves. The claim is that the demand for impartiality is not consistent with the human tendency to give more weight to the agent's own interests than the utilitarian principle allows. This observation about human nature can be made in more or in less pessimistic terms. In Kant, as we have seen, the terms are pessimistic. This is not because we desire our own happiness.[6] It is true that he thinks that because we are *finite* rational beings, and not pure rational beings, we cannot have duty as our sole incentive. This is not yet, however, the reason for his pessimism. For we can become the sorts of people who are happy in doing our duty, and the inclinations and virtue can be brought progressively closer together.[7] This is true, even though Kant wants to distinguish his position from the view that happiness simply consists in knowing that one is doing one's duty. I suggested in Chapter 3 that Kant has in mind, rather, that the person of virtue

---

[5] I have discussed the question of how radical the difference is in Hare and Joynt (1982) 163–83. In particular, I have discussed the relevance to this question of the two-level moral theory of R. M. Hare, described briefly in Ch. 1 above. I considered the thesis that the wealth of a rich individual or a rich nation should be given away until the point where personal or domestic need is as great as that of the people to whom the money or food might be sent. I concluded that the demand is not as radical as that, but is more threatening to our present standard of living than most of us in the rich part of the world are comfortable with. For a reply to the objection that the demand is too high, see Singer (1993) 242–6.   [6] *KpV* 24 (25).

[7] I discussed in Ch. 2 the suggestion that the battles continue even after the revolution, though the final result of the war is the victory of the good will.

has the faith that a life of virtue will be consistent with a happy life; but this will not be because the two terms have collapsed into one, but because Providence has seen to it that the first is rewarded by the second. On Kant's view, it is possible to have as one of my desires the desire to do my duty; it is not possible, however, as a finite being, to have this as my only desire. Fulfilling the demands of duty will not, then, by itself produce happiness. But I can have faith that it is consistent with my happiness, given the way the world is ordered.

The reason for Kant's pessimism, however, is not that we desire our own happiness in everything we desire, but that our initial condition (before the revolution of the will) is one of *preferring* happiness to duty. In this condition our inclinations diverge from duty, and we will act in accordance with duty only in those cases where this is a means to what we most want for ourselves. In our initial condition, our own interests tend to have more motivational force for us than the utilitarian principle allows. There is a bias in favour of our own interests. This should not be misunderstood as a claim about selfishness. The term 'interests' is deliberately inclusive, so as to allow that not all the interests we have are selfish ones. It is possible for me, for example, to have an interest in saving the lives of starving Somalis. But still we are prone to give more weight to our own interests, just because they are ours, than the utilitarian principle allows. We are beings who can have interests in what the utilitarian, or R. M. Hare's archangel, would prescribe in our situation, but we do not naturally have *only* these interests. Unfortunately we are motivated more by the other interests than the utilitarian principle allows, even where we know what the utilitarian principle requires in our situation. We therefore have a problem which Kant would put in terms of 'ought' and 'can'. If it is the case that I ought to do something, it must be the case that I can do it. This does not mean merely that I must be able to do it *if* I want to do it, but that I must be able to want to do it.[8] The problem is how

---

[8] Tom Carson, in a reply to a previous draft, claimed that my reading of 'ought implies can' is incompatible with determinism. The question at issue is whether there is a defensible form of compatibilism which allows *both* that I am able to want x or want not x at some time t *and* that I am determined by heredity and environment to one of these states rather than the other. I think there is such a form of compatibilism, but I do not want to argue that here. The reading I give of 'ought imples can' is one I share with the optimist, so it is not an issue for this project. See Kagan (1989) 274. See also Wolf (1990) 99.

Practical Reason can be practical; that is, how it can prescribe to me, or be binding on me. For if I am, as Kant thinks, under the sway of my desires as a whole (before the revolution of the will), the desire to do my duty will not have the requisite force to overcome my other desires. At least, it will not regularly have that force. It is not clear, then, that I am able to want most of all to do my duty; at least, it is not clear that I am able to do so regularly. But then if it is not the case that I can, it is not the case that I ought; and Practical Reason, which prescribes a life of duty, will not be practical or prescriptive *for me*. Impartiality is, for the utilitarian, in the same predicament as Practical Reason for Kant. If everything we desire is filtered through the bias towards our own interests, how can we come to be motivated by the desire above everything else to do what impartiality requires?

b. A UTILITARIAN REPLY

There is a utilitarian reply which construes this claim as an objection to utilitarianism.[9] The reply is that humans do in fact have the resources to empower themselves to live by the moral demand. Let us call the proponent of this view 'the optimist'. The optimist starts by asking us to consider the nature of prudence. Prudence allows me a greater concern with my own interests than the utilitarian principle would allow. But it insists that I should be unbiased towards my present as opposed to my future interests.[10] If I am prudent, in other words, I will not give greater weight to what I now want to have now, just because I can get it now. There are some qualifications that have to be made immediately to this claim about prudence. In many cases I have more control now over securing what I want now than over securing what I now want to have in the future. In those cases it is consistent with prudence for me to prefer the present effort to secure the present interest over the present effort to secure the future interest. Moreover I know better now what my interests are, and it is consistent with prudence to prefer securing an interest now since I

---

[9] The reply comes in Kagan (1989).

[10] There is an ambiguity in the phrase 'future interests', between interests I now have in future states of affairs and interests I will then have in those states of affairs. See R. M. Hare (1981) 101–6 for the distinction between now-for-then and then-for-then preferences. In the present context, I am talking about now-for-then preferences. There are complicated questions which I am not addressing here about what prudence requires for then-for-then preferences.

am more sure that I have it. But with an equal probability of success in securing a present and a future interest, and with equal knowledge that the two are indeed my interests, prudence requires me not to prefer the present interest to the future. It is, so to speak, impartial between times in the way the utilitarian principle is impartial between people.

The optimist points out that I can be moved by the thought of what prudence would prescribe, even if I am not presently moved equally by the future interest. I may dread going to the dentist, because of what I know he is going to do with his drill. I also know that the long-term health of my teeth is more important than the temporary discomfort in his surgery. The fear of the immediate pain may master me for a while, but I can be won over in the end by the thought that abcesses are worse. One reason why this works is that there is a continuum of vividness to paleness that accompanies the holding of belief.[11] A vivid belief glows, we might say, and a pale belief recedes. Very often beliefs about present interests (or the very near future) are more vivid than beliefs about future interests (or the more remote future). What can happen is that by attending to the future interest (for example by imagining it in detail), I can make the belief about it more vivid. By seeing the significance of the present lack of vividness of that belief, I can be moved to attend to it in a way that increases its vividness. This is because I know that if all my beliefs were vivid, including especially my beliefs about my future interests, I would be motivated to do as prudence requires. Here we have a way of saying both that we are by nature biased in favour of the present *and* that prudence (which is impartial between present and future as such) can be prescriptive for us. For despite the bias, we can be motivated by the thought of what we would be motivated towards if we were prudent.

The optimist then returns from prudence to morality. He claims that we can say about morality what we have just said about prudence. We can concede that we have a bias, this time towards our own interests in general rather than our present interests as in the case of prudence. But the optimist thinks we can also say that

---

[11] There are limitations on how *many* of our beliefs can or should be vivid. But we can construct the notion of a being without our limitations (e.g. some sort of god) as an ideal case. For a discussion of how much information we should have, see Brandt (1979) 70–87.

morality (which does not have this bias) is binding on us. For we can overcome the apparent gap between the 'ought' and the 'can' by appealing to the fact that we can be motivated by the thought of what we would be motivated by if our beliefs about the interests of others were as vivid as our beliefs about our own interests. Just as our beliefs about our present interests tend to be more vivid than our beliefs about future interests, so our beliefs about our own interests are characteristically more vivid than our beliefs about the interests of others. The optimist makes a counter-factual claim: If all my beliefs were vivid, I would tend to conform to the impartial standpoint (to what the utilitarian principle requires).[12] This claim occupies the same place in the structure of the argument as the previous claim about prudence: If all my beliefs were vivid, including especially my beliefs about my future interests, I would be motivated to do as prudence requires. It is because this counter-factual claim about prudence is plausible that I can be motivated now by the thought of what I would be motivated by if I were prudent. In the same way, because of the counter-factual claim about morality (if it is true), I can now be motivated by the thought of what I would be motivated by if I were moral.

But is this counter-factual claim about morality true? The optimist gives us several considerations in favour. First, it is in fact easier to sacrifice my own interests for others as I acquire more vivid beliefs about their interests. This can be true, for example, when I form a close and long-lasting relationship with someone. I can start to feel in my bones what she needs from me, and this makes it harder to resist her claim on me. The converse seems to be true as well. Distance makes it harder to sacrifice my own interests. This is why some relief organizations have schemes which enable the donor to take on a particular recipient, often a child, whose photograph will be sent to the donor at regular intervals with reports about her progress.

---

[12] I have stated the counter-factual claim, as Kagan does, without using degrees of vividness. It should be distinguished from the claim (1), 'If we made our beliefs about others considerably more vivid, we would tend to do what the utilitarian theory demands', and from the claim (2), 'If we made our beliefs about others maximally vivid, i.e. as vivid as we can possibly make them (given the limitations of human nature), then we would tend to do what the utilitarian theory demands.' I think the falsity of (1) follows from the arguments in this chapter. (2) will be trivially true if 'vividness' is taken in the second way I distinguish below, and false if 'vividness' is taken in the first way. I owe this distinction to Tom Carson.

Moreover, we can be moved towards our duty by imagining in detail the plight of the people we are affecting by our decisions.[13] All this suggests the moral power of vividness; it suggests that we are more likely to be able to sacrifice our own interests in favour of others if we come to see vividly what their interests are.

c. THE TROUBLE WITH OPTIMISM

This reply by the optimist is not, unfortunately, persuasive. The problem is with the counter-factual claim about morality. It is not at all clear that if all our beliefs were vivid, especially our beliefs about the interests of others, we would tend to conform to the impartial standpoint. One way to see this problem is to think more about vividness. This is a metaphor which tends to disguise the difference between two different ways in which our belief-holdings vary. One continuum is the degree of clarity and distinctness attending a belief which we hold.[14] The second is the degree of wholeheartedness with which we care about the belief, or the degree of importance we attach to it.[15] Take as an example my belief that it is in Aunt Fanny's overall interest to be given a chocolate éclair. Suppose also that the éclair is the last one on the plate, and Aunt Fanny and I both want it. Perhaps she wants it more than I do, because she has just returned from a long trip to Slobovia, where she could not get any. I can imagine her pleasure to myself with different degrees of clarity and distinctness. I can also attach different degrees of importance to her pleasure. These two continua can diverge. I can be quite clear about her pleasure, but not care about it much at all.

The counter-factual claim about morality is that I will tend towards the impartial judgement if my beliefs are vivid. If we understand this claim in terms of clarity and distinctness, I think it is

---

[13] Consider Mrs Do-as-you-would-be-done-by in Charles Kingsley's *Water Babies*.

[14] This is the sense given to 'vividness' in Brandt (1979) 60.

[15] Kagan explains that pale beliefs are beliefs 'to which we only pay lip service' (1989: 283). This is the second continuum. He gives the example of a person who is asked whether he learnt anything at a lecture, and replies, 'She didn't convince me of anything I didn't already believe; but I didn't really *believe* it before.' This person's beliefs may have been clear before, but now they become important. On the other hand, the example of a pale belief he starts from is the belief that 'a billion is a thousand million'. It may be possible to make this into a vivid belief by '[contrasting] the length of one million dollar bills stuck end to end with the corresponding span of one billion dollars'. This sounds more like the first kind of continuum.

false. Understood this way, the claim is about *cognitive* short-comings.[16] The failure of belief is a failure to understand with clarity and distinctness how my choices will affect other people. It is true that much insensitive action is generated by this kind of failure. It does not follow, however, that as my beliefs fail less in this way, I will be more inclined to sacrifice my own interests in favour of others. And even if this did follow, the counter-factual claim about morality might still be false. For this claim is not merely that my tendency towards impartiality increases with increased vividness of belief. The claim is that with vividness of belief, I will have an overall tendency towards impartiality. We could put the difference between these two positions quantitatively. The claim is not merely that vividness of belief will increase my tendency to impartiality from n% to n + 1%. Rather, it is that with vividness of belief my tendency to impartiality will be greater than half. Consider first whether understanding vividly Aunt Fanny's potential pleasure is likely to *increase* my tendency to give her the éclair, if it is the last one on the plate. Surely this depends on my relation to Aunt Fanny? If I am generally malignant, or if I hate her in particular, then understanding her potential pleasure more clearly will increase my tendency to take the éclair myself. But even if we grant that greater vividness of belief (understood cognitively) increases the chances that an agent will sacrifice his or her interests, it does not seem likely that it will increase them sufficiently for us to judge the new probability greater than half.

The claim is supposed to be universal in the sense that it attributes a counter-factual tendency to *everybody*. Surely there are some misanthropic people who are either indifferent to the interests of others, or enjoy causing them distress? This may seem an extreme type, rarely to be met with. Perhaps most people are benign, at least to the degree that if they really understood the effects of their choices on others, they would be more likely than not to sacrifice their own interests when these conflict with the interests of others. What gives me pause, however, is the thought that people who know each other very well continue to do great harm to each other deliberately. Within families one person's desire for power and control can make family life a misery for the others. Or think of children who have been together for several years at school, and know precisely how to

---

[16] See Kagan (1989) 286, 289, 299, 301.

torment each other. They establish a hierarchy, like the pecking order of chickens in a coop, and make the lives of those at the bottom of the hierarchy continually miserable. It is not merely the love of power which interferes with benevolence, but also the typical responses to the love of power by its victims; envy, fear, and resentment.[17] What the reader should do is to imagine as richly as possible some type of human relation in which there is detailed knowledge by the parties of each others' interests, and then fill in an account of the contempt and cruelty often found there.

Sometimes the lack of benevolence is disguised by a deliberate blindness. Our beliefs about the interests of others can be made paler by design. It will not necessarily be conscious design, but we will slip into the habit of seeing things in the way it is in our interest to see them.[18] Those who do not feel the force of the demand to give generously to famine relief may not be vividly aware of the suffering they are failing to prevent. But they may have chosen not to be vividly aware of it.

The optimist may hope to derive comfort from this strategy of induced paleness.[19] He may think it shows that the person who is using the strategy knows that if she did allow the beliefs about others' interests to become vivid, she would have a tendency to sacrifice her own competing interests. Perhaps it is because she knows this, and wants to avoid the sacrifice, that she adopts the strategy. She turns off the television when the pictures of starving children come on, because she does not want to be moved to contribute to saving their lives.

This may sometimes be the case. But it does not follow that if only we could secure vividness of belief, we could secure the tendency to impartiality. For the strategy of induced paleness is only one of the techniques available to the person who wants to get his own way and at the same time pretend to himself to be benevolent. Another

---

[17] The cathedral close at Barchester, as Trollope saw it, is an instructive example. Trollope was himself at the bottom of a pecking order at school, and knew what he was describing. See Glendinning (1992).

[18] Iris Murdoch likes to describe people of this type in her novels. She talks of the sober truthful mind, which says no 'to the prompt easy visions of self-protective self-promoting fantasy' (1977: 79). I will consider in Ch. 5 the case of a man who wants his own way in a family and pretends that his desires are simply stronger than those of his spouse, or the other members of the family.

[19] There is also a self-deceptive strategy of induced vividness. See Watson (1975) 214.

technique is rationalization in terms of some normative principle which takes the appearance of objectivity, but derives its motivational power for him from its convenience as a disguise for self-interest. Racial superiority is the most obvious case, but there are many others. I can pretend to myself that my wishes deserve to be given priority because anybody deserves this who can trace back his ancestry as far as I can, or who has accumulated as much wealth as I have.[20] With the support of such a principle, self-interest can survive vividness of the agent's beliefs about the interests of others. There are other strategies as well, such as the strategy of induced crisis. I can pretend to myself that I will get back to what I know impartiality requires once I am through the temporary crisis which threatens to undo my life completely; no one can be expected to think about Somalia when his whole life is at stake. There is no reason to suppose that overcoming one technique of partiality will succeed in overcoming all of them. There may be an underlying bias which has numerous techniques of self-persuasion at its disposal.[21] The optimist hopes in the strength of what we can call 'the counter-factual motivation', that is, our motivation by the thought of what we would be motivated by if all our beliefs were vivid. But in the case of these techniques of partiality the counter-factual motivation has already been overridden. The battle is, so to speak, already lost.

So far, I have been speaking on the assumption that we should understand vividness cognitively. As I said earlier, however, vividness is a metaphor which conceals an important distinction. On the one hand there is the clarity and distinctness attending a belief, and on the other hand the degree of importance we attach to it. It is true that I will tend towards impartiality if I attach a great deal of importance to my beliefs about the interests of others, *and* I am also committed to being moral, in the sense in which this requires impartiality. It is also true that commitment to morality is likely to make me think my beliefs about the interests of others important. But there are various kinds of case in which it is possible to think my beliefs about the interests of others important, and not be committed to acting morally on the basis of those beliefs. It is possible, for example, to think those beliefs important *because* of their relevance

[20] Or 'any citizen of a boot-shaped country'. See Mackie (1977) 85, and above, Ch. 1 n. 7.
[21] There is a catalogue of such techniques in James (1961) 320 f.

to morality, but still not be committed to morality. I may agree without reservation that Aunt Fanny has a strong interest in the éclair, and I may even agree that there are no competing interests with equivalent moral force. But I may still take the éclair myself. Perhaps I am not committed to morality at all, or I might be committed to some version of morality which does not require impartiality. I will say more about this latter possibility in Chapter 6. Or I might have a weak commitment to morality, so that it survives competition with some of my interests, but not my love of desserts. I may have a blind spot. Perhaps I am otherwise a good person, but I am greedy about desserts. Some thinkers have held that virtue is unified in the strong sense that I cannot have one virtue without having all of them.[22] If they are right, then this kind of case would not be possible. Though I shall not argue for it, I think they are wrong.

The counter-factual claim about morality is that vividness of belief brings with it the tendency to impartiality. If we understand vividness in terms of the importance attached to a belief, the claim will be that I will tend to give Aunt Fanny the éclair if I think it is important that this is in her interest. This seems likely to be true if I am already strongly committed to impartial morality, and quite uncertain if I am not. One reason for thinking that it is uncertain, if I am not so committed, comes from the considerations I have already mentioned about the love of power, and the typical responses to it. Imagine, for example, that Aunt Fanny is advanced in years, has very few resources of her own, and has been staying in the family for several years. The other members of the family may become quite accustomed to the thought that something is in her interest, and even that this is significant because it means she deserves it, impartially and abstractly speaking, but so what?

d. THE OPTIMIST'S RESPONSE

There is a response to the kind of objection I have been making.[23] Suppose we concede that most agents do have some motivation to

---

[22] Aristotle seems to have thought this, following Socrates (*NE* 6. 12, 1144^a29 ff.). See also Kant, *Rel.* 26 (31) and Mulholland (1991) 84 f.

[23] Kagan's reply (1989) is in two stages (though the objection he is replying to is not as strong, I think, as the one I have made in the text). First, he claims that even if

overcome their bias towards their own interests. This would be consistent with Kant's view that there is a seed of goodness which survives even in the most hardened of criminals.[24] This seed of goodness is a responsiveness to the call of duty, and Kant is giving a reading of the claim that 'they who in other aspects of life seem least to differ from brutes still continue to retain some seed of religion'.[25] Kant's claim is actually stronger than the concession I supposed, which is not that *everyone* has such a seed of goodness but that most people do. It is consistent with this concession that some agents have entirely lost such motivation.

The optimist then argues that it follows that most agents have the motivation to *try* to be impartial. He thinks that this shows that the gap between the moral demand and our natural capacities can be bridged, and that therefore what he construes as an objection to utilitarianism can be overcome. For the pull towards self-interest, which he acknowledges, is not on his view *endorsed* by most agents. Suppose we think in terms of an inner battle between the pull to self-interest and the motivation to try to be impartial. The pull to self-interest, he claims, is sufficiently weakened by the agent's unwillingness to endorse it, so that the motivation to try to be impartial can prevail.

e. THE FINAL WORD

This response is inadequate. The first point to note is that if what I said earlier about rationalization is correct, there may be an endorsement by the agent of the pull to self-interest. The agent may justify giving greater weight to her own interests on the specious grounds of some normative principle adopted (perhaps unconsciously) because of its power to disguise the real motivation in play.[26] Thus

there is a residue of bias towards self-interest that survives making one's beliefs about the interests of others vivid, this residue is small. Here the dispute seems to be empirical. The second stage of the reply is not empirical, but conceptual, and I describe it in the following text.

[24] *Rel.* 41 (45). [25] Calvin, *Institutes*, I. iii. I.

[26] This will not be a good objection to the optimist if he requires only that we act *in accordance with* a principle of impartiality, not *from a motive* which is impartial. For the distinction, see *Gl* 65 (398). But at least in one form of the theory, utilitarianism requires that we train ourselves so that we come to have the disposition to act *on* principles of various kinds, including the utilitarian principle itself. See R. M. Hare (1981) 191 f.

Kant argues that our fundamental motivation, the maxim of our action, can be opaque to us.[27] We may think that we are acting for the greater glory of God, or for democracy, when in fact we are disguising (perhaps unconsciously) our own interest. If the pull to self-interest can be endorsed under the disguise of a supposedly objective normative principle, it will not be weakened in its conflict with the motivation to try to be impartial.

There is a second point to be made here. Suppose a fanatical tenor thought that everyone should sing like Caruso. We might object that most people do not have the capacity to do so. It is foolish, we might say, to tell them they ought to try to do what they cannot. He might reply, 'But they can *try* to sing like Caruso,' and he might think this shows that the gap between the demand and their natural capacities can be bridged. Now *trying* is a hard notion to analyse. The question is whether we can try to do what we know we will never be able to do by our own efforts. I think we cannot, at least with one kind of trying. Robert the Bruce learnt from the spider, 'Try, try, and try again,' but he learnt because the spider in the end succeeded. There has to be a point in the trying. What is slippery in the example of the fanatical tenor is the phrase 'like Caruso'. Even a small improvement in technique may make the voice sound more like Caruso than it did before. In this sense everyone can sing (more) like Caruso. But if the fanatical tenor was urging more than this (and, being fanatical, he probably was), he is justly rebuked for being hopelessly unrealistic. We should distinguish two kinds of trying. With one kind, if I am trying to do A, I must have in mind actually achieving the doing of A in my own person by my own efforts. With the second kind, all that is necessary is that I envisage a marginal improvement in my performance on a continuum which has the doing of A at one end of it.

Most of us can manage to be less partial, less biased towards our own interests, if we try.[28] It makes sense, then, to urge us to try to be impartial. But this is is the second kind of trying distinguished

[27] *Rel.* 61 (68). See Niebuhr (1932) 93, who argues that ordinary people 'project their egos' upon the nation, and are more devoted to the quest for national power the more their own 'lusts for power and prestige' are thwarted by their individual circumstances. I discuss this claim in Hare and Joynt (1982) 30–3.

[28] Kant sometimes denies that we can make *any* improvement, when under bondage to radical evil. For discussion of the difficulties which this doctrine raises for him, see Ch. 2 above.

above. Impartiality as it is construed by the utilitarian principle requires *no* bias towards the agent's own interests. Since not all our interests are selfish, the principle requires no bias even towards an agent's unselfish interests. I may feel drawn, for example, to meet the needs of the starving people of Somalia, but impartiality does not allow me to give more weight to this concern just because I feel drawn to it. I have been claiming that impartiality in this sense is beyond natural human capacities. If this is right, I cannot try to be impartial in this sense with the first kind of trying, because I cannot have in mind actually achieving this level of impartiality in my own person by my own efforts. Trying to be impartial in this sense with this kind of trying would be like trying to jump to the moon.

Does this show, however, that it is not the case that I ought to be impartial in this sense? May I argue, 'It is not the case that I can be impartial in this sense, and therefore it is not the case that I ought to be'? Kant is writing in the Christian tradition which has consistently urged believers to be what they cannot by their natural capacities become. Thus Augustine says, 'God bids us do what we cannot, that we may know what we ought to seek from him'.[29] Jesus himself says, 'Be ye, therefore, perfect, even as your Father, which is in heaven, is perfect.'[30] But this perfection is not something we can achieve by trying to achieve it. One way to see this is to note that, if I was right in Chapter 3, moral faith is required for perseverance in the moral life. This makes it possible to combine our interest in our own happiness with our commitment to morality. But moral faith is not something I can acquire by trying to acquire it. It is something that some people seem to have and other people seem not to have. The source of it is mysterious, though it is no doubt related to whether people are unconditionally loved as children by those who have primary care for them. In the tradition that I will be discussing in Chapters 8–10, faith that God will keep his promises to us is a gift from him. It may look as though Augustine is denying the principle that 'ought implies can' when he says that God tells us to do what we cannot do. But the principle is in fact preserved; for what is impossible is not our *doing* what God bids, but our doing it *without*

[29] *On Grace and Free Will* 16. 32.
[30] Matt. 5: 48. This chapter, and this verse in particular, is a favourite of Kant's. In *Rel.* no other chapter is quoted so frequently. See *Rel.* 147 (159). See also 1 Pet. 1: 16: 'Be ye holy; for I am holy', and *Rel.* 119 (128).

his help.[31] Jesus does not say, and scripture nowhere says, '*Try* to be perfect'.

I think it is this tradition which lies behind the apparent paradox or antinomy we have reached in discussing the position of the optimist. The thesis of the antinomy is that we ought to be impartial. I have not denied that this moral demand should be taken in the strong sense I have attributed to the utilitarian principle. In Chapter 6 I will discuss a possible modification. The antithesis is that we are not capable of this kind of impartiality by our own natural capacities. The paradox arises if we think that 'ought implies can'. The optimist tries to disarm the paradox by denying the antithesis, by puffing up our capacities. The tradition that provides the context for Kant's discussion of this question takes a different tack. It admits a work of grace. Kant finds himself forced to appeal to grace also, though he thinks we cannot fit it into our theoretical or practical reasoning. 'Hence we can admit a work of grace as something incomprehensible, but we cannot adopt it into our maxims either for theoretical or for practical use.'[32] My strategy in this book is to point back to the tradition in which this question arose, in order to suggest philosophically unfamiliar resources for answering it.

The argument of this chapter has been complicated, and it is probably worth recapitulating the stages by which I reached the present point. I started with a claim about utilitarianism, that it is too demanding to fit natural human capacity. This might be construed as an objection; if it is not the case that we can will as the utilitarian principle prescribes, then it is not the case that we ought to so will. The optimist does construe the claim as an objection in this way, and he replies to it by starting from the notion of prudence. We can be motivated now, he says, by the thought of what we would be motivated by if we were prudent. It can be true, therefore, both that we ought to be prudent and that we are presently biased in favour of present interests against future ones. The optimist then applies this line of reasoning to morality. We may presently be biased in favour of our own interests against those of others. But (he claims) if all our beliefs, especially those about the interests of

---

[31] As I argued in Ch. 1, the point is not merely that God's help is *possible*; for in that sense, since God is omnipotent, it is possible to jump to the moon with his assistance. Rather, the point is that God makes his assistance available for doing what he asks us to do.　　[32] *Rel.* 49 (53).

others, were vivid, we would have a tendency to act from the impartial standpoint, as morality demands. Unfortunately, however, this counter-factual claim about morality by the optimist seems to be false. I argued this for the two different meanings I think can be given to 'vividness of belief', both for the clarity and distinctness with which a belief is held and for the importance attached to it. In the case of the second meaning, it is only if a person is already committed to impartial morality that vividness of belief will tend to produce impartial action. The optimist responded that we can still *try* to act from the impartial standpoint, even though we may have a bias towards our own interests. I objected in two ways to this claim. First, I pointed to the fact of rationalization. The pull to self-interest can be endorsed under disguise; in this way its power in the internal battle against impartial morality can be increased. Second, I claimed that the notion of trying is itself problematic; it does not make sense to urge us to try to be impartial in the sense of trying that requires envisaging ourselves as achieving this level of impartiality in our own persons by our own efforts.

The upshot of all this is that there is indeed a serious objection against utilitarianism if it is required to exaggerate human capacities in the way the optimist does. The exaggeration is especially clear in the cognitive interpretation of the counter-factual claim about morality. The optimist claims that if we saw clearly the damage we do to other people, we would tend not to do it. This seems to me false to experience. Utilitarianism is not required to exaggerate in this way, however. Not all utilitarians do, R. M. Hare, for example, is a utilitarian who takes a different approach to the moral gap, which I described in Chapter 1. Utilitarianism is the inheritor of a tradition, expressed for example in Kant, according to which living by impartial morality requires a *revolution* of the will. Utilitarianism could be construed as a theory, like Kant's theory in the *Groundwork*, about what our lives would be like after such a revolution; but then the theory needs a supplement about how human beings can get to the position in which the demand of the utilitarian principle can be lived.

5
CENTRALITY

THIS chapter, like the previous one, will discuss problems in the current philosophical literature which arise from failing to recognize the existence of what Kant calls radical evil. Here, however, I will raise an objection, not to the optimist's counter-factual claim about morality, but to a different principle, which I will call 'the strength-of-desire principle'. This is the principle that we can satisfy the requirements of justice by giving initial preference in moral decision to the stronger of two desires, independently of whose that desire is. I will conduct the argument of this chapter in four sections. First I will raise an objection to the strength-of-desire principle, namely that it cannot account for the importance we give to the centrality of a desire in a person's life. I will then discuss three different responses to the objection along with the difficulties attending each one. It is not my intention in this chapter to give an answer to the objection, but to show how various current answers to it suffer from failing to recognize what Kant calls the propensity to evil. I am also not going to try to establish that there is such a thing as the centrality of a desire. Some theorists think that the whole notion of the unity of a person, and hence the centrality of desires to a person, is a piece of disreputable metaphysical baggage which we are better off without. Even if they are right, however, we still have the notion, and it is the connection of this notion with fairness that I am trying to understand.

a. THE OBJECTION

According to the strength-of-desire principle, if two people are in competition for some good, and the first desires the good more strongly than the second, the good should be awarded to the first, other things being equal. Thus Peter Singer says, 'To decide impartially, I must sum up the preferences for and against going to dinner with my friends, and those for and against visiting my father.

Whatever action satisfies more preferences, adjusted according to the strength of the preferences, that is the action I ought to take.'[1]

Here is another example. Suppose the day has arrived for a family to leave on its holiday and the father desires very intensely to leave the house, packed and ready, at a time agreed to beforehand by the family. The agreed time comes, and the house is not yet ready to leave by the mother's standards. She cares about leaving the house tidy, which will make them all a little late; but she feels this concern less intensely than her husband feels his desire to be on time. The concern might be moral on both sides. There may be someone at the other end who will be kept waiting if the family is late. There may be some other family coming to stay in the house, and the mother wants to leave it nice for them. But the question of the morality of these desires is not what I want to raise. My question is whether the father's desire should prevail simply because he desires more intensely. Or would this be in some way unfair to the mother?

I want to propose that it is unfair to give this weight to how much a desire is felt.[2] There are some people who simply feel their desires very intensely. We might call them 'Tiggers'. This intensity is a brute fact about them; they were just born with an unusually powerful motor, or were caused to be this way by some feature of their childhood upbringing. The intensity does not mean, in particular, that their desires are integrated to any significant degree; it simply attaches to their desires one by one. Other people, although they feel their desires less intensely, are more reflective about themselves, and know the structure of their own desires fairly well. They know at least roughly how important it is to their lives as a whole that their various desires be satisfied. We might call them 'Eeyores'.[3] The unfairness of the strength-of-desire principle is that

---

[1] Singer (1981) 101. The case he is imagining is that he is about to dine with three friends when his father calls saying he is ill and asking him to visit.

[2] Could we reduce the moral demand presented by the world's starving people by observing that starvation causes lassitude, and hence less intense desires? See Rawls (1985) 244: 'Thus, citizens are to recognize that the weight of their claims is not given by the strength and psychological intensity of their wants and desires (as opposed to their needs and requirements as citizens), even when their wants and desires are rational from their point of view.' Some principle is needed to limit the strength-of-desire principle. It will not be simply the principle of formal justice, which counts each person as one and no person as more than one. The strength-of-desire principle is held, by its adherents, to be justified by the principle of formal justice; since it gives equal moral weight to equal strength-of-desire in *any* person's desires.

[3] I owe these terms to Robert Gay.

it discriminates in favour of Tiggers over Eeyores. We could put the point in terms that Callicles from Plato's *Gorgias* would recognize. The strength-of-desire principle encourages people to have as many strong desires as possible.[4] Given the principle, morality will then require other people to give way. It may be that some of those who do live by very intense desires have encouraged this intensity in themselves as a result of recognizing this point. The strength-of-desire principle seems to encourage the development of the kind of person who makes life less happy for other people.

b. THE MINIMALIST VIEW

I shall call the first broadly utilitarian response I want to consider 'the minimalist view' because it makes do with the minimum of additional theoretical resources. It starts by taking the 'strength' in the strength-of-desire principle to be a measure of either intensity or the tendency to action. 'Intensity' here will be a term of phenomenology, of internal experience. On the hydraulic picture of motivation it will correspond to pressure, but *felt* pressure. 'Tendency to action' will be a behavioural measure. A desire, on this measure, is stronger to the degree that it tends to result in action other things being equal.[5] The relation between felt intensity of desire and the tendency to action is rather obscure. It is not always the desire we *feel* most intensely that we end up acting upon. But if strength-of-desire were to be measured solely by the tendency to action, it would not be possible in advance to determine what weight to give to a desire on the strength-of-desire principle. There are two different phenomena here, with no reason in logic why they should correlate. I will simply assume a correlation, knowing that it does not always obtain, since the difference between these two ways of thinking about strength-of-desire does not affect my argument.

---

[4] See Plato, *Gorgias* 492a: 'A man who is going to live a full life must allow his desires to become as mighty as may be and never repress them.'

[5] There is a good discussion of the relation between the tendency to action and *experienced* intensity in Brandt (1979) 25–32. He says that something is 'valenced' for an agent if his central motive state is such that if it were then to occur to him that a certain act of his then would tend to bring that thing about, his tendency to perform that act would be increased. Brandt then denies that when something is occurrently valenced, and is before the mind, there has to be a correlate in experience to the valence. This is partly because our behaviour is influenced by desires which are entirely unconscious and partly because experience does not seem to vary in intensity with the known corresponding valences.

Sometimes the strength-of-desire principle, in the minimalist's interpretation, can be applied without any sense of unfairness. Suppose I have to decide whether to give the remaining painkiller to the person with the greater or the lesser pain. Fairness seems to require following the principle that the more intense pain deserves the remedy, other things being equal.

What does the strength-of-desire principle, on this interpretation, say about the case of the family leaving for its holiday? If the principle simply gives greater weight to the father's desire because of its felt intensity, there will be an objection that this is unfair to the mother. The minimalist does not need to leave the matter here, however. He can say that we need to look at the whole set of desires that each party has. Perhaps the father's desire to leave on time is stronger but isolated from his other desires; whereas the mother's desire is closely integrated into the whole pattern of her desire, so that defeat here will spell partial defeat for large numbers of other desires connected up with this one.

One way to spell out this notion of integration is to appeal to the difference between first-order desires and second-order desires, which are desires about desires.[6] There can also be third-order desires; indeed there is no theoretical limit to this regress. Suppose I want to be a courageous sort of person, and that courageous people standardly feel the desire to stay in battle and not flee.[7] Then my desire to be courageous is at least a desire to have these praiseworthy desires; it is a second-order desire for first-order desires. As a first approximation, the minimalist can say that a central desire is one that is endorsed by a higher-order desire. For example, my desire not to flee in some situation will count as central if it is endorsed by my desire to be a courageous sort of person. If a first-order desire is endorsed in this way, then acting from that desire will standardly (though not necessarily) be endorsed as well, and preventing action from the first-order desire will frustrate the second-order desire as well. As Aristotle says, virtue is a disposition not only to feel desires of a certain kind but to take actions of a certain kind. To enlarge on the initial example of this chapter, the mother may want not to be

---

[6] See the use of this distinction in Frankfurt (1971). See also Frankfurt's later view (1988b).

[7] See Aristotle, NE 3. 6–9. But his account is much richer than this, involving fear and 'confidence' and love of the noble. See Pears (1980) and J. E. Hare (1988).

the sort of mother who is mindful only of the needs of her own
family. Her desire to leave the house nice will then count as central.
This means that if she has to leave the house dirty, she is frustrating
not only the desire to help the family she thinks she should have
helped, but also the desire to be a certain kind of person. If she is an
Eeyore, her desires for her life will be highly connected. Especially
her central desires will be linked up with a host of other second-
order and third-order desires, which she will be frustrating. For
example, she will want to be the sort of person who sticks with her
ideals under pressure. The father, on the other hand, might have
inherited his aversion to being late from a period of his upbringing
(say, his schooling) during which lateness was severely punished.
The aversion might be a kind of deposit from this earlier period.
Such deposits might, it is true, be connected up deeply, even if
unconsciously, with a person's other desires.[8] But they need not be
so connected; in Tiggers I am supposing they are not.

The minimalist can give greater weight to desires that have
purchase over other desires in the way this mother's desire does. The
minimalist can even give precedence to such a desire over another
desire which is, in isolation, stronger in the minimalist sense than
the first one. He might often give precedence to Eeyores on this
reasoning. Because their desires are more self-consciously connected,
frustration of one carries with it the frustration of many. With
Tiggers, on the other hand, though their individual desires are
stronger (in the minimalist sense), less damage may be done to the
whole structure of their desires by the frustration of each desire
singly. The minimalist will be able to give 'central' desires (like the
mother's) greater weight, even if they are not 'stronger', because he
can allow a trade-off between one strong desire and several weaker
ones.

But this move by the minimalist to accommodate the sense of

---

[8] Wollheim (1984) 197–225 offers a Freudian account of the growth of the moral
sense. Much of the talk about internal battle, in Kant and in this book of mine, is
usefully seen against the background of Wollheim's remarks about the asceticism of
morality. On Freudian theory much of Kantian morality is a deposit from an early
introjection. But Wollheim does allow for an evolved morality, a morality beyond the
superego. It is interesting to compare what he says about this evolution with
Kierkegaard's remarks about the transition from the ethical to the religious life, which
I shall discuss in Ch. 8.

unfairness produced by the example fails. Consider what happens to many people during adolescence. It is a period of very intense desires which are not well integrated with each other. The stage of life is mercurial, with rapid swings of mood between high and low; the highs are higher and the lows lower than they were before and will be after. This is to say, I think, that both the desires and the aversions are more intense. Adolescents are living through a period of maximum potential desire-satisfaction and aversion-avoidance. They would be, if they knew about it, following Callicles' advice.

There is a contrasting character I will call 'the fifty-year-old'. In her motivational structure the desires and aversions are flattened out, but connected with each other into a more coherent pattern.[9] Perhaps it is significant that these two features (flattening-out and connectedness) go together. Perhaps as a person gets to know herself better, her conflicting desires start to wear each other down; so that what is left is a structure with desires that are weaker in themselves but fit each other better. Intensity of single desires in a fifty-year-old is somehow suspicious, as though it puts the person's maturity in question. There can still be strong commitment, but it is more to the structure as a whole than in an adolescent, with more tolerance for the frustration of individual desires.

Suppose, by waving a magic wand, I could accommodate all the desires and aversions of the adolescent or all the desires and aversions of the fifty-year-old for what should happen to them one afternoon. I should by minimalist reasoning prefer the adolescent. One way to picture this is to suppose that I could make myself into either one of them, with all of that person's desires and aversions accommodated, but not both. Which should I choose? I will maximize desire-satisfaction and aversion-avoidance if I prefer myself as an adolescent. Consider some aversion, such as being bored at a children's piano recital. This is an aversion which I can imagine myself having both as an adolescent and as a fifty-year-old. But as an adolescent, I feel as though I am going to die if I have to stay in the room a moment longer. As a fifty-year-old, I am still bored but I reflect that I gave this same kind of pain when I was a child, and minded it less when my own children were on stage. I can laugh at myself a little more, and take myself less seriously. This

9 Hume records that young people read Ovid, and that when they get older they read Horace; he is recording a natural progression from passion to moderation.

means in part that there is a second-order desire not to give very much weight to any first-order desire without reflection. This also suggests that the very connectedness which provided the initial minimalist response about centrality also makes boredom for the fifty-year-old more tolerable.

There is another aspect of maturity, it is true, which tends in the opposite direction; people who know themselves better will have more trust in their initial instincts about what they really want. Perhaps these two aspects are combined as follows. This character I am constructing, the fifty-year-old, knows more easily than the adolescent what she really wants and what kind of person she is and wants to be. She also knows from experience that there is considerable substitutivity in achieving these things. This means that she knows there are many alternative routes to achieving what she wants, and therefore it is usually less crucial to secure any one of them. On the other hand, because she knows more easily than the adolescent what these routes are, she knows when she does have to secure one of them. The point is that there are many *different* kinds of link between lower-order and higher-order desires. This is true even if we restrict our attention to higher-order desires which are, in a general way, in favour of or *for* lower-order ones. Endorsing a desire is one such link; but amused toleration of a desire is another, and so is weary acquiescence in a desire. The notion of connecting a lower-order desire to a higher-order one does not yet capture what is important in centrality. We need to be able to say what kind of link we are talking about. The point with the adolescent and the fifty-year-old is that for many lower-order desires (such as the desire not to go on listening to the children's piano recital) the fifty-year-old is more likely to be able to tolerate their frustration because of the link with her higher-order desires. If I could relieve my boredom at one stage or the other, minimalist reasoning should therefore lead me to give preference to myself as an adolescent. But it would be unfair to discriminate against fifty-year-olds in this way.

The minimalist might reply that adolescence is after all *not* for most people a period of maximum desire-satisfaction and aversion-avoidance. This may be because in the world as it actually is, the desires of the adolescent can hardly ever be satisfied. The intensity of those desires therefore translates into intensity of frustration. The reason for this is that the desires are either in conflict with each other, or would, if satisfied, lead to too much distress for other people.[10] If, therefore, I am trying to choose in the real world whether to satisfy the desires of the adolescent or the fifty-year-old, I should choose the fifty-year-old; in this way I will tend to maximize desire-satisfaction even though the adolescent's desires are more intense.

Even if this is right, however, it is because of contingent features of the adolescent's situation. The account in terms of higher-order desires does not yet allow the minimalist to give weight to centrality as such. There are too many different ways in which a person can have desires for desires. The connection of some lower-order desires to higher-order desires does not yet give us a reason for giving preference to those lower-order ones. The appeal to higher-order desires does not capture the notion of identification with a desire, which is one thing we need if we are going to understand why the mother's desire in my initial example deserves weight because it is *central* to her.[11] It is possible for an agent to have second-order desires for first-order ones and still not identify with the first-order desires; and possible for her to have first-order desires with which she identifies without having second-order desires for them. Identification is not so much having a desire for a desire, as having a desire (first-order or second-order) in the right way. We still need to characterize what this right way is.

What is the distinction between desires I identify with and desires I do not? To put this the other way round, what does it mean to think of my desire as external to me? We need here an account which does the work of the traditional Christian account of sin. Paul in Romans makes the point this way:

Sin, seizing the opportunity afforded by the commandment, produced in me every kind of covetous desire. . . . I do not understand what I do. For what I want to do I do not do, but what I hate I do. And if I do what I do not want to do, I agree that the law is good. As it is, it is no longer I myself who do it, but it is sin living in me. I know that nothing good lives in me, that is, in my

[10] I suggested earlier that one reason for the difference with the fifty-year-old is that her conflicting desires have, over the course of thirty years, worn each other down; this implies that the desires of an earlier stage were in conflict with each other.

[11] This objection is made by Watson (1975) and also forcibly by Wolf (1990) 28 f. I am going to claim that identifying with a desire is not yet giving centrality to it, which requires in addition attaching importance to the desire.

sinful nature. For I have the desire to do what is good, but I cannot carry it out.[12]

There is a complex and rich body of doctrine here. What is relevant for present purposes is that Paul distinguishes two sets of desires he has: there are the desires produced by sin, and the desires which he identifies as what *he* wants. Intensity and the tendency to action can belong to members of either set.[13] Some of the desires produced by sin are, moreover, second-order, such as the desire not to have the desire to submit to God's law. This is the way sin seizes the opportunity afforded by the commandment.[14] Without the commandment, I could not have the desire not to have the desire to submit to it. In Paul's time, for example, the early church was characterized by the practice of radical generosity: 'They had all things common.'[15] This gave sin the opportunity to work within Ananias and Sapphira, who deceptively kept back part of their estate.[16] The desire to spend their resources on themselves was not in itself sinful. But faced with the call to give most of them away and live in faith, the desire to keep them took on a different character. It became the denial of this call, and hence the desire not to have (or follow) the desire to heed the call.

One way to make the distinction between the two sets of desires is to point to the difference between authority and power. Those with authority are entitled to obedience even if they do not receive it. Those with power do receive it, even if they are not entitled to it. The person I want to be and thus the desires I want to have can be authoritative for me, even if they are not the most intense or the

---

[12] Rom. 7: 9, 15–18 (New International Version). But the whole chapter is the necessary context, and is embedded in a complex argument which extends over Chs. 1–8. I am assuming that Paul is talking in Rom. 7 about himself after conversion, though some interpreters have denied this.

[13] With this passage taken in isolation, it is true, Paul sounds as though he has no tendency to act on the desires that he identifies as *his*; but he is describing himself here in the flesh *as* a slave to the law of sin during the episode of failure, not in the mind (*nous*) *as* a slave to God's law.

[14] See Augustine's discussion in *Confessions* 7, which contains continual ref. to this passage. The connection with faith comes, for example, at the final moment of conversion where he takes up and reads Rom. 13: 14, which ends 'and make not provision for the flesh in concupiscence'. He says, 'immediately I had reached the end of this sentence it was as though my heart was filled with the light of confidence'. I shall say more about sin as the denial of the call of faith in Ch. 8, in ref. to Kierkegaard's account of 'dizziness'.   [15] Acts 4: 32.

[16] The story of Ananias and Sapphira follows immediately in Acts 5.

most likely to lead to action (the most powerful). Paul thus introduces the passage in Romans by saying that we were once under the jurisdiction of the law of sin, from which we have been released by dying to what once bound us; the law of sin may still have some power, but it no longer has authority. His view is the original of Kant's translation, discussed in Chapter 2, that there has been a decisive shift from the old man to the new man, even though there may still be habits left over from the old way of life.

Here is one way, then, to characterize what it means not to identify with a desire: it means regarding the desire as sinful. This description has the merit of avoiding too piecemeal a distinction, as though our desires could be isolated from each other into single good or bad units. Sin is a nature, a large-scale pattern of desires. We can see this if we look back to the character of the fifty-year-old. In comparison with the adolescent, she has come to terms with herself. She has come to see that the parts of herself she dislikes are, some of them at least, the bad side of parts of herself she likes. For example, she is good at concentrating on her academic work, but this also means she is often not very perceptive about the needs of the people around her. She has started to see the desires which she does not want to have less like isolated intruders, and more as spreading out widely in the stable network of her character. Moreover the parts of herself she does like seem less purely honourable than they did, and more mixed up with the rest. Now it is possible to characterize all this as mere accommodation, as throwing in the towel. Perhaps she does not have the energy any more for the fight for self-improvement. On the other hand, it is also possible to characterize coming to terms with oneself as wisdom and maturity.

Does the fifty-year-old endorse the whole of herself, or should she do so? There is a difference between endorsing and *acknowledging*. She can acknowledge a trait or a desire, in the sense that it is no longer seen as an isolated intruder, but none the less admit that it forms part of a pattern of traits or desires which tend to lead her astray. 'God', she may say half-humorously, 'isn't finished with me yet.' The fifty-year-old, whose character I am constructing, still has what she recognizes as familiar faults. But she sees herself more nearly as a whole than she did, and therefore does not blame her failures on isolated desires or traits of character but on the whole package turned in the wrong direction. She tends to be proud or ashamed of the whole package as it issues in one kind of action or another. There is thus a distinction like the one Paul discusses in *Romans* between what she wants and what sin in her wants, a distinction which is not readily applied one desire at a time. Because she sees more of the connections between her desires, she can see how complicated and pervasive are the influences of both sin and good. She can see how much of herself can go both ways. She does not simply divide herself up into black and white units, desires she approves of and desires she does not. But she will not say that to understand all is to pardon all, either for herself or for others. Seeing the complicated connections between her desires does not mean *endorsing* them all in the sense of seeing them both as her own and as good. It will mean *acknowledging* them, in the weak sense that more and more of them are seen as a familiar part of the whole package, not isolated intruders (even while admitting that she would be better off without some of the desires which she acknowledges in this sense). With this distinction in mind, we can now introduce a third idea, *identifying with* her desires, in the sense of acknowledging them *and* not wanting to change them or have them changed. Identifying with a desire is stronger than acknowledging it, on this account, and weaker than endorsing it, since she may identify with many desires which she sees can be good or bad, depending on how they are connected up with other desires into a larger-scale pattern. It may be that she does not want to change a desire, or have it changed, even though she would like to change the pattern in which it is connected with other desires to produce harm for herself or other people. Sin, in Paul's sense, is often widely and subtly diffused in a life. I can have a desire for the last éclair on the plate, to return to the example in Chapter 4, without yet having anything to be ashamed of. This is what Kant says about many of the desires for my own happiness. But if the desire is structured into the sort of pattern of desires which Kant calls being under the evil maxim, I may refuse to identify with the pattern and the desire as structured that way. Perhaps my love of desserts blinds me to the fact that somebody else, my Aunt Fanny, deserves the éclair more than I do. Sin is a familiar enemy, a pattern that I can both acknowledge and refuse to identify with.

This is a very rough classification. My point so far is that the minimalist cannot rescue the strength-of-desire principle from the charge of unfairness by appealing merely to the distinction between higher-order desires and lower-order ones. An account of fairness to the mother in my initial example needs an account of what it is for a desire to be central. Even if we could provide an account of identification and endorsement, we would still not know what centrality meant; for centrality requires, in addition, that she finds the object of the desire *important* to her life as a whole. Could the minimalist give the following account of importance: 'within the class of desires I endorse, the desires I find important are the ones for which I have a higher-order desire which also generates a large number of other desires I have'? One major difficulty here is understanding how to count desires. If I have the desire to catch the bus in ten minutes, do I have in addition the desire not to be late for the bus, the desire to be at the bus-stop in less than eleven minutes, and so on? This difficulty prevents simply adding up the number of desires generated. But there is a plausible idea that some desires control a larger share of my life than others, and that the way they do this is by determining other desires. For example, the desire to be a good pianist may include the desire for the desire to spend hours of every day practising (though this is also an example where the term 'desire' seems inadequate; do I *desire* the fifth daily hour of practice?). Perhaps importance could be measured by how many decisions in one's life a second-order desire controls? On this account we could call the desire to be a good pianist an important desire, since it controls the lower-order desire to practise today after lunch, which itself controls the desire to play over this bar for the thirtieth time today. This account is not right, however. My second-order desire to be a well-mannered sort of person may control hundreds of daily and predictable interpersonal transactions; but it may still be less important to me than the desire to be brave, even though the opportunities for what I count as bravery are very rare and irregular. We cannot get to the idea of importance simply by adding up the number of decisions controlled. This would be, if anything, a measure of power rather than authority. No doubt there will be higher-order desires involved in the importance to my life as a whole of some desire which I endorse. But we cannot explain this importance in a desire simply by pointing to the existence of a higher-order desire which accompanies it.

Decision theorists have a variety of ways to get a person's preference ordering, by asking, for example, what she would sacrifice for what else. But coming high on a preference ordering will not by itself count as centrality in a desire. There are too many different ways in which people prefer things. If we try to apply the strength-of-desire principle without adding an account of what it is to identify with a desire, endorse a desire, and attach importance to a desire, we will be pretending to be able to say what we care about morally in distributing between people, when in fact we cannot yet do so.

c. THE NATURALIST VIEW

The second view I will consider is what I will call 'the naturalist view', because of its reliance on a view of human nature. I am taking the view from James Griffin's *Well-Being*. The strength-of-desire principle is interpreted differently by this view because 'strength' is measured differently. On this view we should assess the strength of desires not in the sense of felt intensity, or tendency to action, but 'in a sense supplied by the natural structure of desire'. How do we know what the natural structure of desire is? Griffin starts with a theory of prudence, an account of what makes human life good. He sets up a list of prudential values, which he calls 'the common profile' because it provides a picture of normal human desires. 'Virtually all persons, when informed, want to live autonomously, to have deep personal relations, to accomplish something with their lives, to enjoy themselves.'[17] The common profile includes both the prudential values themselves and their importance relative to each other, that is, a hierarchy between them. Individual differences between people affect the degree to which and the manner in which a particular person can realize one or other of these values, but any normal person will conform to the common profile in spite of such differences. The various prudential values on the list are not said to be reducible to one super-value, units of which could then be totted up to give the eventual decision about what to do. But the decision is still said to be a matter of maximization.[18] Since the items on the list and their relations are what constitute general prudential value for humans, *informed* desire will be desire that corresponds to this hierarchy. The strength of a desire, then, can be measured by the relative place of the desire in this hierarchy, and the hierarchy itself

---

[17] Griffin (1986) 114.
[18] 'The finally effective magnitudes are fixed by global desires. Desires form a hierarchy, and the whole idea of a hierarchy of desires brings the prudential policy of maximization along with it' (ibid. 145).

can be described as both 'the natural structure of desire' and 'the informed preference order'.

This view gives a good response to the objection from unfairness that I have been talking about. The naturalist will not discriminate against Eeyores in favour of Tiggers. This is because mere intensity or tendency to produce action will not be sufficient to determine strength.[19] As long as I am normal, my informed global desires will correspond to the natural hierarchy. There will not, then, be any problem about a divergence between what is central to me and my strongest desires. We can thus at the same time preserve the strength-of-desire principle (interpreted in the naturalist way) and overcome the objection from unfairness.

There are, however, serious objections to the view, of which I will mention two. The first is that the list is parochial, and, if it is made more inclusive, incoherent. I have already given the four main items on the list, namely autonomy, deep personal relations, accomplishment, and enjoyment.[20] A fifth is understanding (knowing about oneself and one's world). Since this list is supposed to be constitutive of the global prudential values of any normal human being, incompleteness is a serious weakness. I think what is immediately noticeable about the list is how much it leaves out. To give two examples of general headings that should be there, there are no communal values and no religious values. The other important omissions are power and prestige, and I will come back to these in the second objection.

For Socrates, it was a central value not merely to have a flourishing personal life but to be part of a flourishing *polis*. Indeed, this misstates the case. For him, the institutions (*nomoi*) of his *polis* were like his parents in that they formed his identity. His full name included reference to his city: 'Socrates, son of Sophroniscus, the Athenian'. The most important relations to him were not deep personal relations but civic relations.[21] A second major omission is

---

[19] Griffin makes use of an objection he ascribes to Roslind Godlovich: 'The desires I feel most intensely could be satisfied by your constantly imperilling my life and saving me only at the last moment' (ibid. 315).

[20] The complete list puts autonomy under the general heading 'the components of human existence', and adds (under that heading) the basic capabilities that enable one to act, and liberty (the absence of obstacles to action in those areas of our life that are the essential manifestations of our humanity).

[21] Griffin gets closest to this in his discussion of fraternity (ibid. 301 and n. 39). But he analyses this as 'a kind of free, easy, naturally concerned relation between

religious values. Suppose my deepest value is disengagement from the world, or a life of union with God, or the flight of the alone to the alone, would I be abnormal? By the standards of much contemporary Western psychiatry, perhaps. But do we want to be tied to the presuppositions behind this body of practice?[22]

The list is liable, therefore, to the charge of parochialism. It is the list, to put it harshly, of an individualist, achievement-directed, secular Westerner. The objection is not, moreover, to incompleteness alone; it is to incoherence. The introduction of communal and religious values brings conflict into the list. This is not just conflict in ranking between values, but presents the threat of displacement from the list itself. The desire for achievement or accomplishment, as the list defines this value (making something valuable of one's life and not just frittering it away) may well be *incompatible* with disengagement.[23] The desire for autonomy (setting one's own agenda) may be incompatible with some ideals of citizenship.[24] Would the Zen master characterize himself as aiming at understanding himself and his world? These general prudential values have to be given detailed treatment if they are to function well in giving us a measure of strength. To the extent that they are given such detail, they are likely to reveal conflict. This objection to the particular list does not itself show that there is no list that is both substantial enough to give a measure of strength-of-desire in individual decision-making and sufficiently general to give the desire structure of human nature. The objection suggests, however, that we have to be careful not to exaggerate our capacity to describe the content of such a list.

The second and most important objection is that the list is too benign. It omits goals which we actually have, and which control

persons.' He does not say, though he may intend, that this kind of relation is within a community one may not have chosen to be born into; and that membership of such a community is for many normal human beings one of the highest prudential values.

[22] Griffin's response to the point about religious values is to deny that these are in the ordinary sense prudential values at all (ibid. 83). He suggests that they belong to a different category. The trouble is that they do not belong in his account of moral values either, and they are thus not given a place in his account of decision-making. What matters is not whether we call them 'prudential' values, but whether we allow that they can be the central values in the desire hierarchy of a normal human being.

[23] Ibid. 29. See Kierkegaard's account in *EO* i, 'The Rotation of Crops'.

[24] Aristotle is, to our ears, surprisingly unconcerned about autonomy in this sense, though very concerned with freedom as opposed to slavery. See J. E. Hare (1988).

much of our behaviour, but which are not (in the form in which we often have them) consistent with living morally. Foremost among these are power and prestige. The naturalist claims to give us a list of our main prudential values, of what we think (after reflection) makes life go well for us. Unfortunately there are items which belong on the list, even with full knowledge of the facts and of logic and of the relevant concepts, which both have tremendous shaping power over our actual decisions and are inconsistent with life going so well for other people. In Chapter 4 I discussed what Luther calls the lust for power. Kant is in the tradition of Luther's doctrine of the bondage of the will; he holds that human beings, as soon as they enter into each other's company, are beseiged by envy, the lust for power, greed, and the malignant inclinations bound up with these.[25] It may be that the desire to control and dominate others is at least as strong a desire (in the minimalist sense) as the desire to understand oneself and one's world. The first desire often lies behind the motive power of the second. It is true that people are often ashamed of the extent to which the desire for power shapes their lives, but that shows *conflict* in the list; it does not show that power does not belong on the list in the first place. The desire for prestige, for being admired by other people, controls large areas of our decision-making, far larger than we like to admit. But like the desire for power, it requires for its fulfilment that other people not have as much success in attaining it as we do ourselves.

As I suggested in Chapter 4, we need a theory of the springs of action which gives room for rationalization. If power is indeed an important goal for many people, it may appear under disguise in the accounts such people give to themselves and others. Griffin's terms for the prudential values in the common profile may survive, for some perfectly normal people, but with the content distorted. This is what has happened regularly to terms of evaluation, from the use by Augustus of the language of the Republic to the twentieth-century use of terms like 'socialist' and 'democratic'.[26] It is a history that

---

[25] *Rel.* 85 (93).

[26] For an illuminating example, see Thucydides's description of what happened to moral language in Corcyra during the Peloponnesian war. 'Words had to change their ordinary meaning and take that which was now given to them. Reckless audacity came to be considered the courage of a loyal ally; prudent hesitation, specious cowardice' (*History of the Peloponnesian War* 3. 82–3).

Orwell projected into the future, in *Nineteen Eighty-four*, with the ministries of Truth and Justice. Consider, for example, the abusive relations that have been tolerated in the name of deep personal relations. We should not be misled in constructing the list of prudential values by the names which people offer for them.

These two objections are internally related in an interesting way. It is because the naturalist has a benign list of prudential values that he thinks we do not have to make an existential choice of values or go beyond prudence and morality to religion. The values on the list are, for him, given by our human nature. If the list contains disreputable items as well as respectable ones, this makes it more likely that those interested in the moral life will have to make a radical choice of values, or 'decisions of principle'.[27] The naturalist does want us to have control over the central features of our fate; that is part of having autonomy. But he does not think that we can control what our central prudential values are, since these are given to us by nature.[28] What *should* be within our control, on the naturalist's view, is the adoption and implementation of the plan that we adopt to secure the values on the list nature gives us, and the careful definition and clarification of what these values are. It is possible in theory, he thinks, to have radical argument about what these basic values are; but this would require stepping back far enough from our ordinary concerns so that they became not serious, or mattered much less than we ordinarily think. Once we are engaged in life, on this view, the natural values will take over. But then, he asks, what could make us step back in this way, or disengage? Could the thought that we are going to die, or that the constant increase of entropy ensures the vast death of the solar system? He argues that this would imply that the basic values are the sorts of thing that require unlimited time if they are to matter at all, and he sees no reason to believe they are that sort of thing.[29]

This is another example of the naturalist's brisk attitude towards religious questions.[30] But if our nature is, in theological terms,

---

[27] The phrase is from R. M. Hare (1952) 56–78.

[28] Griffin (1986) 70.

[29] Griffin suggests that the radical questioning of a prudential value does not even make sense. Such questions are probably 'steps into confusion, steps off the edge of coherent talk about values' (ibid. 66).

[30] Contrast the attitude towards the radical questioning of value in T. S. Eliot's 'East Coker' lines 112–26. I will quote just one image from this passage, 'Or as, when

fallen, we may have to make a radical choice between different values that our nature supplies. We may have to choose between what Kant calls the predisposition to good and the propensity to evil. The question addressed in the first division of this book will then arise; how is this kind of choice possible? There are, I think, many occasions for the radical questioning of value. One author who gives particularly vivid narratives of such questioning is Kierkegaard. He contrasts in *Either/Or* the aesthete with Judge William (the ethical man). I discuss the pair in detail in Chapter 8. The aesthete likes to look at his life in the way the lookout in the crow's-nest of a ship observes the storm lashing the deck. He does not want engagement, merely interesting observation. Especially, he does *not* want deep personal relations, and he does *not* want to achieve anything with his life, and he does *not* want autonomy if that is taken to mean responsibility for decision. He is not, therefore, by the naturalist's list, a normal person at all; and that is just what Judge William observes. The judge insists that autonomy and marriage and a job to which one is committed are universal demands of human nature. But then the judge finds himself in difficulties rather like the aesthete's; he finds himself unable to lead the life he has set for himself, and he ends up seeming as impoverished from the perspective of the religious life as the aesthete seemed from the perspective of the ethical. The point is that the aesthete's and the judge's values can be questioned radically, both from below (on Kierkegaard's scheme) and from above. It may be that Kierkegaard simply does not make sense here. But how would a modest philosopher know this, without first going through the challenging exercise of trying to see the question through the eyes of Kierkegaard's narrators?

d. THE RATIONALIST VIEW

We need, then, a view which allows centrality to be considered in moral decisions alongside strength of desire in the minimalist sense, but which does not depend on too benign a view of human nature. Central desires need to be given weight independently of the desires' intensity or tendency to lead to action, if we are going to avoid

---

an underground train, in the tube, stops too long between stations | And the conversation rises and slowly fades into silence | And you see behind every face the mental emptiness deepen | Leaving only the growing terror of nothing to think about'.

discriminating against Eeyores. But nature as the naturalist construes it does not give us the notion of centrality we need. In the discussion of the minimalist view, I distinguished between three increasingly specific ingredients in centrality: identifying with a desire, endorsing a desire, and attaching importance to a desire. In this final part of the chapter I will look at a third view of centrality which focuses on the first of these ingredients. I will call it 'the rationalist view', drawing it from Susan Wolf's *Freedom within Reason*.[31] On the rationalist view, there is a kind of 'deep' identification with a desire, or ownership of it, which allows us to hold a person responsible for an action which comes from such a desire, and thus enables us to apportion deep praise or blame to the action. We can apportion such praise and blame if we can determine whether the person whose desire it is possesses the ability to act in accordance with Reason. In this part of the chapter I will look at this notion of deep ownership.

To see why the rationalist takes the line she does, we can start with two examples of desires that I have but are not deeply mine in the required sense. I have been hypnotized by a master hypnotist so that I want to stand up and sing the national anthem whenever I smell pizza. When I subsequently smell pizza, and find myself with a strong desire to get to my feet, the desire seems inexplicable to me, or alien. Or perhaps I am a kleptomaniac, and find myself one day in a shop putting a pen-set from the shelf into my pocket rather than into my shopping basket. These examples are different in several ways, but they are alike in that I come to act on a desire which, as it were, bypasses my will. In a full treatment of this notion, the idea of the will would need to be clarified; and the coherence of the idea that the will issues in free action would have to be defended. All this is too ambitious a task for now. I will rely on the compatibilist tradition in Hume, and before Hume in Calvin, which distinguishes between

[31] Wolf is not a utilitarian, but for a utilitarian account which makes some of the same moves, see Brink (1989). An important difference between the way I am using Wolf's ideas and the way she uses them is that she is defending a notion of responsibility and freedom, whereas I am discussing a notion of centrality. But the kind of responsibility and freedom she is defending depends on the notion of the agent being the 'deep' source of the content of his or her will. If Wolf succeeds in this, she will also have an account of what it is to identify with a desire in such a way that the desire deserves to be given weight.

necessity and compulsion.[32] Both examples, we can say, deprive us of a kind of liberty we normally have, so that we are compelled to act.

It is tempting to say, in the light of these examples, that I identify with a desire deeply if it does not bypass my will, or if its influence on action goes through my will. What would this mean? Perhaps we can distinguish between an agent's values and the rest of the agent's desires.[33] To value something, on this account, is to think it good or to think there is some reason to want it. Alternatively, to value something is to endorse the desire for it. Not all desires are endorsed; take Wolf's examples of the desire 'to drown one's baby in the bathwater', or the desire 'to smash the face of one's squash competition with one's racket'. Endorsing or valuing is thus more than merely acknowledging a desire, in terms of my distinction in Section c. Can we now say that I identify deeply with a desire if the object of the desire is additionally something I value? This is not yet enough. For it is possible that I may be alienated from what I value just as, in the previous examples, I was alienated from what I desired. This is harder to see. But consider the following examples. Suppose I think I am Napoleon. I not merely dress as he did, tucking my arm inside my waistcoat, but I speak in late-eighteenth-century French and think ceaselessly about strategies to revenge myself on Wellington. Or suppose I am living in a world in which Big Brother has taken over the programming of peoples' lives, so that I am not merely hypnotized to desire one thing when given one stimulus (such as the smell of pizza), but programmed to a coherent set of desires that covers virtually all the situations I am likely to find myself in. Or suppose, finally, that I was the victim of severe and continual abuse when I was growing up, and am now no longer able to form loving relations with people. In all these cases, I will do valuing which is not, in a sense hard to define, authentic. The third

---

[32] Hume, *A Treatise Concerning Human Nature*, 407; Calvin, *Institutes*, II. iii. 5.

[33] See Watson (1975). Another treatment of the distinction is by Taylor (1989) 4 f. Taylor distinguishes a class of what he calls 'strong evaluations', which 'involve discriminations of right and wrong, better and worse, higher or lower, which are not rendered valid by our own desires, inclinations, or choices, but rather stand independent of these and offer standards by which they can be judged.' See also Brink (1989) 78: 'And we typically invite others to share our attitudes and prescribe courses of action because we hold the (defeasible) belief that these attitudes and courses of action are correct or valuable.'

case is the hardest. If I form the judgement that someone who is apparently helping me is in fact untrustworthy, I am valuing; I am evaluating the person in terms of what I care about and what matters to me. But my capacity to make appropriate valuations of people has been severely damaged. This is true even though there may be nothing in the rest of my desires and values which is inconsistent with this particular valuation; or at least, if there is anything, it may not be accessible to me or to anyone else.

The rationalist therefore makes the move which defines the position. She says that the agents in these three examples are not able by their own powers to act or choose in accordance with Reason. What is meant by 'Reason' here is 'whatever faculty or set of faculties are most likely to lead us to form true beliefs and good values.'[34] The idea is that an agent is responsible for a decision if it is made in light of all the reasons there actually are for doing and for not doing it. In the terms I have been using, the rationalist could say that an agent deeply identifies with a desire if the object of the desire is something she values *and* at the time of her valuation she is able to act or choose in accordance with Reason in this sense. The rationalist claims that we are inclined to say the three agents in the examples are alienated from their valuations *because* they have been blinded to the reasons for acting that Reason would give them.

The thesis of the present chapter is that the rationalist's account does not allow for radical evil. To put this another way, she exaggerates our natural capacities to live a moral life. In this respect, her account suffers from the same kind of objection as the previous two. If responsibility for an action requires us to be able to be cognizant of every reason for and against it, none of us will ever be responsible. Only God has the right kind of mind for that kind of task. The rationalist is aware of this objection, and concedes that we do not have the requisite powers of reflection and imagination, the requisite breadth of knowledge, or the requisite amount of leisure.[35] She therefore revises the account downwards: what is necessary is

[34] Wolf (1990) 53. There is a preference in the rationalist account for the language of moral realism, such as 'tracking' values, or 'seeing' them. It is not my purpose here to discuss whether this preference is defensible.

[35] Ibid. 142. Wolf sees the ability and inability to act or choose in accordance with Reason as due to the presence or absence of intellectual powers within the agent (ibid. 71). She does not consider the possible combination of natural inability and divine assistance.

that we recognize and appreciate a set of reasons sufficient to show which action or choice would be right. I am free and responsible *enough*, accordingly, as long as my blindness to some other reasonable alternative does not lead me to acts of intolerance or prejudice. This is still, however, a very strong condition on responsibility: I am not responsible if the reasons I entertain for an action are not sufficient to show the action would be right.

Note that the failures allowed on this account are cognitive failures or deficiencies of time. In this respect, the rationalist's account is like the optimist's in Chapter 4. What I suggested there was that cognitive failures can be a product of moral failures. This is straightforwardly true in cases like that of the abused child, where the moral failures of others can cause a disposition to valuational failure in their victim. I have in mind something less straightforward: an agent's *own* moral failings causing her to be blind to certain moral considerations (or reasons for action). This is clearest, perhaps, in cases of deterioration. A person can start off on a course of action at the beginning of which she is still open to doubts about its legitimacy; but by the time she is fully engaged in it, she can only dimly 'hear' those doubts. They do not any longer have the kind of authority for her which would deter her from overriding them. It is instructive to study the deterioration of conscience during the conduct of a war. Strategic bombing was considered impermissible at the beginning of the Second World War, and widely practised by both sides at the end of it.[36] What considerations a person is open to depends in part on what sort of person she has allowed herself to become. The rationalist position is that a person is responsible for an action only if *at the time of performance* she possesses the ability to act for the sake of the reasons there are in favour of the action and against it.[37] But a person can get into bad habits; and when she does, she can become insensitive to some of the considerations there are against an action. She gets used to seeing things the way it becomes in her interest to see them. Is she then not responsible for her actions? I think we should say that she is responsible, and also that she deeply owns the desires she comes to have. This is true even though she can no longer act or choose on the basis of the reasons

---

[36] See Hare and Joynt (1982) 91 f. Iris Murdoch's novels are full of characters who have deteriorated in their moral perceptiveness.

[37] Wolf (1990) 90 and n. 7.

there are against her pattern of action, because she can no longer hear those reasons except as a vague and perhaps irritating memory of the kind of person she used to be. People can become used to a life of senseless violence and cruelty. We exaggerate their surviving moral capacity if we say that all those whom we hold accountable are at the time they act capable of acting or choosing on the basis of the standards against which we judge them.

We can now generalize this point to failings a person has from the beginning, and not merely failings into which she deteriorates. What she can hear or see as a reason for her to act depends not merely on her cognitive abilities and the time available, but on her moral sensitivity. We should allow for the possibility that there are considerations which should move us to action, and which are even necessary to show us which action or choice is right; but we have grown up ignoring them. To soften up the opposition to such an admission, consider the case of the slave-owner in 1750. He grows up in a world in which slavery is taken for granted. He is perhaps the decent and compassionate sort of person who rebelled against the institution in the following century. But given his moral formation at the beginning of the eighteenth century, can we say that when grown up he possessed the ability to act in accordance with the reasons there are against slavery? Even Kant, who surely understood about the dignity of human beings, argued that a man who commits a crime can be made 'the property of another, who is accordingly not merely his master but also his owner'; serfs and slaves are 'men without personality' (i.e. without rational will).[38] Now we should ask about ourselves whether we are not likely to have grown up ignoring some moral consideration in some comparable way. If the reason that would be necessary for us to avoid some wrong pattern is not accessible to us, given our moral formation, we are not (by the rationalist account) responsible for our failure to avoid that pattern.

The consideration of cultural blindness should be a cause for

---

[38] *MM* 66 (241), 139 (330). If we accept the view that there is still a seed of goodness in all humans, however depraved, and that this is a vestigial awareness of the moral law, then we might say that the slave-owner has had to suppress an uneasiness about slavery, perhaps when he was very young. But by the time he is an adult, he can no longer hear this concern. Kierkegaard suggests that history can accumulate the difficulty of opting for the good. Haufniensis (the pseudonymous author) denies that every individual plays 'his little history in his own private theater unconcerned about the race' (*CA* 34). See Quinn (1990) 242.

hesitation about our moral capacities. I want to move to a cause for humility drawn from the consideration of what Kant calls 'the perversity of the human heart'.[39] The rationalist's position requires, as I have interpreted it, that a person who deeply owns her desire must be able to act or choose by her own powers in accordance with Reason. Kant's view of the human heart, on the contrary, is that there is 'a propensity of the will to maxims which neglect the incentives springing from the moral law in favour of others which are not moral.' Moreover there is an insidiousness in this propensity; for the human heart tends to deceive itself in regard to its good and evil dispositions, and to picture itself as meritorious when it is not so. All humans still have, in his view, the seed of goodness in them, so that they can hear, at least faintly, the call of the moral law. Kant wants to say they are therefore correctly held accountable when they do not heed the call. But he thinks that they are not able to overcome the propensity to evil by their own devices, because 'the extirpation could occur only through good maxims, and cannot take place when the ultimate subjective ground of all maxims is postulated as corrupt'.[40]

Suppose we now return to the moral demand on the people living comfortably in the rich parts of the world to sacrifice a significant portion of their wealth for the sake of the starving in the poor parts of the world. Most people who fall under this demand do not live by it. Is this because they are not aware of the suffering they could help to alleviate? No, they are at least dimly aware of it. If they are not *vividly* aware of this, it is because they have chosen not to be vividly aware of it. Perhaps this is too strong. They have got trapped in a world in which the normal expectations for standard of living make radical sacrifice inconceivable. In what sense are they *able* to act or choose in accordance with the demand? They cannot by their own devices overcome the suffocating influence of 'common sense'.

Take another example. For a utilitarian, the moral demand includes the secular equivalent of what are called in theology 'the evangelical counsels'; for example, we are to love our enemies. The mere fact that someone has deliberately harmed me in the past does not alter the fact that, if I now meet him, I should give him what he needs if I can.[41] But in what sense am I able to act or choose in

---

[39] *Rel.* 25 (30), 32 (37).   [40] *Rel.* 32 (37).
[41] See Luke 6: 29: he has taken my cloak, and I offer my coat.

accordance with this demand? The Christian tradition divided on the issue at the Reformation. Some held that the evangelical counsels are appropriate for those with a special call, like monks. Some held that they are appropriate for all, but that special grace is required for their implementation. Neither side held that we have the capacity to live by these demands by our own devices. This was because of a realism about the countervailing pressures towards favouring what Kant calls the dear self.

On Kant's view, we can hold people responsible even if they cannot themselves overcome the desires which obscure the call of duty. In the terms used earlier, we can say that they deeply own those desires. This is so because they do still hear the call, even if indistinctly. Some combination like this would account for what would otherwise be puzzling. On the one hand, we see people constantly failing by the moral standards they and we uphold at least verbally, and we want to hold them and ourselves responsible and accountable for such failures. Yet there seems to be something inevitable about their and our failing; it is not just that we have cognitive limitations as human beings, but that we seem to have moral limitations as well. There are two attitudes which seem internally coherent, though contradictory to each other.[42] The first is a moral idealism, which holds people straightforwardly capable of living morally good lives and therefore accountable for their moral failures. The second is a cynical realism, which holds that we are straightforwardly incapable of virtue and therefore not to be blamed for its absence. Neither of these positions seems satisfactory, however, for we want to combine parts of each; we want realism *and* accountability. The question is how to combine the two coherently. The rationalist insists that the responsible agent must be *able* to act and choose by her own powers in accordance with Reason. But this is too optimistic. What we need is a theory which both allows that morality is possible for us, and does not exaggerate our natural capacities. One theory of this kind is that the morally good life is possible for us, but not by our own devices.

The rationalist's strategy for understanding responsibility is to move back from desiring to valuing (because not all desiring is deeply owned), and then to move back from valuing to Reason (because not all valuing is deeply owned either). The main objection

---

[42] See Niebuhr (1941) ch. 9.

is that she has stopped too soon. For the reason we actually operate with, the faculty which leads us to form our beliefs and values, does not reliably track the True and the Good. It is possible, certainly, to posit a faculty with an honorific capital letter, Reason, which *is* reliable. But then our access to Reason is not reliable. If we postulate this super-faculty, we can say, with Kant, that it survives in all of us, so that we are all accountable for our moral failures. Another option is to disagree with Kant about the survival in all people of the seed of goodness, and to admit that for cases like the man who thinks he is Napoleon, or the exploited worker in *Nineteen Eighty-four*, or the abuse victim, it has not survived to the degree necessary for accountability. In either case, we should not go on to say that for those in whom it survives, accountability means that they can by their own devices act and choose in accordance with it. This does not fit with the experience of the overwhelming difficulty, even in the best of circumstances, of leading a morally good life.

6

REDUCING THE DEMAND

I HAVE claimed that there are two strategies, other than invoking God's assistance or some substitute, for removing the gap between the moral demand and our natural human capacities.[1] The first strategy is to exaggerate our capacities, and this was the subject of Chapters 4 and 5. The second strategy is to reduce the demand.[2] I will concentrate in this chapter on attempts to claim that impartiality is not always required in moral judgement. These attempts can be seen as driving a wedge between the two formulations of Kant's categorical imperative which I discussed in Section *a* of Chapter 1. Impartiality is a construal of the first formulation. On this construal a moral judgement commits the agent to making the same judgement for any situation which is the same in its universally specified description.[3] Thus if I make the judgement that I should take my Christmas holidays in the Bahamas, and if this is a full-fledged moral judgement by Kantian standards, then I am committed to saying that anyone who is in my sort of situation (fed up with marking papers, starved for the sun, able at least barely to afford it, etc.) should do the same sort of thing. In the present chapter I will use the

---

[1] Some material in this chapter has also appeared in J. E. Hare (1995a). I want to thank my commentator at the American Philosophical Association meetings, Julie McDonald, for her comments on a previous draft.

[2] As with the first strategy, there are many non-philosophical examples, such as 'I'm OK, You're OK' literature and the rational emotive therapy of Albert Ellis; see Roberts (1993). There are people who do not seem to feel the force of universal moral obligations at all, or who have local allegiances and refuse to see them as constrained by universal moral obligations. There are appalling examples in various parts of the world which have disintegrated into tribal war. The 1970s and 1980s have been characterized in the USA and in Western Europe as decades of 'me first', in which there was widespread deterioration of the commitment to universal morality. My project, however, is to consider more narrowly philosophical attempts to reduce the moral demand.

[3] It needs to be added that the situation needs to be the same only *in the morally relevant respects*. But this qualification requires detailed discussion which is not germane to the topic of this chapter. For present purposes we can say that any respect is relevant which affects the well-being of any of the parties who would be affected by the agent's acting on the maxim whose moral permissibility is being considered.

term 'universalism' for this construal of the moral demand and the insistence that *all* moral judgements must be impartial in this sense. The second formulation of the categorical imperative is that we must always treat humanity, whether in our own person or the person of another, as an end in itself, and never merely as a means. Kant thought that these two formulations were formulations of the same supreme principle of morality. In this chapter, however, I will consider the possibility that we may be able to treat another person as an end in herself without being impartial in the sense required by the first formulation. If so, there may be a kind of moral judgement which is not moral by the universalist's standard. In Kant's formulation, what we respect as an end in itself is autonomy or rational will. But as I analysed this formulation in Chapter 1, it had the effect of requiring us to share as far as possible the ends of others, or to make them *our* ends. In this chapter I will explore the thought that we can make the ends of another person *our* ends not because she is a centre of rational agency, but because she is related to us in some special way. The important question for the book as a whole is whether, if we allow this, we have reduced the moral demand; I will argue that we have not. It will not matter so much whether we have a new class of judgements which we should *call* moral.

Several objections to universalism in ethics have been made by recent moral philosophers. I will concentrate on some objections made by feminists. Non-feminists have objected on overlapping grounds.[4] I will distinguish four objections; and I will claim that although they are valid objections to some types of universalism, they are not valid objections to the type of universalism I have defined. I will then give a fifth objection which I will claim to be valid against universalism as defined. This objection will not derive from feminist premises, but I intend it to be compatible with them. If the objection is valid, we should accept the 'particularist' thesis that not all moral judgements are universalizable, though many may be. I will argue that this particularist thesis does not, after all, reduce the moral demand.

---

[4] For a discussion of some differences in emphasis between feminist and non-feminist objections to universalism, see Marilyn Friedman (1991a). By 'non-feminist' I do not mean 'anti-feminist'. I will return to feminist ethics in discussing the atonement in Ch. 10 below.

a. FOUR FEMINIST OBJECTIONS

The Objection from Specificity

The first objection is that moral judgements must often be specific, whereas the universalist requires them to be general. I will start with Carol Gilligan and Nell Noddings. Gilligan discusses the Kohlberg tests for moral development, which gave the result that women characteristically did not reach the higher stages that men reached.[5] One such test was the Heinz dilemma, a story about a man whose dying wife needed a particular experimental drug which was supplied by only one researcher, at a cost Heinz could not afford. The questions Kohlberg asked his subjects concerned whether Heinz should steal the drug after negotiations to buy it had broken down. Kohlberg's highest moral stage required seeing the dilemma in terms of self-chosen ethical principles and their ranking, such as respect for the dignity of human beings as individual persons. Gilligan claims that there is another equally valuable kind of moral thinking (she calls it 'care' thinking) where the rival claims are weighed not in the abstract, in terms of the relative priority of the principles behind them, but rather in the particular. She says that this kind of thinking tends towards 'the reconstruction of the dilemma in its *contextual particularity.* Substance is given to the skeletal lives of hypothetical people. Insistence on the particular shifts their judgement away from the hierarchical ordering of principles and the formal procedures of decision making that are critical for scoring at Kohlberg's highest stages.'[6] Nell Noddings says that if we care, 'what we do depends not upon rules, or at least not wholly on rules—not upon a *prior determination* of what is fair or equitable—but upon a constellation of conditions that is viewed through both the eyes of the one-caring and the eyes of the cared-for'.[7] She also says that the ethic of caring itself 'will not embody a set of universalizable moral judgments'.[8]

---

[5] See Gilligan (1980) 306. Gilligan herself, unlike some others in this literature, wants to preserve a universal morality.

[6] Ibid. 311. I do not want to enter the hotly debated empirical question of whether women in fact tend in their development towards care thinking and men towards justice thinking.   [7] Noddings (1984) 134.   [8] Ibid. 28.

But the objection to an account of morality as a system of general or abstract rules is not yet an objection to the requirement of universalizability or to universalism. There are two distinctions here that need to be distinguished. The first is the distinction between general and specific, and the second is the distinction betweeen universal and particular.[9] A principle is universal if it is stated in purely universal terms, without singular reference. I shall say that it is particular if it is not. A situation can be described in universal terms and still be described in minute and completely specific detail.[10] There can also be general particular judgements, like the claim that all Americans are morally good. This looks universal because of the 'all', but it makes singular reference to America. The distinction between specific and general is, unlike that between universal and particular, one of degree. In order to count as general a principle must abstract from some of the detail of the situation to which it prescribes. There is no determinate answer to the question of just how much detail is allowed in a general principle; but the direction of the answer is clear. The principle that you should not kill is more general than the principle that you should not kill except in self-defence, which is more general than the principle that you should not kill a person in self-defence unless you know he is intending to kill you, and so on.

Now contextual particularity, as Gilligan and Noddings describe it, seems to be a matter of specificity, of detail. They want moral thinking to be sensitive to all the nuances of the situation in which the caring person and the cared-for person find themselves. It is rules which abstract from these details that they do not like. But a maxim can be universal and yet concrete, in the sense of mentioning (in universal terms) anything that distinguishes this situation from any other.[11] In this first objection there is, then, a valid point against any account of the moral demand which fails to acknowledge the

---

[9] This distinction between the distinctions can be found in R. M. Hare (1981) 41, and more fully in R. M. Hare (1972-3). The term 'universal' can be used in other ways, but this is one familiar philosophical use.

[10] It may be that the notion of *complete* specificity does not make sense; but at least I can go on giving more and more detail, and there is nothing in the requirement of *universality* to stop me.

[11] Kant wanted moral maxims to be simple and general, but this is not a requirement of the categorical imperative as I have interpreted it. See Ch. 1, Sect. *a*.

need for sensitive moral perception of the relevant details in particular situations. It may be that the required sensitivity is not, itself, a rational capacity, in Kant's sense.[12] But we do not yet have a valid objection against universalism as I have defined it.

The Objection from Empathy

There is a second objection, already present in the first quotation from Noddings above, that caring requires taking on the perspective of the other person. Michele Dumont says, 'Care of its very nature must be particularized, that is, it must be a response to what a particular person actually needs or wants or what will serve a particular relationship. From the care perspective people are perceived as having access to others *in their own terms*.'[13]

As far as I can see this objection is not valid against the kind of universalism defined above. Treating another human being as an end requires, for Kant, treating her as the *author* of universal law. In the *Groundwork*, when he comes to his examples of how to apply the categorical imperative, Kant says that we have as far as possible to share the ends of the other persons affected by our actions. What limit does he mean to impose by the phrase 'as far as possible'? In the *Metaphysics of Morals* he adds that we should consider whether the ends of other persons are themselves morally permissible, and that we are not morally bound to share the ones that are not.[14] To determine whether another person's maxim passes the test of the categorical imperative requires an understanding of that maxim in the other person's own terms. It may well be beyond our powers to do this completely. In Kant's view we do not even know the fundamental maxims of our own actions, let alone the maxims of others. It is not a valid objection to universalism as such, however, that it does not consider the perspectives of those affected by an

[12] See Blum (1991). Kant himself recognizes a faculty of judgement, and holds that rational agents may lack any natural talent for distinguishing whether something does or does not stand under a given rule; see *KrV* A132 f. = B171 f.

[13] Dumont (1988) 8.

[14] One place to see this is the fragment of a moral catechism at *MM* 481 (269). Except for this restriction, Kant's principle is that each person's true needs must be left to each to decide for himself; see *MM* 393 (197). See Mackie (1977) Ch. 4 and Singer (1988) 147–59. On Mackie's view, morality is supposed to screen out many preferences of the people affected by an agent's decision. He argues against the view that morality initially considers all preferences alike, and then rejects some of them as interfering with the preferences (moral and otherwise) of a majority of others.

agent's actions; for there is nothing in universalism as such to prevent this.

There is, again, a *version* of universalism which is liable to this objection. Kant himself supposed that we could state the maxims of morality in simple and relatively general formulas, though I have laid out his view in a way that ignores this feature of it. If we followed his lead in this, and then screened out the preferences of others that did not conform to these formulas, we would be guilty of not 'caring' in Dumont's language. Probably we are guilty of this much of the time in our moral thinking. This does not show that universalism is wrong, however, but that we are failing by the universalist standard (as I have described it). If what I have been arguing in this book is correct, we should expect that our ordinary practice would not match up to the moral demand.

The Objection from Personal Ideals

A third objection is that universalism is not sensitive to the existence of divergent personal ideals. Margaret Walker says, 'The Moral Particularity Thesis allows certain individuating and defining features of an agent's life . . . to matter where they do in some cases in a way that is not universally generalizable.'[15] She has in mind that different people have different views about what is morally most important. To one person it may be her sense of indebtedness to her parents, while to another it may be her loyalty to her profession. Walker takes such particulars to be discretionary, in the sense that morality does not require the same responses from those facing the same sorts of situation. Two different people facing the question of whether to care for an elderly parent at home may reach different answers on the basis of such discretionary considerations.

But is her position inconsistent with universalism as defined at the beginning of this chapter? The key is to discover what is meant by 'universally generalizable' in the quotation above. Walker goes on to allow the difference between particularity and specificity. She then says, 'Irreducibly particular judgements consist in an agent's assigning to particularized grounds a discretionary value (compatible with generally acceptable orderings of generic value) in the act of affirming a certain moral position on their basis.'[16] The phrase within parentheses here suggests that Walker has in mind a

---

[15] Walker (1987) 171.   [16] Ibid. 177.

screening procedure. She wants to allow the moral agent discretion, but only within certain limits. This seems right; an account of morality should not countenance *any and every* view about what is morally important. But then we are left with a theory of moral permissions which apply to everybody, and an area within these permissions which is discretionary. Is *this* theory inconsistent with universalism? As far as I can see, it is not. Kant himself distinguished between perfect and imperfect duties on the grounds that imperfect duties can be fulfilled in a multitude of different morally permissible ways. It does follow from universalism that a judgement of moral permissibility for one agent commits the maker of the judgement to the same judgement of permissibility for any agent in the same sort of situation. But Walker would not, I think, want to deny this.

What kind of universalism would be liable to her objection? One which thought that there was only one right answer to every question about what a person should do in a situation of a certain sort, where the situation was defined independently of the person's own aspirations. This might not seem a plausible view, but it is in fact common in practice. We proceed morally as if our own discretionary personal ideals were morally necessary for everyone else.

The Objection from Close Personal Relations

There is a fourth objection, from the tension between universalism and close personal relations. Lynne McFall says, 'Impartiality is incompatible with friendship and love'.[17] She argues that friendship requires, at least for many people, unconditional commitments; moreover these commitments are identity-conferring, in the sense that they determine what counts for an agent as a reason for acting and they are not themselves justified by reference to other commitments. But, she says, unconditional identity-conferring commitments, except to impartiality itself, are inconsistent with impartiality. 'Can a utilitarian have friends?' she asks; and she answers, 'Yes, but not of his own.' What generates the incompatibility is the utilitarian's refusal to refer in his maxims to himself, and therefore to the people related to him, as legitimate objects of special interest; in other words, the utilitarian's universalism as I have defined it.

[17] McFall (1987) 16.

The notion of friendship as an identity-conferring commitment is introduced by McFall, however, as an example of the kind of commitment all of us have unless corrupted by philosophy. All of us have unconditional commitments in the sense that there is nothing we can foresee that would cause us to violate the commitments; the corruption of philosophy comes in when we are invited to consider bizarre examples where the commitment could not be sustained. But there is nothing in impartiality that requires a willingness to violate, say, a friendship in some actually foreseeable circumstance (though such violation may be required in examples imagined by philosophers). Kant observes in *The Doctrine of Virtue* that it is no violation of impartiality to spend more time with the people we care about, or to look after them in circumstances or in ways in which we would not look after others.[18] It is in principle possible for a far-seeing agent to prescribe a set of universal principles, best for all parties impartially considered, in accordance with which she spends time with her friends and meets their needs and also spends time with others and meets the needs of others. If the objection is about universalism as such, it is not successful.

There is, however, a version of universalism which would be vulnerable to this objection. As things are, it may be said, there is not time enough and there are not resources enough to meet the commitments of friendship *and* to meet the moral demand of service to strangers. If the universalist were to say that whenever I could do more good to anybody else (given finite time and resources) than to my friend, I may not help my friend, he would be vulnerable to McFall's objection.[19] The universalist who is going to survive this objection has to make some distinction of levels, one example of which is R. M. Hare's distinction of intuitive from critical moral thinking, described in Chapter 1.[20] I will say more about this reply from the distinction of levels in the following section of this chapter.

---

[18] *MM* 246 (452). R. M. Hare likewise insists that preferential treatment of those close to us can be justified at the critical level (1981: 135 f.).

[19] Cottingham (1986) argues that impartiality does not allow me to sit up all night with my sick child, 'if I could be making a greater contribution to human welfare by helping any other child who may be in greater need of care and attention.'

[20] There are other examples which can play the same role in this argument, though they differ in other respects. See Marilyn Friedman (1991*b*).

b. A FIFTH OBJECTION

Particular Moral Judgements

I now want to defend myself the thesis that there are moral judgements that are not universalizable; that is, that there are moral judgements from which singular terms are not eliminable. This defence will not rely on support from any of the previous four objections.[21] I will call moral judgements of this type 'particular moral judgements'. I am going to discuss judgements that prescribe action, even though there are equally important moral judgements (about character, for example) which do this only indirectly.

It is helpful to see particular moral judgements as intermediate between prudence and universalizable morality. They are like prudence in that they do not eliminate singular reference. My prudential judgements contain essential reference to myself and my interests. But note that what I prescribe for myself in prudence *is* standardly specified in universal terms, or at least can be. Suppose I make the prudential (not the moral) judgement that I ought to take a holiday in the Bahamas. I am committed by this judgement to the

---

[21] This fifth objection is similar in some ways to an objection mounted by Blum (1980). Blum defends a view that he calls 'direct altruism', which denies that in order to be morally good an action must be (or be regarded by the agent as) universalizable. He draws our attention to the cognitive dimension of the altruistic emotions; in particular, they involve the attitude of regard for another person for his or her own sake. The difference between altruistic emotion and reason is that the latter requires universalizability and the former does not. This is because, Blum says, the altruistic agent (acting directly from altruistic emotion) 'may simply fail to give thought to whether his action has this sort of universal validity' (p. 89). Blum does not distinguish, as I am going to do, between universalizing a whole judgement and universalizing the terms in different positions within the judgement. I also differ from him in not wanting to tie the objection to the moral *sentiments*. There can be non-universal moral judgements, in my sense, without these deriving from sentiment, moral or otherwise. Finally, even if we grant that Blum is right, against Kant, that the moral sentiments have moral value in themselves, it does not follow that where altruistic emotion generates an action, this is enough for the overall moral commendation of the action. It might follow, for some altruistic emotion, if Kant were right that the well-being of all humans could be the object of moral emotion (*MM* 264 (473): 'one who takes an affective interest in the well-being of all men'). But it is not clear what is the difference between this and what Kant calls respect for the moral law, 'a feeling produced by an intellectual cause' (*KpV* 76 (73)). It may be that the altruistic emotions have moral value in themselves, but that they are not, so to speak, autonomous; they are not sufficient by themselves to license overall moral commendation of the actions that spring from them.

judgement that I ought to take this sort of holiday whenever I am in this sort of state.[22] This prudential judgement gives me a (prudential) *reason* for my action, and the reason is given in universal terms even though it applies to *me*: 'whenever I am starved for the sun, bored with marking, etc.' Particular moral judgements are like judgements of prudence in both these ways. They contain ineliminable singular reference, in this case to some other particular person as well as to myself, and what they prescribe I should do for that person is specifiable in universal terms. I ought, let us say, to go and visit my friend, because he is feeling wretched and would value my company. Again this judgement gives me a reason, this time a moral reason, for my action. If this is a particular moral judgement, I am not committed by making it to the judgement that I ought (or even am morally permitted) to visit *anyone* thus situated (even any other friend). But I am committed to the judgement that I ought to visit *him* whenever he is in that sort of state and I can help him. So particular moral judgements are like prudence in these two respects. But they are also like universalizable morality; for they override self-interest in the interest of another person. They are, though not in Kant's sense, treating another person as an end in himself or herself.

It is helpful also, I think, to distinguish four positions within a prescriptive judgement, and see how universalization relates differently to them.[23] The first two are the position of 'addressee', the person to whom the judgement is addressed, and the position of 'agent', the person whose action is being prescribed. Frequently, the addressee will not be explicitly mentioned, and frequently, the addressee will be the same as the agent. But neither of these features is always the case. The addressee and the agent are the same, for example, in the Ten Commandments, which were addressed initially to the people of Israel, who were in a particular covenantal relation with God. But when God tells Joshua before Jericho that the seven priests should bear before the Ark seven trumpets of rams' horns, the addressee and the agent are different.[24] Third, there is the position of 'recipient', the person to whom the action is to be done. The people of Israel are told, for example, to leave sheaves in their fields at harvest for the aliens and strangers within their gates. Finally, there is the position of the 'action', which is what the

---

[22] See Parfit (1984) 149 f.   [23] This list is not exhaustive.
[24] Josh. 6: 4.

speaker judges should or should not be done by this agent to this recipient. Leaving sheaves in their fields at harvest is what the lawgiver tells the people of Israel to do for the aliens and strangers.

It is usual to think that universalizability has to be a feature of the terms in all four positions at once, but this is not so. Universalizing a term is replacing it with purely universal terms; but it is possible to do this at some positions in a judgement and not at others. To soften up opposition to this claim, consider the case where the term in the addressee position is not universalizable. This is quite often the case with moral judgements. Thus, the prophet is chosen by God to give a particular message *to a particular audience*: 'O house of Israel, . . . Hate the evil, and love the good, and establish judgement in the gate.' The prophet is not thereby committed to addressing this same judgement to anyone else who is like the people of Israel in universally specifiable repects.[25]

The Ten Commandments, I think, are a case where the terms in the addressee and the agent positions are not universalizable. This is a complex exegetical and theological question. I think God is initially prescribing to the particular people he has selected, and he has not selected them because of their universal characteristics.[26] The Ten Commandments are part of his covenant with the people of Israel. They are probably supposed to apply eventually to all human beings. My point is that for the universalist, they have moral value *only* when applied to all people. This is why Kant thought the Jews did not have a moral relation to God; he thought their claim to a special relation with God disqualified them from setting up the universal church. If I am right about Christianity, however, it too has a kind of particularism in it which Kant wanted to find in Judaism, but not in Christianity. In traditional Christianity, as I understand it (though here I may depart from my ecumenical ambition), there is

---

[25] Amos 5: 1–15; see also Amos 7: 14–15; 3: 9–10. It is an interesting question whether there is always a person in the addressee position, even if this is implicit; and it is unclear whether, if there is, we should include the occupant of this position in the judgement itself. It might be claimed that we should not, because there is a complete thought if the term is removed; but this cannot generally be used as a criterion for exclusion. For my purposes it is useful to draw attention to the position of addressee, because it illustrates the variability of moral judgements in respect to the universalizability of the terms in the different positions within them.

[26] See Deut. 9: 4–6. For the connection of the Ten Commandments with the covenant, see Exod. 34: 28: 'And he wrote upon the tables the words of the covenant, the ten commandments.'

particularism not merely in God's covenant with Abraham and the covenant with David, but also in his covenant with the particular people he chooses through election to graft as Christians onto the vine. If it is right that the Ten Commandments are initially part of the covenant, then they will not initially be *moral*, on the thesis of universalism. On the other hand, the term in the action position is already universal. The people of Israel are not to commit adultery at *any* time or in *any* place.

Another biblical example will illustrate the non-universalizability of the term in the recipient position. A lawyer asks Jesus which is the greatest commandment in the law, and Jesus replies, 'Thou shalt love the Lord thy God with all thy heart, and with all thy soul, and with all thy mind. This is the first and great commandment. And the second is like unto it, Thou shalt love thy neighbour as thyself. On these two commandments hang all the law and the prophets.'[27] In the first and greatest commandment the term in the recipient position is not universalizable. The command is not prescribing that the believer should love anyone who is the same as God in universally specifiable respects.[28]

What I am claiming, then, is that there is a class of moral judgements which are like judgements of prudence in the following respect: they are judgements in which the terms in addressee and agent and recipient positions are not, but the term in the action position is, necessarily universalizable. Why do I want to insist that particular moral judgements are *moral*? For Kant they are not moral, because they are not universalizable. Three points should be made against him. First, he is not here speaking for the ethical tradition as a whole. For Aristotle, our moral relations are always to the members of this family or this *polis*. The universalist may claim that the special relations that we ought (morally) to honour *can* be justified on universalist grounds. I will come to this claim in a moment. The present point is that the need for such universalist justification is a recent part of the tradition. In Greek philosophy and also in Judaism and Christianity we have examples of relations which

---

[27] Matt. 22: 36–40.

[28] This is especially clear in the Hebrew commandment which stands behind this command, 'I am the Lord thy God, which brought thee out of the land of Egypt, from the house of bondage. Thou shalt have none other gods before me' (Deut. 5: 6–7). The God of Israel is here making a claim of special relation to his own people.

are held to override in their importance any other relations, and which are embodied in what I have called particular moral judgements. I gave the Ten Commandments as an example. Second, particular moral judgements can exemplify what seems to me paradigmatic of morality, namely regard for another person for his or her own sake. To put the point this way is to claim that the two formulas of Kant's categorical imperative given in Chapter 1 can diverge, though not in Kant's own account of the second formula. The requirement of treating another person as an end and never merely as a means can be met by a judgement which fails the requirement of universalizability (if this is taken as a requirement on all the terms in a judgement). Finally, it is characteristic of moral judgements that they give *reasons* for action that treat others as ends in themselves. Because the term in the action position is universal or at least universalizable we can talk of particular moral judgements (in my sense) giving reasons for action. They give reasons because they tell me that whenever my friend Joe, for example, is in a particular kind of difficulty, I should try to help him. As long as these last two features of particular moral judgements are recognized, it becomes a terminological question whether to call them 'moral' or not.

Caring for Another Person for her Own Sake

Not all judgements with universalizable terms in the action position are particular *moral* judgements. Only those judgements count as moral which express care or regard for another person for his or her own sake. But this is a difficult phrase. In Kant, I care for another person for his own sake when I respect his practical rationality. In Aristotle, I do so when I love his *nous*.[29] But it may not be possible to say what it is about a person that I care about when I care for her for her own sake. It is true that there will be numerous descriptions of the person to whom I am related by a special relation, and that some of these descriptions can be given in some contexts as an answer to the question 'why *him*?' or 'why *her*?' For example, he is my friend, or she is my daughter. But it is characteristically not under this

---

[29] *NE*, 9. 8, 1168^{b}35. See Vlastos (1981) 31 on Plato's account of love, which 'does not provide for love of whole persons, but only for love of that abstract version of persons which consists of the complex of their best qualities'. See the excellent discussion in Price (1989) 97 f.

description that the response is evoked within a special relation. Perhaps I give up my Friday evening to go to my daughter's student recital. To say that I do this because she is my child is to impoverish, even to demean what I do. At a soccer match I am specially moved by her distress when she is the goalkeeper and she lets through the ball. Why? Because she is my child? This will often be right as a *causal* account of my response. But it is wrong as an account of the phenomenology of the relation. When asked the question, 'Why do you do these things for her?' it will often be untrue to the relation to reply, 'because she is my child (or wife, or friend)'. Rather, I do them for her own sake.

Is there, then, no description which could be the basis for a universal extension (to *any* person in just those circumstances)? Here we can be agnostic, just as we can for prudence. Is there some unique set of universally specified descriptions that identifies me as *me*, and could not identify anyone else, so that I could at least formally universalize my maxims of prudence?[30] John Lucas asks, 'Should a person be loved for himself alone?'[31] As he says, we get into difficulty either way. If we say it is a person's characteristics that constitute the reason why he should be loved, we seem to be denying his unique individuality. 'You only love me for my yellow hair.' On the other hand if we say, 'You are loved not for your characteristics but simply because you are you,' this divorces your 'youness' from all your characteristics, including those 'which we naturally think of as being most expressive, if not constitutive, of personality'. Lucas's solution is to think of a person as a Leibnizian monad, possessing an infinite number of features, partially ordered as regards importance and knowability. Any account, then, of what makes a person lovable will be based on some initial segment of this infinite list; and the real basis of our love will very likely be more than we can give in the account. Lucas may be right. But there are other alternatives. We could suppose bare particulars, or transcendental egos, or (my preference) that the individual is individuated by a unique set of characteristics, some of which are *not* themselves universally specifiable because they contain ineliminable reference to other individuals or particular regions of space and time. In any case, caring for another person for her own sake, on this account, relates

[30] I say 'at least formally' because universalization may be just a cover-up. See Mackie (1977) 85.
[31] Lucas (1976) 64.

me to another person whose identifying descriptions, if there are any, I do not know.

Here are two examples of particular moral judgements which come from actual experience with American friends, though the names are changed. An activist feminist (call her 'Amy') is bringing up her adolescent daughter alone, since her husband is doing graduate work in another city. She believes strongly in the local cause she is fighting for, and in the importance of her presence at the demonstrations and planning sessions which the cause demands. When she considers her situation impartially, she concludes that she does more good by going to the meetings than by staying at home. But she also makes the particular moral judgement that her daughter needs her at home. Or a man (call him 'Tom') has taken early retirement, partly in order to look after his family. He and his wife have at home their daughter, who is a full-time nurse, and her two children (she and her husband have separated) and Tom's father-in-law, who requires constant attention especially at night. Tom has been offered a job as director of a BA course in management at a local Christian college. He is a devout Christian, and he finds when he asks himself if he will produce more fruit for God's kingdom if he takes the job, the answer is that he will. But he makes the particular moral judgement that God is calling him to meet the needs of his family and he should stay at home.

The universalist will claim that universalism can account for the moral value of special relations, such as those between Amy and her daughter and Tom and his family. To make this point, we can return to the two-level theory of R. M. Hare, outlined in Chapter 1 Section *b*.[32] A two-level theory like his can provide a moral justification at the critical level (where the moral thinker is an act-utilitarian, ideally with total information and complete impartiality) for the judgement at the intuitive level that parents should give precedence to the interests of their own children. 'Parent' is, after all, a universal term.

---

[32] See R. M. Hare (1981) 137: 'If we ascend to the critical level and ask why [the intuition that the mother's partiality should be praised] ought to be [inculcated], the answer is fairly obvious. If mothers had the the propensity to care equally for all the children in the world, it is unlikely that children would be as well provided for even as they are.' A helpful art. relating R. M. Hare's two-level theory to particularity in moral relations is Adler (1989). He is replying to Blum (1986) and (1988). There are other two-level theories which allow impartiality at one level to be consistent with partiality at another. See Hill (1987), Railton (1984) 153–5, and Gewirth (1988).

Such a universalist will say that this is just another case where utilitarianism is made to seem counter-intuitive by an oversimplified view of what utilitarian moral thinking is like; for at the critical level we are looking at the general acceptance utility of intuitions, and children (and aged parents) will in general be better looked after if people in Tom's or Amy's situation act on their family-biased intuitions.

But this two-level account distorts the experience of what it is like to be in these special relations. There is a way to make this objection which is easy for the universalist to meet. The objector might say that within special relations the parties do not and should not look for impartial justifications for their actions in addition to the considerations that arise directly out of the relations themselves.[33] The objection, stated in this way, is that the mother who, in the classical kind of example, chooses to save her own child from the flames rather than some other child does not need to wait for impartial moral justification of her choice; in such a case, seeking impartial justification would be untrue to the special relation between mother and child. The universalist can reply, however, that the two-level theory does not require *waiting* for an impartial justification in such cases. It does not require moral agents to entertain in their deliberation all the moral reasons there are for their actions. A mother may have internalized the impartial justification for mothers giving preference to their own children, and this line of reasoning need not (and probably should not) intrude on her thinking at the time of crisis.

This reply is not enough. The trouble is that when Amy and Tom try to think morally at the critical level, they find the judgement coming out in favour of going to the meetings, or taking the job. The two-level universalist may indeed be able to come up with impartial justifications for special relations, but these justifications will not work for situations in which critical thinking would prescribe overriding what these special relations seem to require. The critical level can justify judgements at the intuitive level that give preference to special relations; but it also justifies *overriding* these intuitive judgements when doing so will produce the most good, impartially considered. Amy may be thinking morally as well as she is ever able

---

[33] See Blum (1986). Williams (1981) 18 talks about the agent having 'one thought too many'.

to think, not in a crisis situation that leaves no time for reflection or in a situation of acute temptation where she will be likely to rationalize. She may reason to herself that she should go to the meetings because she will indeed be achieving the most preference-satisfaction by so doing, counting each person as one and no person as more than one. She has a role in the movement that no one else can play, and the movement will, if it is successful, improve the local living conditions of women significantly. Thinking this way, she is willing to prescribe that not only she, but any person in a morally similar situation, should do the same. But Tom and Amy can *also* see it the opposite way round, giving precedence to the particular. When they do this, it seems to them that if the critical level cannot come up with a justification for their preference for the family in their specific circumstances (and not merely in general), so much the worse for their thinking at the critical level. Their trouble is that there does not seem to be any neutral ground from which to evaluate the two ways of looking at the moral situation. To insist on a universalist justification for one choice over the other would be to beg the question. Gilligan makes reference in this context to the ambiguous figure which can look like a vase, or like two faces turned towards each other, but which cannot look like both at the same time. She uses this as an illustration of the relation between care thinking and justice thinking.[34]

The question is what moral value is left to the particular moral judgement (in the sense I have given) in cases where it conflicts with the universal judgement. To the universalist it will seem that Amy's feeling that she should stay with her daughter (if she has got the critical thinking right) is an intuition which arises from a disposition that is in general right for her to have, but which in this specific circumstance needs to be overridden. The universalist can go on to allow that it is perfectly appropriate for Amy to feel badly when she overrides her intuition, even though she is morally justified in overriding it; for the disposition which produces these feelings of guilt is itself a disposition she is morally justified in having. I have argued, however, that there is a kind of judgement properly called 'moral' which cannot be dismissed in this way. It is not derivative in its moral value from justification at the critical level, as the universalist describes this.

[34] See Gilligan (1987), esp. 30 f.

I do not know of any non-question-begging way to rule out particular moral thinking from being properly described as *moral*.[35] In this section I have claimed that there is a type of judgement which is not fully universalizable, but which deserves to be called a moral judgement because it preserves the typically moral character of caring for another person for her own sake. The only ways I know to rule out this type of judgement as not properly moral beg the question in favour of the universalist. In the following section I will try to say more about the relation between this kind of moral judgement and the requirement of impartiality.

c. THE MORAL DEMAND IS NOT REDUCED

Extreme Particularism

If it is wrong to confine moral judgements to those which are fully universalizable (universalizable in all their term-positions), it is also wrong to confine moral judgements to those that are particular in my sense. This point has been made by several feminist writers. I will not try to prove that we have moral obligations to all the other human beings affected by what we do. It would beg the question to say that morality is fully universalizable, and therefore cannot be limited in its reach to those in a special relation to the agent. I will, however, make three points against what I will call 'extreme particularism', the view that all our moral obligations are expressible in particular moral judgements.

Nell Noddings is an extreme particularist in the degree to which she identifies morality and caring. She says, 'I am not obliged to care for starving children in Africa, because there is no way for this caring to be completed in the other unless I abandon the caring to which I

---

[35] There are indeed question-begging ways. Here is one of them. The universalist may appeal to the principle that if I ought to do something, it is morally permissible for me to do it, all things considered. Suppose we grant for the sake of argument that there are two kinds of moral obligation: we can say 'I ought (as a universal obligation)' and 'I ought (as a particular obligation)'. We can abbreviate these as 'I ought (u)' and 'I ought (p)'. By the description of these kinds there will be some times when I cannot do both what I ought (u) and what I ought (p). But then, the universalist will say, we will not know that if I ought (u) to do something, it is permissible for me, all things considered. But this objection begs the question. If there is such a thing as what I ought (p) to do, then it is *not* the case that whatever I ought (u) to do is morally permissible for me, all things considered.

am obligated.'[36] She rejects the notion of universal caring, though she thinks we should maintain an internal state of readiness to try to care for whoever crosses our path.[37] To care, in her account, is to act not by fixed rule but by affection and regard; caring is a rich relation between the 'one-caring' and the 'one cared-for', calling for 'a displacement of interest from my own reality to the reality of the other'. This kind of relation is only possible for an agent within a comparatively small group of other people.

Suppose we grant that morality calls for care, in the rich sense Noddings gives to this term. It does not follow that morality allows us, in caring for others in this way, to violate the rights of people who are outside the caring relationship. I may not, for example, run over a slow pedestrian when rushing my daughter to the hospital. This is a negative or perfect duty, in Kant's sense. There are also positive fully universalizable obligations which we have towards people with whom we are not in a caring relationship. The Good Samaritan, for example, encountered by the side of the road a man who had been attacked by robbers and left for dead, and who was outside the Samaritan's own tribal group.[38] There was no antecedent attachment of affection or regard. We should, according to Noddings, maintain an internal state of readiness to try to care for whoever crosses our path. But what is the status of this 'should'? It is not itself an expression of affection or regard, but an expression of the commitment to remain open to those feelings. To make sense of this commitment we need to appeal to some feature of the situation which calls for those feelings, even when they are not actually present. To some degree the extreme particularist can accomplish this end. She can say that special relations (of family, or friendship, or profession) call for a caring attitude, even when it is not present. Moreover there may be widening circles, so that moral progress allows caring for people under a progressively less restricted description.[39] If so, we can think of progressively wider relations

---

[36] Noddings (1984) 86.   [37] Ibid. 18.   [38] Luke 10: 33.

[39] Hierocles, an orthodox Stoic of the second cent. AD, 'drew a picture of a man at the centre of a number of concentric circles. In the innermost he stands himself, with his body, and the satisfaction of his physical needs, in the next are his parents, brothers, wife and children, then more distant relatives, then members of his deme (ward or village), of his city, of neighbouring cities, of his country, of the human race. Hierocles suggests that we should try to contract the circles, treating e.g. uncles like parents: the ultimate aim would be to treat all men as our brothers.' See Sandbach (1975) 34.

calling for feelings of affection or regard when they are not present. But the extreme particularist cannot agree all the way with Stoic *oikeiosis* or 'appropriation', which requires 'the feeling that all mankind belongs to us'.[40] Universal caring is what Noddings is concerned to deny.

Here are the three points against extreme particularism. First, the institution of morality we are familiar with does include fully universalizable obligations. Large numbers of people use the moral words like 'ought' in a way which commits them to such obligations. In this sense morality *does* include negative obligations not to harm strangers and positive obligations to meet their needs; and if 'we' use the word 'ought' in this way, then we are committed in this way. There is still the question 'Are we *right* to think we have these obligations?' But what is the sense of 'right' in the question? If the question is whether the institution of morality can be morally justified, it can be answered by a two-level theorist at the critical level of moral thinking; it is good that people think at the intuitive level in terms of fully universalizable obligations. But if the question is pushed back, so that it asks for a moral justification of *critical* moral thinking, the two-level theorist will say the question has lost its sense. There is a question that can still be asked with sense, however, though not by the universalist. The question is what share of our moral thinking should be occupied by fully universalizable moral thinking. I will come back to this question in a moment.

The second point against the extreme particularist is that the consequences of the disappearance of fully universalizable morality would be serious. There is a widespread sense of having negative obligations (such as the obligation not to run over the slow pedestrian) and positive obligations (to needy strangers) which are fully universalizable. I do not mean that the term 'fully universalizable' is widespread; it is a term of philosophical jargon. But there are hundreds of thousands of people who hear about the needs of the victims of wars or famines or hurricanes, and feel they should respond just because it is human beings who are suffering and need their help. Even so the response is a long way from being adequate to meet the need. There are, it is true, resources in the world for meeting the material needs of most of these victims. But the distribution of these resources to meet the needs will occur only if

---

[40] Cicero, *De Finibus* 3. 63.

the sense of fully universalizable obligation grows stronger.[41] This is not yet an argument that the resources *should* be distributed to meet the needs more adequately; I am only pointing out that the consequences of the disappearance or the weakening of the sense of obligation to needy strangers will be significant. Many more needs will not be met.

There is another way to put this.[42] People's resources for favouring the people they love are distributed in a vastly unequal manner. From the universalist standpoint, some preference for those in special relations is justified; but partiality is always in danger of defeating its own justification. Partiality is justified, for the universalist, because it contributes to the protection of those who are vulnerable. But if partiality is unconstrained, it leads to reducing the number of people who can be adequately protected by partiality. If those who have extra resources (where 'extra' has not yet been defined) feel comfortable using almost all of them to meet their own needs and the needs of the people they love, most of the most vulnerable will not in fact be protected even by those who rightly feel a special obligation towards them. Again, this is not an argument in favour of the existence of non-partialist obligations, for it presupposes there are such.

The third point against the extreme particularist is that special relations, like those of friendship and family, are liable to certain kinds of internal corruption from the lack of the sense of justice.[43] Dividing up morality into 'care' for the private and 'justice' for the public sphere damages both spheres. I will not here make this argument both ways, but I will concentrate on the damage to the private sphere.[44] Relations within families or between friends need regulation by justice of an impartial kind. This is clear when the issue is sexual or physical or emotional abuse, or treating family or friends as unpaid servants. But this is not the point I am trying to make. The opponent of the universalist will rightly object that

---

[41] No doubt many contributors do not see themselves as under obligation, but as going beyond obligation. I am making the empirical judgement that if more people felt under obligation, more resources would be sent (rather than e.g. more people giving up on meeting their obligations at all). In fact it will take action by governments to accomplish adequate redistribution, not merely action by individuals. But getting governments to act requires changes in the attitudes of large numbers of individuals and groups within the wealthier countries.

[42] See Marilyn Friedman (1991*b*) 818–35.

[43] See Piper (1991) for a sustained argument that compassion requires impartiality.

[44] See Van Leeuwen (1993) Chs. 12–13.

justified partiality towards friends and family (i.e. caring for those in special relations as ends in themselves) is not likely to lead to such evils, and is in fact likely to diminish the danger of them; what leads to these dangers, she will say, is not partiality itself but the lack of accountability within private relations because of the (often false) *assumption* by society at large that the people involved are in fact caring for each other. Society at large, this opponent will say, leaves the private sphere largely unsupervised, because of the assumption that the people within these relations will look after each other's interests; if they do not do so, that is not because the parties are displaying justified partiality to each other but because they are failing to do so.

My present point, however, is that the people within special relations need also, for each other's sake, to treat each other impartially. They need to look at each other not merely as objects of special favour, but also as human beings deserving no more and no less than any other human beings. This is again an argument that presupposes, rather than giving a reason for, the existence of universal obligations. It is important, for example, for a mother to treat herself as (at least) equally valuable with her children. This is important for her own sake, but also important for the children. There may be a temptation for her to give such preference to the interests of those in her family that she ceases to treat herself as a person with her own dignity. This temptation is as present in friendships as it is within families. If the needs of her friend become too vivid, and her desire for his well-being too strong, she can forget what is due to herself.[45] There is, as it were, a baseline of respect for herself as a person with dignity. Strangely, if this line is crossed, she ceases to be able even to give herself to another, because she is not (so to speak) there to give. This language is metaphorical; but this does not mean that it is inaccurate. There is a difference between choosing as an equally valuable person to give herself to another and merely being (as it were) absorbed by the needs of the other. In the second case what she is giving has lost much of its power to help.

The recipients of preferential treatment also need to be aware of this baseline; if they are children, they need to be shown it. There is a danger in being loved unconditionally that one starts to confuse the quality of the gift with the quality of the recipient. The recipient can

---

[45] Piper (1991) uses the term 'vicarious possession'.

start to think of herself as naturally fitted to be treated this way, and to expect this treatment from other people as part of the proper order of things. Children need to be shown that they are not more valuable in themselves than their siblings, their parents, and the other children in their classes at school. It can be a startling lesson for a child who has been the apple of his mother's eye to discover that his mother is not willing to put pressure on his teacher to get him into a team, or even to make a scene in the shop to get him the last remaining construction set of the kind he wants for Christmas. It is a valuable part of the lesson that it comes from his mother, because he can start to learn to integrate the relations he has to people at home and the relations he has outside. But even within the home, he needs to learn the barriers beyond which he may not push. He needs to learn to respect his mother's privacy and her interests apart from him; that she is (in short) her own person as well as his mother.

How are Universalist and Particular Morality Related?

If it is granted that we have both kinds of moral obligation, both those expressed in particular moral judgements and those expressed in fully universalizable moral judgements, is there any way to make progress in answering the question of what *share* of our moral thinking each kind should have? I will call these two kinds of obligation 'universal obligations' and 'particular obligations'. For the present chapter, the important question is whether admitting the existence of particular obligations reduces our obligations overall, and hence reduces the moral demand. I think that it does not. There is one premiss which would lead to the conclusion that the moral demand is reduced; but I do not see good reason to accept it. The premiss is that particular obligations take precedence in general over universal obligations. If this were true, then we could reduce our moral obligations by eliminating many of those universal obligations which conflicted with particular obligations, in the sense that we could not meet both of them given limitations of time and other resources. Why would anyone accept this premiss? The argument might be made that the special moral relations in which an agent stands are what give point to the agent's life; without them her life is not worth living for her.[46] The argument would conclude that it is

---

[46] Williams (1981) 16 talks of how 'a commitment or involvement with a particular other person might be one of the kinds of project which figured basically in a man's

not reasonable to ask her to sacrifice these relations, even for the sake of universal morality. But it does not seem to be generally true that people in the sorts of position Amy and Tom are in, in my examples, are choosing between universal moral obligations and what is required to make them want to go on living at all. There may indeed be such cases, but many of the conflicts between universal obligations and particular obligations may be quite trivial. In any case, it is not clear what the argument is which shows that it is never reasonable to ask a person to sacrifice what makes life worth living for him. The argument might be rephrased to say that a person's special relations are what constitute her as the agent she is; asking her, then, to sacrifice these relations does not adequately reflect the nature of persons and personal agency.[47] On this view, it is inconsistent to ask someone to be an agent and make this kind of sacrifice. But it does not seem generally true that people in the sorts of dilemma faced by Amy and Tom are denying their identity as agents if they choose to do what universal morality prescribes. For some people, putting their desires and interests under the constraint of universal morality is a way of making those desires and interests their *own*. We are left, then, with these two kinds of moral demand, and with no convincing argument that in general, when there is conflict, the particular moral obligations should win. Suppose the Good Samaritan is hurrying along the road to Jericho to get back to the bosom of his family, because he has been on a long trip and his children need him at home. The positive universal obligation to help the needy stranger can still take moral precedence.

Another possibility is that universal obligations take precedence over particular obligations. This might be by a kind of lexical or regulative priority; perhaps universal obligations provide a screen through which desires and interests have to go before they can even enter deliberation.[48] But this seems true not of universal obligations

life in the ways already sketched.' See the discussion of the relevance of 'ground projects' to personal identity in Kagan (1989) 258 f.

[47] I take the phrase from Kagan, ibid. 262. See McFall (1987).

[48] I am influenced here by Barbara Herman's notion of a 'deliberative field'. She argues that 'there is no obvious or necessary incompatibility betwen impartial ethics and the value of attachment' (1992: 58). But her idea is that the moral agent 'normalizes' desires and interests by (Kantian) moral principles before the desires and interests even enter into deliberation, and this gives the Kantian moral principles

in general, but of a narrow class of them, including but not limited to Kant's class of perfect duties. It is not clear that universal obligations in general take precedence over particular obligations. This is the relevance of the cases of Amy and Tom. Adding particular moral obligations is merely that; it does not subtract any of the universal moral obligations we already knew that we had. In this way the moral life is made more difficult, not any easier, by giving particular moral obligations non-derivative moral weight.

There is one way to mitigate the extra difficulty, though not to remove it. The tension between universal and particular obligations derives in part from the absence of intermediate institutional arrangements between the family and the large-scale bureaucracies of government or national church. In Aquinas, and before him in Aristotle, the discussion of our obligations to strangers took place against the background of assumptions about the kind of community they were living in, and its relations to those outside the community. Part of our difficulty now, exacerbating the tension between universal and particular obligations, is that there have been huge social changes which separate us from the world of Aquinas and Aristotle. We have far greater connection with the rest of the world, both in how much we know about it and in how much we can affect it by our actions. The demand of the neighbour's need now pours in from all over world. Aquinas can say that alms-giving is obligatory, not merely good and beyond the call of duty; but several conditions have to be met. First, he says, the giver must have surplus goods left over after satisfying his needs and the needs of those over whom he has charge. Second, the recipient must be in urgent need. Third, the recipient must need this particular giver to help him, if he is to receive the help he needs.[49] Aquinas concedes that these conditions may be met in a situation 'when one is bound rather to give aid to a stranger, for example if he is in extreme need, than to one's own father who does not happen to be in such straits'.[50] After this

---

lexical (or regulative) priority. I would want to add that what I have called particular moral relations can have lexical priority of the same kind, though I think she would not agree.

[49] *Summa Theologiae* Ia-IIae q. 32 a. 6. See Spoerl (1994). Aquinas is justifying giving precedence to one's family; not luxuries, however, but 'enough to keep himself with his children and dependents alive.' Aquinas would probably condemn much of the expenditure of the middle-class Westerner.

[50] *Summa Theologiae* IIa-IIae q. 31 a. 3.

concession it is striking that he does not feel the burden of the large numbers of people in the rest of the world who are in extreme need. Does he not know about them? He seems to have the confidence that the needy people he does know about, the poor and the stranger in the gate, will be adequately cared for if the community he belongs to exercises its responsibilities within 'the order of charity'. His word for neighbour (the recipients of our kindness, or mercy, or alms-giving) is *proximus*, the one next to us. We have lost this sense of the contiguity of the recipients of our usual charitable donations. We usually do not know who they are, and (if we are giving to them through taxes, or some large organization such as Oxfam or the Red Cross) we do not know the people who are administering assistance to them by means of our resources.

It is still possible, however, to belong to a community which itself sends out people to meet the needs of the suffering in remote parts of the world. If the community is small enough, I may know the people who are going out. Even if I do not know them personally, I may feel connected to them because we are members of the same community. What can happen then is that they create outreaches of the community in the parts of the world where they go to help. In the world to which Aquinas was writing, people mostly knew the people they were helping. They did not have to feel the overwhelming burden of the need of those in the rest of the world whom they could be helping but were not. We cannot go back to that. But it is possible for me to feel connected, through those who go out on my behalf, to one part of the world rather than another. This diminishes the burden, because part of the moral stress is the anonymity of all those millions of suffering people. The scale of the problem, compared to my individual circumstances, brings a sense of powerlessness and defeat. If I can know that my community is connected for the reasonably long term to a group of villages in, say, Bangladesh, this gives me a sense of which problems in the world are, so to speak, my problems. It destroys hope if I think of the individual conscience with all the world's needs arrayed against it. I can be more hopeful if I belong to a community which is together trying to meet a deliberately chosen set of needs. It is best here not only that I know and feel connected to some of the people that are being helped, but that I know and feel connected to the people who are providing the help.

Being part of a community which is meeting the needs of strangers helps in other ways with motivation. There is a picture of this in the Deuteronomic law.[51] The picture is one that has itself strongly influenced a whole succession of communities, such as Calvin's Geneva or the Bethlehem community of the Moravian Brethren, which have shared the feature that the community is seen as the place where the needs of strangers are met. In the Deuteronomic law the lawgiver sets up obligations not merely between the members of the community but to needy strangers outside it. There are three ways in which he encourages the members of the community to meet these obligations without exaggerating the sense of their own virtue. First, if the community will observe the laws he gives them (for example the law about the cancelling of debts every seven years), there will be no poverty. He recognizes, however, that the laws will not all be kept, and therefore there will be poverty; and he commands the people to take this opportunity for generosity. The first point is that the context for the generosity is that the community has failed its obligations to keep God's law. The generosity comes out of a confession of communal sin, not a sense of self-righteousness. Second, the lawgiver is talking to well-to-do land-owners whom he holds ultimately not responsible for their own prosperity; they have themselves been saved from the position of aliens and needy strangers by God's gift and they are always liable to return to that position. The Israelites are to imitate God's kindness to them in their need by being kind to others. They should not think of themselves as giving away what they deserve to keep, but as giving what they have been given by God's grace. The generosity comes out of gratitude. Third, their meeting the needs of the poor is a requirement if their community is to continue to be the recipient of

[51] For the treatment of the alien in this body of law, see van Houten (1991) 77 f. See also Weber (1952). Some relevant texts (quoted in the New International Version) are Deut. 24: 19–22: 'When you are harvesting in your field and you overlook a sheaf, do not go back to get it. Leave it for the alien, the fatherless and the widow . . . Remember that you were slaves in Egypt. That is why I command you to do this.' See also Deut. 15: 4–5, 11: 'However, there should be no poor among you, for in the land the Lord your God is giving you to possess as your inheritance, he will richly bless you, if only you fully obey the Lord your God and are careful to follow all these commands I am giving you today . . . There will always be poor people in the land. Therefore I command you to be openhanded toward your brothers and toward the poor and needy in your land.' Probably Jesus was referring to this passage when he said, 'The poor you will always have with you, but you will not always have me' (Matt. 26: 11). Perhaps he was suggesting his continued presence in the poor and needy.

God's blessing. God's people are in a covenant with God, and if they do not obey the laws he gives them they are breaking the covenant. The generosity is a condition of future blessing.

The picture in Deuteronomy cannot be applied directly to the contemporary world. It can, though, be more easily approximated if there are intermediate institutions, communities with a sense of covenant which are intermediate between the contemporary institutions of family and national safety-net or international relief organization. The great advantage of these intermediate structures is that those who participate in them can see themselves as part of a community which is together meeting its obligations to the needy strangers outside the community. Because their shared resources are so much greater, they can see themselves together meeting significant needs; there is not the sense of hopelessness that attaches to individual efforts to help.[52] On the other hand, if the community is relatively small, the individual contributions are not swallowed up in an anonymous bureaucracy. This is an idealized picture, but it is still a recognizable one. In the culture at large, however, the tension between the obligation to needy strangers and the obligation to intimates now seems acute. One reason for this is that to a large extent in the Western world the communities which had these intermediate structures in place have disappeared.

These remarks about intermediate institutions are not designed to make situations like those of Amy and Tom in the previous examples any easier. Adding particular obligations to universal obligations is simply adding; it does not remove the universal obligations we already have. In cases like Amy's and Tom's it makes the moral question of what do harder; and I do not know of any general rule for how to proceed in such cases. For the argument of this book as a whole what is important is that adding particular obligations does not reduce the moral demand.

[52] Derek Parfit (1984) 85–6 makes the point that the world is now so interconnected that we need to make some changes in the way we think about morality. In particular, we need to learn to care morally about the very small effects each of us has on a very large number of other people. What he calls 'Common-Sense Morality' (our old way of thinking about morality) works best in small communities. He may well be right. One response is to try to meet more of our obligations to strangers within the structure of small communities, and the morality that works best in them. This will be hard to achieve; and even if it is achieved it will not remove the need to think morally in new ways because of the interconnectedness that Parfit describes.

7

SUBSTITUTES FOR GOD'S ASSISTANCE

IN this chapter, I am going to look at three attempts at a naturalistic ethics, those of Donald Campbell, David Gauthier, and Alan Gibbard.[1] These three authors do not engage in either of the two strategies discussed in Chapter 4–6 for dealing with the gap between the moral demand and our natural capacities; they do not, that is, try either to diminish the moral demand or to deny that we have an in-built tendency to give more weight to our own interests than impartiality allows. Rather, these three authors can all be understood as aiming at what Donald Campbell calls 'a scientific mediational normative ethics', in which both the moral gap is recognized and some non-theological substitute for God's assistance is introduced to close it. In all three cases what closes the gap is some machinery external to the agent's will, as it were an invisible hand, which transforms egotists into useful members of society. I will mention some difficulties with these accounts, but I am not claiming to show that there is no naturalistic substitute for God's assistance that succeeds. In particular, I will not discuss any of the de-theologized or Marxist versions of Hegel, which hold out the prospect of redemption through history.

a. SOCIAL EVOLUTION

Campbell is not a philosopher, but a social psychologist. His work has been influential in philosophy, however, both in evolutionary epistemology and in evolutionary ethics.[2] He is straightforwardly a naturalist, in the sense that he wants to do away, like Herbert

---

[1] I have chosen these three figures as a sample, but there is a large literature in evolutionary ethics which I have not tried to cover.

[2] For his views it is necessary to consult a series of articles: Campbell (1975), (1978), (1979), (1982), (1984), and (1985). I am grateful to him for comments on an earlier draft of this chapter, and for several years of good philosophical conversation.

Spencer, with 'a supernatural transcendent authority'. Belief in such an authority is not, he thinks, compatible with contemporary science.[3] On the other hand, he asserts that the religious tradition which does believe in such an authority has enduring social value. This is a value which is produced, he thinks, by the mechanisms of social or cultural evolution, which has a wisdom beyond that of the priests who transmit its messages through the religious tradition. He thinks that what he calls the 'preachments' of this tradition may be necessary in order to reach what he calls 'the bio-social optimum'. In his presidential address to the American Psychological Association he puts the point in terms of a two-system analysis of some specific moral precepts. The two systems are the biological system, at the level at which biological selection is working, and social system preaching, which he says is necessary to counteract the biological bias towards egotism. He says that on a scale from absolute selfishness to absolute altruism, the biological system tends to selfishness (though not absolute selfishness), the social preachments (including the religious tradition) towards absolute altruism. The social function of the preachments is to bring about the bio-social optimum, roughly half-way between the biological optimum and absolute altruism. The function of the religious tradition within the larger class of social system preaching is to allow worship, which grounds the worshippers' norms in something outside the worshippers themselves.

There is thus a tension between Campbell's naturalism and his acknowledgement that the preachments of the religious tradition need to continue for good social reasons. He seeks to lessen this difficulty by arguing, on evolutionary grounds, that it is just as rational to follow religious traditions which one does not understand as it is rational to continue breathing air before one understands the role of oxygen in bodily metabolism.[4] He realizes, however, that it can be argued against him that the naturalist does not merely 'fail to

---

[3] Campbell (1975) 1104: 'On grounds of deep intellectual conviction, I speak from a scientific, physicalistic (materialistic) world view. The evolutionary theory I employ is a hard-core neo-Darwinian one for both biological and social evolution, the slogan being blind variation and systematic selective retention'. See R. M. Hare's remarks about religion and science quoted at the beginning of Ch. 1, Sect. *b* above. The *theistic* evolutionist is not, in my categorization, a form of naturalist. The use of evolutionary accounts is not necessarily naturalist; but I will not discuss this possibility further in this chapter.   [4] Campbell (1984) 25.

understand' the religious tradition; rather, the naturalist thinks this tradition is *mistaken* in its appeals to a transcendent supernatural authority. Campbell therefore proposes a way to translate religious language so that it can both be acceptable to the naturalist and maintain its social effectiveness in promoting worship. Rather than saying 'God is good', he proposes, we should say 'Good is God'. The same translation is proposed for 'God is love' and 'God is truth'. The difference between 'God is good' and 'Good is God' is that 'God' is being used as a kind of name in the first case and a kind of title in the second. Compare the two sentences 'Caesar is good', where we are talking about some particular Caesar, say Julius Caesar, and 'Good is Caesar', where we mean that Good is our ruler. Or compare 'Teacher is evil' referring to one's teacher, and 'Evil is teacher'. What is missed out in these second sentences is *reference* to some particular individual. In this way Campbell's suggestion resembles Kant's practice in translating Christian doctrine within the pure religion of reason. Kant, however, does this as a pure rationalist, not a naturalist. Why does Campbell want to eliminate singular reference? It is not individuality itself he objects to, because he allows that our ecological niche might be a proper object of worship—which is a sort of individual. He wants to exclude the particular individual worshipped in the Christian tradition, because he wants to exclude at least some of the traditional identifying attributes of this individual. Especially, he wants to exclude the attributes which mark this individual as a transcendent supernatural authority.

The question we need to ask, then, is whether the preachments of religion minus transcendence can have the same social effectiveness in bringing about the bio-social optimum. It seems that an essential feature of the effectiveness of the preachments is that the norms preached are not preached as self-generated. It is this externality which gives the preaching its added force, so that it can promote the kind of worship which counteracts the tendency towards the merely biological optimum. Campbell concedes that 'an effective super-ego or conscience may not be achieved by simply preaching scientific analyses proving that everyone would be better off if everyone abode by restraints and social duties. Even if convincingly conveyed, it would still leave it in the rational best interests of any single individual to be a "free rider" or to cheat on the system.'[5] It is just

---

[5] Ibid. 30. See also Campbell (1985) 40.

the features of traditional preachments that go *beyond* such scientific analysis which contain the effectiveness required to overcome these considerations of rational best interest. We shall revisit this point in connection with the work of David Gauthier.

Showing that the norms derive from a source external to the agent (thus allowing worship) does not yet show that the norms have to derive from a transcendent *supernatural* authority. There are many intermediate possibilities. One feature of patriotism, for example, is that it lends norms the authority of the traditions of the agent's country.[6] Campbell proposes the human ecological niche for this sort of role in transcending the individual. He says it can generate a sense of awe, or a sense of a creator with purposes larger than our own, and it can generate prayers to live in accordance with these larger purposes, and a life goal of complete adaptation. But both our countries and our niche are limited as sources of transcendence. Patriotism has geographical limitations, and can lead to disastrously maladaptive behaviour. The worship of the niche has temporal limitations. This is because, as Campbell sees it, the ecological niche is changed by our own actions. Thus he thinks that the advent of the nuclear age has made patriotism maladaptive within our new niche.[7] The niche is always what we *have* as a species done with what we have been given, and this means it is not always a good guide for the future. But the main difficulty with the niche as the source of our norms is that it is hard to give it the role ascribed to God in most of our religious language about salvation. How do we talk about the niche with our religious language of atonement and justification? The best way to see Campbell's suggestion, I think, is to read the ecological niche as an example of the way God-talk might be translated, rather than as a complete specification of such a translation. He hopes that with this example in place, the rest of the translation can be left indeterminate, and we can use the old language for its social effectiveness without understanding how in detail it can be translated into new language which is acceptable to the naturalist.

There are two flaws I want to focus on in Campbell's proposal. The first is that it makes the preachments of the tradition dishonest,

---

[6] Rousseau locates *amour de la patrie* as the sentiment which makes virtue possible, rather than mere natural goodness. See Gauthier (1990) 94.

[7] Campbell (1982) 771.

in a rather peculiar sense. It is not that the preachers are themselves disingenuous. Campbell imagines that they go on doing their business, and having their social effectiveness as before. But the naturalist gives an interpretation to their language which is at odds with what the preachers think it means. Even the naturalist does not know what much of it means, but he has a naturalist translation of enough of it to make the rest tolerable without translation. This is not yet dishonesty. After all, most of our language about tables and chairs is given an interpretation by the physicist which is at odds with what we take the meaning to be. What is dishonest, however, is that the naturalist knows that giving the translation in terms of a naturalist scientific analysis will tend to diminish the effectiveness of the preachments in their original form. The naturalist thus hopes that the preachments have a naturalist translation, but he cannot actually go around giving it even if he finds one. Perhaps he can give it to carefully screened groups of his peers, but he cannot let it get out into the general public. Campbell concedes that the only people who will be helped by the translation are those for whom the traditional language is already dead. Everyone else is better off staying with the traditional language. But he does not come to terms with the fact that the promulgation of his own and other like-minded writing is part of the cause of the decline of the traditional faith.

The second flaw is that the naturalist's theoretical machinery seems unlikely to be able to accomplish the work he wants it to do. This is presumptuous for a philosopher to say. Most of the theoretical work, as Campbell concedes, has not been done yet, and a philosopher is not in a good position to say what work in other disciplines will or will not be successful. But here is an example of the kind of work Campbell has in mind:

If we were to (a) achieve a formal theory of social organization that would specify the individual behavioral tendencies (BT1) that were optimal for maintaining the social complexity of the ancient urban societies of Egypt, Mexico, China, etc. (b) apply the best of modern population genetics to describe the innate behavioral tendencies (BT2) that biological evolution was probably producing in those settings; and (c) compare these two sets of predicted behavioral dispositions, we would then have *in the differences* a theoretical basis for predicting the content of the folk moralizings, moral law, proverbs, commandments, temptations, and sins for each of those ancient high civilizations.[8]

[8] Campbell (1979) 43.

He thinks of social evolution as the mechanism which allows us to predict that the preachments in each society would provide just enough pull towards altruism so as to reach BT1, given the countervailing pull of biology towards BT2. On the one hand is the level of social organization (BT1), including kingship types and elaborate funeral rituals and priestly castes. One problem is the supposition that we can reduce these complexities at the social level significantly by talking about *behavioural* tendencies, as though we could understand what the behaviour was without understanding the underlying theologies and aesthetic standards and moral systems. But if the level of social organization is inseparable from this normative level, then we cannot generate the desired predictions. On the other hand there is the level of biological evolution, producing behaviour (BT2) through the efficacy of blind variation and systematic selective retention. A second problem is to see how biological evolution can be sensitive to differences in social setting, such as the differences between Hittite and Minoan class structures. The main difficulty is with the analogy of social evolution itself. For this to have explanatory force, as Campbell admits, the ingredients of biological evolution should be present: heterogeneous variation, systematic selection, and retention and replication of the variation. But the absence of systematic selection of better functioning is a major reason for doubting that a progressive cultural evolution has taken place, or that the current cultural content has an adaptive function. Moreover the retention and replication of cultural forms has neither the precision nor the completeness of the biological model. Again, I am in no position to say these problems are insuperable; but at least a point about the burden of proof seems appropriate here. In the absence of the kind of work which shows that the kinds of prediction in question can be made, we should remain sceptical about the chances of this project. Campbell, to be sure, has an additional reason for thinking that the project will succeed. He believes, as a naturalist, that in the end this kind of explanation is the only kind of explanation there is. It would, however, be begging the question, in a way Campbell himself does not, to make this an independent argument; to argue that we should expect to find an explanation in terms of social evolution just because there must be one.

b. THE MACHINERY OF THE RATIONAL BARGAIN

One good way to understand David Gauthier's *Morals by Agreement* is to see it as attempting a reply to the difficulty Campbell acknowledged about naturalistic ethics. Campbell said,

But an effective super-ego or conscience may not be achieved by simply preaching scientific analysis proving that everyone would be better off if everyone abided by restraints and social duties. Even if convincingly conveyed, it would still leave it in the rational best interests of any single individual to be a 'free rider' or to cheat on the system. Further analysis could conceivably convince us that awe-inspiring indoctrination was needed, to the (same) degree at least as that which produced morally committed persons such as ourselves.

Gauthier's book is an elaborate argument that it is rational not merely to agree to be moral, but to comply subsequently with the agreement. He argues that, from an evolutionary perspective, we may suppose that the value we find in participation is itself instrumentally related to our insufficiency.[9] There are goods, in other words, which we are insufficient to provide for ourselves without co-operation, and we can justify participation in this co-operation as a means to those goods. Morality is then understood as a set of prescriptions for such participation. Gauthier goes on, however, to deny that morality (and participation) is justified only instrumentally. It comes to have, he says, value for us in itself. I will return later to the relation between the instrumental and the intrinsic justifications.

Gauthier insists, against Kant, that rationality is self-interest maximizing and does not require willing one's maxims as universal law.

Proponents of the *maximizing* conception of rationality, which we endorse, insist that . . . the rational person seeks the greatest satisfaction of her own interests. On the other hand, proponents of what we shall call the *universalistic* conception of rationality insist that what makes it rational to satisfy an interest does not depend on whose interest it is. Thus the rational person seeks to satisfy all interests. Whether she is a utilitarian, aiming at the greatest happiness of the greatest number, or whether she takes into independent consideration the fair distribution of benefit among persons, is of no importance to the present discussion.[10]

[9] Gauthier (1986) 325.   [10] Ibid. 7.

Gauthier thus starts from an initial presumption against the rationality (in his sense) of morality, since this requires a constraint on each person's pursuit of his own interest. He sees society (quoting from John Rawls) as 'a co-operative venture for mutual advantage' among persons 'conceived as not taking an interest in one another's interests'. He cites Hume's example of two persons rowing a boat that neither can row alone. Like Hobbes, Gauthier argues that in the state of nature (our state before we invented society) humans are without morality, and it requires a contract between them to bring morality into being. Such a contract would not be necessary, he says, in a perfectly competitive market, which he labels 'a morally free zone'. This would be a society without externalities in the economist's sense, which occur whenever an act of production or exchange or consumption affects the welfare of some person who is not party or who is unwillingly party to it. Without externalities there would be no free riders or parasites. Morality is then seen as a beneficially co-ordinative practice where the conditions of the perfectly competitive market do not obtain. Morality arises, so to speak, from market failure. Gauthier imagines that this co-ordinative practice is established by a contract. He argues from game theory that the equal rationality of bargainers leads to the requirement for such a contract that the least relative benefit, measured as a proportion of one's stake in the bargain, be as great as possible.[11]

A difficulty with contractarian views is that while they may be able to show that it is rational to agree to such a contract, it is not at all clear that it is rational to comply with one once it is established. Why may not each person rationally join 'in the hope of benefiting from the adherence of others, but fail to adhere in the hope of benefiting from her own defection?'[12] This was the difficulty about 'free riders' and cheats noticed by Donald Campbell. Gauthier proceeds by introducing the notion of a constrained maximizer. This person is not disposed straightforwardly to maximize the satisfaction of her own interests; rather, she is disposed to comply with mutually advantageous moral constraints, provided she expects similar compliance from others. She stops asking on each occasion 'Is this in my interest?' and acts out of the disposition to comply with the

---

[11] A person's stake in a bargain is the difference between the least he might accept in place of no agreement and the most he might receive in place of being excluded by others from agreement. [12] Gauthier (1986) 16.

moral constraints. She does this because she knows that only if she does so is she a candidate for the kind of co-operative agreement that makes possible the co-operative goods she wants. Straightforward maximization is, so to speak, self-effacing. Rational constrained maximizers will also not enter a bargain, Gauthier argues, unless the initial bargaining position is itself constrained by fairness between the bargainers.[13] If his argument works, he has shown that it is rational in his sense to be moral. He ends by claiming that although he has derived morality as an instrument of self-interested rationality, it is not to be seen as purely instrumental; rather, the co-operation which morality enables comes to be valued in itself, and comes to be associated with our affective lives, allowing 'a genuine civic friendship to blossom'.

I want now to evaluate Gauthier's project in the light of the two flaws I claimed to find in Campbell. First of all, it seems that morality becomes on his account dishonest. This is not quite the same dishonesty as with Campbell, because it is the institution itself which becomes liable to the charge, rather than the naturalist philosopher. What I mean is that morality, on Gauthier's construal, presents itself to us in a way that it really is not. Morality does not present itself to us as justifying itself first instrumentally, as a means for the production of co-operative goods by those who do not (at least for the purposes of this thought experiment) have an interest in each other's interests. It is true that Gauthier does not suppose that morality is for *us* a second-best, where the best would be securing those co-operative goods without it. He does not suppose that we are in fact without interests in each other's interests. But he does suppose that morality would be a second-best for God, or any godlike person who was without our human insufficiencies. For example, it would be a second-best if we were to possess a ring, as the ancestor of Gyges did, which could make us invisible. Plato, in telling that story, says that this ring conveyed the power 'to do other things as an equal to a god among humans'.[14] For Gauthier, we normal un-ringed human beings do develop both a desire for co-operation for its own sake, and affective concerns for justice. Nevertheless, 'although rational persons who value participatory

---

[13] In particular, the initial bargaining position must be constrained by the proviso that prohibits bettering one's position through interaction worsening the position of another (ibid. 16).   [14] Ibid. 308.

activities with their fellows will develop an affective concern for essential justice, yet the object of their concern is initially an instrumental value'.[15] What does he mean by 'initially'? This is not a chronological story of moral development, for Gauthier concedes that what comes first chronologically is socialization into the institution. None the less he insists that even though our original preferences and capacities may not be autonomously determined, we have the capacity to alter them by a rational, self-critical, reflective procedure. When we do so, we create 'a society of liberal individuals, free to establish their own goals and to choose their own affective ties with their fellows'.[16] In saying that the value of morality is 'initially' instrumental, Gauthier is doing what he calls 'rational reconstruction'. He is establishing the logical relations between the valuations of the liberal individual.

This is not how morality presents itself. On this matter, Kant is closer to the truth, though we have seen in Chapter 6 other grounds to question his universalism. On Kant's conception, the structure of moral rationality is reversed. It is not that practical reason starts off from the pure maximization of self-interest, and then chooses to bring other people into affective ties and finally to value justice for its own sake. Rather, practical reason starts from a recognition of the self and others as under the moral law. This is not a purely intellectual recognition, but a feeling of respect. In terms of the three-part structure I discussed in Chapter 1, what we recognize in ourselves and others is an imperfect resemblance to an at least possible being who is morally perfect and is construed as the source of the moral law. Morality is here not constructed (by agreement, or any other way), but recognized as the standard to which we are already called.

Gauthier is entirely unsympathetic to this view. He supposes that 'our present self-understanding emerges from the disappearance of the belief that man is a creature, taking his goals and values from a divinely established order'.[17] But who is this 'we' referred to in 'our present self-understanding'? Is it the majority of the human race, the majority of Gauthier's fellow citizens, or the majority of his colleagues? There is an extraordinary imperialism in this 'we'.

[15] Ibid. 344.
[16] Ibid. 339. It is doubtful whether we do in fact choose our affective ties in this way.   [17] Ibid. 354.

It is surely nearer the truth to suppose that most people in the world, even most people in America, hold that humans are creatures; and that even those who do not hold this have inherited a structure of moral thinking that is permeated with this view. If we are talking about morality as a conceptual and practical structure in the culture, it is not true to say that it presents itself initially as having instrumental value in promoting self-interest, where 'self' and hence 'self-interest' are understood in terms of persons who take no interest in the interests of others.

This brings up the second flaw in Gauthier's treatment. Even if we suppose that morality requires to be justified rationally, in Gauthier's understanding of that project, it is doubtful whether he can succeed. There is a large secondary literature on this question; and it is unlikely that any argument of such ambition and scope would succeed in all its details. The consensus of the secondary literature, I think, is that there is much to be learnt from his argument, but that he does not pull it off. I will mention just one large difficulty. Gauthier has to prove that it is rational (in his sense) to be a constrained maximizer, that is, to adopt the disposition to comply only with fair bargains. But whether a bargain is worth pursuing depends on my bargaining advantage in the state of nature and on how many other constrained maximizers I can tell there are.[18] If we consider both advantaged and disadvantaged individuals, it does not seem that it would be rational (in Gauthier's sense) to become a constrained maximizer in either case. The adoption of the disposition to comply only with fair bargains will prevent advantaged individuals from ever profiting from their advantage, when the benefits of doing so outweigh the costs of being excluded from bargaining with constrained maximizers.[19] But the lust for power may be perfectly rational in Gauthier's sense, and it would be rational for those who want it and can get it without becoming constrained maximizers to do so. The adoption of the disposition will also prevent disadvantaged individuals from benefiting from unfair bargains with advantaged individuals in which a lesser, unfair, share of the benefit is available (and where, as before, this benefit outweighs the costs of being

---

[18] Gauthier proposes that we are 'translucent' with respect to our moral dispositions, neither opaque nor transparent: i.e. we can evaluate the disposition of others to co-operate 'not with certainty, but as more than mere guesswork' (ibid. 174).

[19] See Kraus and Coleman (1987).

excluded from bargaining with constrained maximizers).[20] There is the difficulty, then, of seeing how constrained maximization could ever get off the ground. For the costs of exclusion from bargaining with constrained maximizers depend on how many constrained maximizers there already are. Gauthier's theoretical machinery does not seem adequate to carry out the task he wants it to do.

The machinery of the rational bargain is what is supposed to take straightforward maximizers into the institution of morality. It is Gauthier's equivalent of redemption. He discusses, in an earlier article, Rousseau's scheme by which the Legislator creates a society in which people are socialized into virtue by the transforming of their passions. Gauthier's verdict is that the scheme fails, and that Rousseau already half knew this. 'We humans live, as Rousseau, despite himself, finally knew that we must live, unredeemed.'[21] The machinery of the rational bargain is Gauthier's substitute for Rousseau's Legislator, and perhaps Gauthier too is doubtful about its chances of success. For he ends with the recognition that his argument may not work for humans as such, taking them from rationality (in his sense) to morality; but it may work only in a transitional stage of culture, between the defunct sense of man as creature and the sense on the technological horizon of man as artefact, 'constructed through an increasingly known and alterable process of genetic engineering'. Gauthier concedes that man as engineered may not be compatible with the ideas of individuality and autonomy which underly the enquiry of his book. But he ends with the hope of a better conclusion, referring to Nietzsche and the mastery over self we can have by embracing the agreement that brings us into morality. But it is very odd to refer to Nietzsche in this context. What would Nietzsche think of the idea that we could be saved by being led into impartial morality by rational choice theory? The end of Gauthier's quote from Nietzsche is revealing: 'Mastery over himself also necessarily gives him mastery over circumstances, over nature, *and over all more short-willed and unreliable creatures.*'[22] Nietzsche is here talking about mastery over other people. This sounds much more like the view of human beings, and especially other human beings, as artefacts, whose nature can be mastered by

---

[20] Consider e.g. the situation of the inhabitants of the island of Melos, described in Thucydides, *History of the Peloponnesian War* 5. 84.

[21] Gauthier (1990) 109.   [22] Nietzsche, (1967) 59–60 (emphasis added).

those who control the technology in the interests of the Will to Power. If anybody did have such power, he would be like the godlike ancestor of Gyges, and immune to Gauthier's argument. In other words, Gauthier's view of morality is closer to the demise of Kant's liberalism and autonomy than Gauthier himself acknowledges. This is what we would expect if Kant's ethical theory depends on postulates which Gauthier rejects.

c. EVOLUTION AND THE MORAL EMOTIONS

Allan Gibbard, in *Wise Choices, Apt Feelings* gives a highly plausible account of the relation between morality and evolution. The connection he draws is like Donald Campbell's except that he does not rely on the notion of social or cultural evolution. To think an act morally reprehensible, he says, is to accept norms that prescribe, for such a situation, guilt on the part of the agent and resentment (or anger) on the part of others.[23] This guilt is, in the terms I used in Chapter 1, subjective guilt, the feeling of failure rather than the actual failure to do what is morally good. A moral judgement that an act is wrong is then the expression of the acceptance of such norms. Suppose we agree that this analysis of moral judgement as 'norm-expressivist' is correct.[24] Gibbard can then say that these moral emotions are not under the control of reason. We can feel the emotions even though we do not have any 'deep background rationale' for them; in particular even though we do not have a deep background rationale for our culture's notion of guilt.[25] We can then use evolution to explain how it may be as natural to follow the norms without understanding them, as it is (in Campbell's words) 'to continue breathing air before one understands the role of oxygen in bodily metabolism'. Guilt, Gibbard says, meshes with anger. This is why he thinks guilt is a good thing. He thinks we are going to have anger in any case, because this seems to be pervasive across cultures and humans are probably biologically conditioned to it; but anger makes co-ordination, and hence the goods attainable only through co-ordination, more difficult. Guilt, he suggests, leads to actions that

---

[23] Gibbard (1990) 47. The progenitor of this account is Adam Smith's view that morality concerns the propriety of the moral sentiments.

[24] It is consistent with R. M. Hare's notion that moral judgements are prescriptive, as defined in Ch. 1 above.   [25] Gibbard (1990) 315.

mollify anger; it leads to apology, for example, and reparation. Evolution gives us guilt, and hence the possibility of co-ordination. Evolution is thus, for Gibbard as for Campbell, the substitute for God's assistance in overcoming the moral gap; but Gibbard makes the account more plausible by not relying on social evolution and by adding a highly sophisticated account of the nature of morality and moral emotion.

Guilt and resentment are, on this view, feelings or emotions, and Gibbard gives two different pictures of what emotions are. On the first picture, we can think of an emotion as genetically determined. Darwinian forces have selected a physical state of the organism which stands behind a particular syndrome. A syndrome is a pattern of typical overt expressions responding to certain kinds of events, and issuing in special kinds of action. Gibbard gives as an example of such a syndrome the dog barking in response to territorial intrusion, and then attacking the intruder. An emotion (on the first picture) is whatever state of the organism stands behind such a syndrome of behaviour. It may not even be 'felt' at all as a distinct internal episode. Unfortunately, guilt does not seem to fit this picture well, as Gibbard admits. For the emotions which he thinks fit this picture well, like anger, are not culturally specific in the way that guilt seems to be. 'Shame or something like it appears everywhere, and so does anger, but guilt seems culturally special. Many languages have no word for guilt, and so if the people who speak these languages do feel guilt they cannot say so.[26] Yet if guilt and shame are distinct biological adaptations to the human condition, then they were widely present as human nature evolved, and they should appear distinctly in a wide range of present cultures.'[27]

This leaves us, then, with the second picture of emotion. On this picture, the distinct emotions people can have are largely a matter of

---

[26] Strictly, what needs to be shown is not that some cultures do not have a *word* for guilt, but that they do not have the *notion* of guilt. Williams says 'Yet we have another word, "guilt", for which the Greeks had no direct equivalent' (1994: 88), and he goes on to argue that this is a deep cultural difference.

[27] Gibbard (1990) 140. For an account of guilt which claims that it is a universal human emotion, see Westphal (1987). See also Rom. 1: 18–23. But Westphal does not distinguish between shame and guilt, and what he thinks universal is the category of purity and defilement; see esp. Ch. 6. Strictly, an evolutionary account of something (call it *x*) does not require that *x* be selected by adaptation. Rather, *x* can be genetically linked to something else which *is* selected by adaptation even though *x* is not.

their own conceptions; and these conceptions will vary sharply from one culture to another.[28] If we take, though, the second picture of the emotion of guilt which Gibbard offers, in which the self-attribution of the agent is crucial, we should ask *why* we have the notion of guilt in our cultural repertoire, and other cultures do not. It is the evidence of this cultural difference that forces the move to the second picture. If 'guilt' were more pervasive across cultures, we could (Gibbard thinks) think of the feeling as a biological adaptive syndrome. This is what he would prefer to be able to say. I have suggested that our morality has been partly structured by theological assumptions. This gives us a hypothesis for why our culture contains the notion of guilt. The explanation is that our culture has been formed within the framework of a monotheism that holds God to be the upholder of the norms by which nature and human life are governed, to see clearly our motivations and reasons for acting, and to be himself offended when we break those norms not only in what we do but in what we care about.[29] If this hypothesis is right, we should expect to find the notion of guilt in those cultures which have been deeply influenced by such a monotheism; for example, we

[28] It seems plausible that the self-conception of a person who feels guilt will standardly involve normative concepts like being to blame or being at fault. Thus, in reply to Scanlon, Gibbard says that the need to be able to justify one's actions to others 'is a part of the workings of guilt and exoneration.' (1990: 272). He says that guilt seems *incoherent* when joined to the thought 'with the same opportunity, let me do it again' (p. 300). But if the guilt is incoherent with a positively normed prescription, this should be because it already contains a negatively normed one. Gibbard has to show that he can avoid this conclusion. For if to feel guilty is to feel as if one were at fault, the account of moral judgement will be circular in a way he wants to deny. Gibbard concedes that if the feeling of guilt invoked the concept of fault, this would make his account circular. He says, 'The full concept [of fault] gets its shape from a connection with norms. The protoconcept at most helps define feelings of guilt. Feelings of guilt can then be invoked, with no circularity, to define a full concept of fault' (p. 149). But we are nowhere told what a 'protoconcept' is.

[29] See Ps. 51: 4: 'Against thee, thee only, have I sinned, and done this evil in thy sight, that thou mightest be justified when thou speakest, and be clear when thou judgest.' See also Jer. 17: 9–10: 'The heart is deceitful above all things, and desperately wicked; who can know it? I the Lord search the heart.' Nietzsche accepts this genealogy, and hopes that the death of God will also bring about the end of guilt. 'The advent of the Christian God, as the maximum god attained so far, was therefore accompanied by the maximum feeling of guilty indebtedness on earth. Presuming we have gradually entered upon the *reverse* course, there is no small probability that with the irresistible decline of faith in the Christian God there is now also a considerable decline in mankind's feeling of guilt' (1967: 90–1).

should expect to find it in cultures deeply influenced by Judaism, Christianity, and Islam.

Most cultures have something like anger in their repertoire, says Gibbard, and they also have something like shame. What is the difference between guilt and shame? He suggests several differences, but the most basic seems to be that guilt is a response to the voluntary *doing* of wrong whereas shame is a response to inadequacy or blemish in what one *is*. Guilt, he says, is the consciousness of lack of proper motivation; shame is the consciousness of lack of proper resources.[30] We could thus make a rough comparison of the two by thinking of guilt as a specialized form of shame: shame occasioned by the lack of proper internal resources in the will for a good action. Putting the comparison this way makes vivid the question I want to ask: Why should a culture specialize in this way? We need to explain why the lack of inner motivation for a good action should become salient. Having done this, we can then suppose that the emotion survives in people who no longer accept that deep background rationale. After all, we still talk about the sun rising and setting. Our language is full of such traces.

These last two paragraphs have the air of armchair history. The hypothesis needs to be checked against the evidence. But suppose it is right, what if anything follows about evolution and the source of morality, in the sense of the acceptance of norms for guilt and resentment? If we think of guilt in terms of Gibbard's second picture, we should not expect there to be a genetic basis for guilt. Rather, there will be genetic programming 'for broad abilities to pick up the emotional script one's culture provides' and to play it through.[31] But then, if evolution is to be the fundamental explanatory mechanism, we need a connection between evolution and the adoption of the religious framework. The naturalist should argue that there is a biological adaptive syndrome behind which stand the physical states which we call the broadly religious

---

[30] Gibbard (1990) 138. See Williams (1994) 89: 'What arouses guilt in an agent is an act or omission of a sort that typically elicits from other people anger, resentment, or indignation. What the agent may offer in order to turn this away is reparation; he may also fear punishment or may inflict it on himself. What arouses shame, on the other hand, is something that typically elicits from others contempt or derision or avoidance. This may equally be an act or omission, but it need not be: it may be some failing or defect.' [31] Gibbard (1990) 296.

emotions. This should be plausible, on Gibbard's account, because the disposition to worship gods is pervasive across cultures in the way that anger is. Atheism is as rare culturally as Gibbard suggests that guilt is.[32] This is especially plausible if we turn our attention to the hunter-gatherer societies, in which Gibbard thinks the Darwinian forces exercised their selective pressures. The naturalist might provide in this way an account of the origin of guilt which is sensitive to its theological background.

One advantage of including the theological background I have mentioned is that it provides an account of why some cultures should have guilt in their repertoire, and others not. There are also some loose ends in Gibbard's account which the theological background helps to tie. Gibbard mentions the danger that guilt will cause us 'to dwell on some things more than makes sense'.[33] 'Sometimes', he says, 'we are too fully engaged in misdeeds, our own and others'; we may need to treat them as water over the dam.' But how are we supposed to do that, without *condoning* those misdeeds? This is a question Kant answered with a theory of atonement, and I will discuss it in Chapter 10. Second, Gibbard mentions the broadly moral feeling of the world 'as morally ordered, as standing watch and punishing transgressions'.[34] Such language is clearly derivative from a theological background. Kant derives from this sort of consideration his postulates of practical reason, including the existence of God, and I discussed his argument in Chapter 3. Third, Gibbard acknowledges that 'on one formulation, morality has won us when we love neighbor as self'.[35] If we understand this, with Butler and Mill, as disinterested universal benevolence, there is a difficulty about whether this would indeed be the best reproductive strategy, as a Darwinian origin should suggest. Gibbard mentions the possibility that '*being known* for charity might somehow have tended indirectly to promote one's reproductive chances'.[36] But we should find this reply as troubling as Glaucon and Adeimantus found the appeal to reputation in Plato's *Republic*. 'Genuine charity', concedes Gibbard, 'is a puzzle: charity may have no apparent reproductive payoff.' But if the naturalist can show there is a biological

---

[32] Atheism seems to arise in those same societies in which, on my hypothesis, we find the concept of guilt. Perhaps the presence of guilt provides a motivation for atheism (i.e. avoidance) which is otherwise lacking.

[33] Gibbard (1990) 295.   [34] Ibid. 272.   [35] Ibid. 257.

[36] Ibid. 260.

explanation behind our religious emotions, he can argue that the theological rationale for the possibility of charity (which I have been detailing in this book) is constructed out of these emotions.

There are, however, two flaws which I have already mentioned in connection with Campbell and Gauthier. First, Gibbard has to suppose that human moral propensities were shaped by something he thinks it would be foolish to value in itself, namely the goal of multiplying one's own genes among later generations.[37] This means that there is a lack of fit between the source of our moral concern and the intentional content of our moral concern, namely what it presents itself as being a concern *about*. Morality is then dishonest in the way Gauthier makes it to be. On Gauthier's account, the 'initial' concern of morality is maximization; on Gibbard's it is reproductive success. If I have been right about the theological assumptions involved in the three-part structure of morality, this makes the lack of fit more vivid. The second flaw will be clear from what I have already said. Suppose that our moral emotions are partly structured, as I have claimed, by theological assumptions; and suppose that, as Gibbard claims, Darwinian forces have shaped directly or indirectly the emotions which are prescribed by the norms whose acceptance is typically expressed by moral judgements.[38] The naturalist who takes the second of Gibbard's two pictures of the moral emotions must give an account of what I have called cultural specialization. One possibility is that the *religious* emotions can be understood in terms of Gibbard's *first* picture, and that biological evolution has selected the physical state which stands behind the human syndrome of worship and prayer. This is the route the naturalist should take, as I have just suggested. But a biological account of the broadly religious emotions will not be enough. If my hypothesis is right, the naturalist needs an account of the features of monotheism which make guilt an intelligible specialization of shame. Is *this* kind of worship and prayer to be given a biological explanation? The argument can be turned on its head. If this is what the naturalist has to show, the task is daunting. There are other possibilities, such as social evolution, or perhaps a Marxist account in terms of social control, or a Freudian account in terms of the discontents of civilization. In any case, the monotheism which on my hypothesis explains why guilt is in our cultural repertoire must itself be explained. I have given no reason to

[37] Ibid. 237.   [38] Ibid. 67.

suppose this cannot be done. Until it is done, however, the naturalist substitute for divine assistance will not have much explanatory power. Until a plausible naturalist account of monotheism is given, we should remain sceptical about the naturalist account of the origin of morality and the moral gap.

PART III

GOD'S ASSISTANCE

8

REPENTANCE

THIS chapter marks the beginning of the third division of this book, which is about what Christian doctrine contributes to the discussion of the moral gap. Any readers who are allergic to theology will find this the most irritating division, though Chapter 9 less so. Chapter 8 is about Kierkegaard's understanding of the atonement. Chapter 9 analyses the notion of forgiveness as this occurs between human beings. Chapter 10 extends this analysis to God's forgiveness of us and his reconciliation with us.

Volume 2 of Kierkegaard's *Either/Or* consists of two enormous letters which a character called Judge William sends to his aesthetic friend, *A* (whose papers form volume 1), and a sermon by a pastor he knows which the judge appends to the second letter. There are thus three kinds of life represented, the aesthetic life by *A*, the ethical life by the judge, and (imperfectly) the religious or Christian life by the pastor.[1] I will try to show that the judge's use of Christian doctrine is very close to Kant's translation of this doctrine within the pure religion of reason. If this is right, *Either/Or*, volume 2, has three merits for the argument of my book. The first is that Kierkegaard gives a vivid picture of what this translated doctrine looks like within a life, the life of the judge. The second is that he gives a critique of this life, both by showing its internal stresses in the judge's own words and by analysing the same stresses from the perspective of the religious life which lies outside it. This critique, I shall say, is that the judge is not able fully to repent. The third merit is that Kierkegaard gives us a way to retranslate the doctrines out of the judge's version of the translation, so that we can see with fresh eyes what the original doctrines mean. I am not suggesting that we

[1] The pastor is not a well-realized character, and I will not for the most part rely on his sermon for an account of the religious life. Especially he does not represent well the dependence of the Christian life upon God. In this chapter I will rely for an account of the religious life on Kierkegaard's writings under the pseudonym Anti-Climacus and under his own name. None the less the pastor's sermon does represent a conflict with the judge's ethical life, and at least a reach towards the religious life.

replace the traditional ways of understanding these doctrines, but that we supplement them with an analogy drawn from a reading of *Either/Or*, volume 2. Section *a* of this chapter describes the stages of the transition Judge William sees from the aesthetic into the ethical life. Section *b* describes the transition into the religious life by using a retranslation of the judge's account, translated back out of a Kant-like pure religion of reason into historical faith. Kierkegaard's own procedure was no doubt the reverse. His description of the transition into the ethical life uses the language of atonement which he originally found in Christian doctrine. But his account is so rich that it will give us an analogy by which to understand that original doctrine afresh.

It is important that Kierkegaard did not intend *Either/Or* to come out under his own name. The work came out under the name of an editor, 'Victor Eremita', who does not see any resolution to the conflict between the ways of life represented. The lives are self-sufficient in the following sense: each has the resources to repel attack from the others to its own satisfaction. The aesthete's life seems to Judge William fragmented and inauthentic; and the aesthete undoubtedly regards the judge's life as boring. But we can see a directionality to the stages as well as their self-sufficiency. There is an internal tendency in the aesthetic stage to break down, as a result of which the movement to the ethical life is made possible. There is the same 'dialectic' within the ethical life; it contains an internal tendency to break down, as a result of which the movement to the religious life is made possible. This possibility is revealed in *Either/Or* by the pastor's sermon added by the judge to the end of his second letter. Kierkegaard's pseudonomy enables us to see these tendencies from the inside, from the way they look to each pseudonymous author from inside each life. He can engage us if we recognize ourselves in these lives. He cannot attain this same effect by merely talking about the directionality from the outside.[2]

---

[2] MacIntyre (1981: 38–42) takes *EO* as a key moment in the failure of 'the Enlightenment project'. He sees Kierkegaard as presenting the aesthetic and ethical lives for our radical choice. The choice is radical, he thinks, because it cannot be based upon any first principles; since any first principle will already be embedded *within* a life, any choice based upon it will beg the question about the merit of that kind of life. According to this view of Kierkegaard, we are simply supposed to opt for one life or another. But this means, MacIntyre thinks, that ethics becomes incoherent, since the principles we opt for cannot have any authority for us. This

a. THE ETHICAL LIFE

Despair

The movement towards despair, internal to the aesthetic life, has itself various stages.[3] The aesthete's life is committed to the avoidance of boredom, to keeping his life interesting. But we can already see in his own papers that he is close to the realization that he is bound to fail. The central paradox is one of control. In order to avoid boredom, the aesthete has to be able to control the way he experiences things. This control requires him not to be too committed to anyone or anything, so as to be able to disengage whenever boredom looms. The aesthete has to avoid, for example, marriage or close friendship or a job he cares about. The trouble is that it is commitment which makes possible the sustaining of interest over a lifetime, or even over six months. The aesthete imagines himself like the lookout in the crow's-nest of a ship, watching the waves crash on the deck below. The ship is his own life, but he is detached from it and watching it from above. What Kierkegaard wants us to see is that the aesthete's disengagement is necessary to him and also dooms him to failure. For the kinds of deep satisfaction that sustain interest in life arise out of the very commitments which the aesthete has denied himself in order to avoid getting bored. Interest is sustained by engagement.

The judge makes this critique of the aesthetic life from the perspective of the ethical life, for example where he describes the life of the Roman Emperor Nero, whose only principle is to satisfy his own desire.[4] Most of us do not have the resources to carry this out; but suppose that, like Nero, we had the whole empire at our command? We could set light to half of Rome in order to visualize more accurately the description in *Aeneid*, book 2, of Troy burning to the ground. The odd thing, says the judge, is that Nero's nature is

failure, he thinks, is already implicit in Kant and bears fruit in the failure of the 'proceduralist' ethics of 20th-cent. analytic philosophers such as R. M. Hare. But MacIntyre has not allowed for the purpose of the pseudonomy in showing indirectly the directionality of the stages. In particular, he does not mention the sermon at the end of *EO* ii. See Piety (1993).

[3] See J. E. Hare (1995c) for a more detailed account of the breakdown of the aesthetic life, and its connection with the language of atonement.

[4] *EO* ii. 184–8.

in fact depression. This is because he is already sated with all the pleasures he can think of. Like a child, he can be distracted for a moment by a new delicacy; but it is too late to achieve continuous satisfaction this way, because he is not a child any longer. A cloud gradually settles over him. He refuses to acknowledge openly to himself that there is nothing now to sustain him, that he is facing unending greyness. This conviction is none the less growing on him. The judge puts this by saying that the spirit is wanting to break through; depression results from repressing the spirit. The aesthete himself sees one last strategy. He describes it in one of his papers, which narrates the search by a panel of aesthetic judges for a fitting occupant for an empty grave somewhere in England, marked only 'The Unhappiest One'. The strategy is to find his own misery interesting, like the young men in Paris who dress in black and expect others to find them fascinating just because of the torment in their souls. Perhaps the aesthete himself is unhappy enough to deserve from the panel the honour of this extraordinary grave. But Judge William is not persuaded. Misery is in fact just misery; merely declaring it interesting does not make it so. The aesthete's strategy is, in effect, a form of atonement. He wants his suffering to be declared by the panel sufficient for his salvation. In theological terms this would be a kind of forensic or external justification. Kierkegaard is making play with the contrast between this hollow victory, which leaves the aesthete in the grave, and Christ's victory, which ends with his resurrection.

The Failures are Taken Over

The judge thinks that the aesthete is ready for the transition into the ethical life. The key, he says, is for the aesthete to *choose* his despair. If he would only admit that he cannot keep his life interesting, then the spirit could break through, and the depression would lift like a cloud. The judge says that the spirit would gather itself together, in this choice, out of its dispersion. Looking back over the small-scale commitments he has made, the aesthete could become conscious that there is nothing that holds them together, nothing that attaches them to how he now sees himself, and so no reason to suppose they could go on interesting him either separately or together.[5] What would it

---

[5] The aesthete might well object. For he does have an absolute commitment, to keeping his life interesting, and all of his other commitments are hypothetical or

be now, in him, that is doing this? The judge says it would be what he has in common with all other humans, after the differences have been stripped away, and all his idiosyncratic preferences and attachments have failed him; what would be left is merely the power to choose or take responsibility for himself. He would thus discover his freedom, and with it the ethical life. He would discover, the judge says, his membership in 'a rational order of things' which can be described as a kind of kingdom, 'a kingdom of gods'.[6]

It is significant that what he would discover is a kingdom of *gods*, for this reminds us of Kant's kingdom of ends (or persons as ends in themselves).[7] The difference is also significant because for Kierkegaard the judge represents not the final destination, but an intermediate stage. Kierkegaard is critical of the judge; and in the same way as he does with the aesthete, he mounts this criticism partly in the judge's own words, and partly in words from a later stage. The central failure of the judge, as seen from the religious stage, is that he does not make the absolute distinction between creator and creature, but thinks he will find God by going deeply enough inside himself.[8] This is why the judge is made to say that the ethical life discovers a kingdom of gods. Putting this as a criticism of Kant's translation of Christian doctrine within the pure religion of reason, we might say that the translation turns humans into gods.

The judge's account also reminds us of Kant's translation of the doctrine of the atonement within the pure religion of reason. Kant

provisional only in the sense that he discards them when they do not interest him any more. He might say to the judge that ethical commitments display the same structure; there is one absolute or categorical commitment to the good, and all other commitments are provisional. The judge would reply that there is a key difference between the two of them: his provisional commitments last, and the aesthete's do not.

[6] Ibid. 292.

[7] Rudd (1993) 71 says 'It is quite frequently claimed that Kierkegaard's ethics is largely Kantian, but this seems to me about as radical an error as it is possible to make in the interpretation of Kierkegaard.' See my review in J. E. Hare (1995*b*). Rudd follows MacIntyre (1981) in his view of Kant, in his treatment of the pseudonymy, and in his attack on contemporary analytic ethics. As long as we do not follow his view of Kant, we can see Kierkegaard as criticizing Kant; not only Kant, however, but Hegel as well.

[8] See Evans (1983) 24–8 and 45–6. There is a difficulty here in characterizing the relation of the ethical life to 'Religiousness A', as described in *Concluding Unscientific Postscript*. Kierkegaard's views no doubt developed, and *EO* represents an earlier account, conceived before the distinction between Religiousness A and B had been worked out.

proposed that the new man, man in his moral perfection (i.e. under the good maxim which subordinates inclinations to duty) suffers on behalf of the old man (who is guilty, having lived under the evil maxim which subordinates duty to inclination). Kant used here the New Testament language of the old man being put to death. His idea was that the new man's suffering is vicarious, since he is not in his own nature guilty, and his suffering makes reparation for the guilt of the old man. The judge makes the same prescription for the aesthete. What is required, as in Kant, is the suffering of the new man on behalf of the old. 'I repent myself out of the whole of existence,' says the judge. 'Repentance specifically expresses that evil essentially belongs to me and at the same time expresses that it does not essentially belong to me.'[9] In what sense does evil essentially belong to me? The judge's point is that in choosing myself as guilty, I collect together all my previous projects out of their dispersion and accept responsibility for them all. In what sense does evil not essentially belong to me? Those previous projects represent a failure of which I am no longer guilty in my new nature, though I take on responsibility for them from my past nature. If I do take on responsibility for them, in repentance, I am (the judge says) *ransoming* myself in order to remain in my freedom.[10]

The ethical agent can now go back into his aesthetic preferences, and either retain them or reject them, but now in the light of the ethical standard which was not previously available to him.[11] He makes, Kant would say, inclinations subordinate to duty. The inclinations now subordinated to duty are for the most part the inclinations that were always there. It is not as though the ethical agent used to like junk food before the revolution of the will, and used to play the trombone, but now likes mung beans and plays the harp. Rather, the ethical agent returns into his aesthetic life and endorses whatever he can. This is how the aesthete can ransom *himself*. The price that has to be paid to make this possible (the

---

[9] *EO* ii. 224.

[10] Ibid. 232. The structure of repentance as the judge describes it is recapitulated (as is much in Kierkegaard) in Heidegger (1962: 325–48) under the heading of the call of conscience.

[11] 'In the choice of myself in my freedom, I grasp myself in my concretion, and thus choose in such a way that in the choice I remain in myself; I array myself in myself' (ibid. 231).

ransom money) is the despair over his life that, when chosen, allows him to recognize his freedom in the first place.

Kierkegaard is thus giving us a description, in the words of the judge, of what Kant's translation of the atonement feels like from the inside. He is also giving us (because of the directionality of the stages) a criticism of this description. I do not mean that he is criticizing the accuracy of the description of how it feels, but that he is criticizing the claim that as described it works. This is a delicate task; by a kind of dramatic irony, Kierkegaard has to write the judge's lines in such a way that the weakness of the judge's position is clear to the audience, but not clear to the judge himself. Kierkegaard is criticizing the claim that a revolution of the will which achieves what the judge thinks it achieves *can* be accomplished in this way. When discussing Kant's version of the atonement, I concluded that he presupposed in his translation that the revolution of the will was possible; and therefore he could not use his version of the atonement (or of the rest of God's work in salvation) to show that the revolution of the will was possible, given the initial propensity to evil. The same is true now of the atonement described by Judge William. It has to presuppose that the aesthete can accomplish his own transition into the ethical life. The transition is supposed to be accomplished by what the judge calls 'repentance', which he takes to mean not just acknowledging his aesthetic failures, but the choosing of something in himself to which evil does not essentially belong. But what if he cannot find in himself any such thing? The failure of the judge is to repent far enough down; he is satisfied with himself prematurely.

Catharsis

The judge thinks that the victory over merely aesthetic despair is made possible by a kind of incongruity. To explain what I mean by incongruity, it will be useful to use a metaphor from the theatre. Kierkegaard loved the theatre himself, and frequently uses metaphors drawn from it. Judge William, however, does not much care for the theatre, and disapproves of the aesthete's delight in it. He notes that the aesthete likes happy endings on the stage but is much less sanguine than the judge about happy endings in real life. The judge puts a kind of curse on him: 'then may it be your just punishment . . . that all playwrights compose nothing but tearjerking plays, full of all possible anxiety and horror that would not allow your flabbiness to rest on the cushioned theater seats . . . but would horrify you until in the world of actuality you learn to believe in that which you want to believe in only in poetry.'[12.] The structure of this curse is that the aesthete is condemned to a kind of catharsis; he is condemned to watch only plays that arouse pity and terror, and the result is supposed to be that he regains a kind of tranquillity in his actual life.

There is an echo here of Aristotle's account of tragedy. If you take people who are in a condition of ecstatic worship (as in the *Bacchae* of Euripides), you place them alone in a neutral environment, and you play to them the same music as is usually used to accompany their worship, they tend to calm down and are relieved from their frenzy. How does this work? One interpretation is that it works by a kind of homeopathy. The frenzy is due to an excess of warm black bile (in Greek, *melas cholos*). If you play the customary music, you warm the black bile again. But without the company of their fellow worshippers, and without the context of the wild mountainside, the worshippers achieve a distance from the feelings aroused by the music. The feelings are acknowledged as present, but the worshipper as it were goes out of gear with them. This is because in the neutral context the worshipper's own basic character is able to reassert itself. She comes to herself. In the same way, in the theatre the emotions are communicated in such a way that a member of the audience both acknowledges that she shares them and preserves distance from them. The degree of sharing and the degree of distance are both variable, and dramatists have various techniques for adjusting both. Catharsis can take place only where there is both identification and distance, so that the emotions can be both acknowledged and put out of gear. The audience has to feel engaged in what is happening on stage, and it also has to know that what is happening is only a play.[13] For catharsis to work, on this account, there also has to be an incongruity between the passions acknowledged and the spectator's basic character. If the spectator is inextricably mired in insane jealousy, for example, the emotions stimulated by *Othello* will not cause catharsis or release but will reinforce the disposition he already has.

---

[12] *EO* ii. 122.   [13] See Bullough (1912) 404–5.

Judge William thinks of the aesthete as going constantly to plays with happy endings as an escape, because of a fear that real life is going to let him down. This fear is that he is not going to be able to sustain his own interest in life, and it generates an endless searching for new artificial stimulations to distract him. The heroic or comic triumphs on stage have this power to charm him for a while. The judge's own view, however, is that interest in one's life is not so precarious within the ethical life. The secret is to discover the robust spirit inside oneself, which is incongruous both with such a fear and with the false heroics on stage. To accomplish this, the judge imagines putting the aesthete under a curse, that the plays and operas cease to have the power to give him escape. He imagines turning all the happy endings into tragedies, so that the aesthete cannot escape the fear even at the theatre. He hopes that without the constant distraction, by acknowledging and facing his fear, the aesthete can see that he was all along pilot of his ship and not merely lookout; it is *his* projects that have failed to sustain him, and will continue to fail for as far as he can see. The threatening side of this admission is that he has to acknowledge himself as having failed at the only thing he cares about, namely keeping himself interested. But the judge's expectation is that in taking responsibility for his own life in this way, the aesthete will discover a position (his freedom) over which the threat of boredom and hence the fear of it has lost its power. When a person has found freedom, he has found 'the Archimedean point from which one can lift the world'.

The judge thinks freedom is connected with the ethical life, because it is 'universally human'. The aesthete's attachments were idiosyncratic, depending on what he thought would give him enjoyment from moment to moment. His commitment to keeping himself interested was not idiosyncratic; but he was not concerned with what *other* people found interesting, except in as far as this impinged on his own enjoyment. On the other hand recognizing the value of his own freedom would provide at the same time a recognition of the value of others' freedom, according to the judge, since it is the same freedom in both cases.[14] This would lead to a respect for others for their own sake which is the guiding

[14] The judge does not elaborate this argument, and it is notoriously hard to spell out arguments of this kind. See Darwall (1983) for criticisms of such arguments in Thomas Nagel and Kurt Baier.

characteristic of the ethical life. The similarities between Judge William and Kant are striking.[15] What the aesthete would discover, by choosing despair, is said to be the universal or humanity in its eternal validity. He would discover duty, which is abstract in the sense that all empirical differentiations have been removed from it.[16] He would discover that this freedom is both universal and individual, because this is what he as an individual essentially is. He would discover the law, the absolute, and that he himself is the law. From the point of view of the ethical he could be reconciled with every human being, because he would prescribe for his own happiness only in a way that was compatible with all others being happy.[17]

The Judge's Failure

The new man in his eternal dignity can now return, the judge thinks, into his aesthetic attachments, selecting which of them to retain and which to reject. One merit of the ethical life, the judge believes, is that it is now possible to sustain interest in one's life, just because keeping life interesting is not now the whole of life's focus and point. All should now be well; except that he discovers that he cannot after all live the ethical life.

The problem that faces the judge at the end of his second letter is that 'in a certain sense every person is an exception'.[18] To see why this produces a crisis for the ethical life it is necessary to look again at the description the judge gives of the point of view from which the ethical agent makes his decisions. This is supposed to be the point of view of the universal human being.[19] It is clear that the judge does not intend here a purely formal test because he gives progressively more content to it. He insists, first, that the ethical agent must work for a living, and not be free from cares about the necessities of life. With respect to what line of work he takes, the ethical agent must

---

[15] I do not want to go further into this question, except to say that I take Kierkegaard to be first recapitulating and then *criticizing* Kant. For a more sinister view see Green (1992).   [16] *EO* ii. 265.   [17] Ibid. 272.

[18] Ibid. 332.

[19] What is this point of view? 'The ethical', says the judge, 'is the universal and thus the abstract' (ibid. 255; see also *PC* 85 f.). It would be a mistake to infer that the judge thinks of the ethical as abstract in the sense of operating a purely formal or logical test. 'Abstract' here means 'not embodied in the social institutions of any particular country'. The ethical, for Kierkegaard, is full of content, and draws not only from Kant but from Hegel. See Hannay (1982) 310–14.

have a calling, though the judge cannot tell him which calling he should have. He has a duty to get married, moreover a duty not to seek out 'an uncommon girl', and a duty to have friends, where the friendship is based on unity in a life-view. These duties are like the rules of Latin grammar which the judge learnt as a boy, and he can remember detesting exceptions to them (like the irregular verbs). Discovering these duties is discovering, as Kant would say, something he can *respect*.

It is striking, then, that Kierkegaard regarded himself as failing in the performance of just these duties. When the book first appeared, it was not known that Kierkegaard had written it, so that its readers could escape this thought. But *we* know that he said to the only member of the church he would allow to his final sickbed, 'I had my thorn in my flesh, and therefore I did not marry and could not take on an official position . . . I could have gotten anything I wanted but in its place I became the exception.'[20] For Kierkegaard himself, the problem of how to live as an exception was the most vivid problem of his life.

The judge concedes that the man who is an exception has placed himself outside the universal, and then appeals, like the aesthete, to the language of atonement. The exception takes his own grief at this discrepancy as his proper punishment, and hopes that he will be reconciled again through this punishment with the universal. 'He will perhaps experience at some time the joy that what caused him pain and made him inferior in his own eyes proves to be an occasion for his being raised up again and in a nobler sense becoming an extraordinary human being.'[21] The exception represents everyone trying to lead an ethical life, 'for in a certain sense every person is an exception'. If the exception can become an extraordinary human being in a nobler sense, all of those trying (and failing) to be ethical can hope for the same ennoblement. We the audience, however, can see that there is no genuine atonement here; as with the aesthete there is only auto-atonement. There are two considerations that the judge introduces in this passage to mitigate his difficulty. The first is

---

[20] From Emil Boisen's notes on conversations with Kierkegaard on his deathbed. See Thompson (1967) 185. This is Kierkegaard's last use of the phrase 'thorn in the flesh'. He first used it autobiographically after visiting a doctor, after which he concluded that his condition could not be dispersed medically 'so that I could realize the universal' (*JP* v. 5913).   [21] *EO* ii. 331.

that the exception has suffered grief, and the second is that everyone else is in the same situation of discrepancy. But do these considerations have the power within the ethical life to reconcile the exception with the universal? Can they bridge the moral gap?

First, the suffering. It is not clear how this suffering can remove the exception's objective or subjective guilt. Kierkegaard himself, if he were in the ethical stage, would be failing his duties to work for a living and to marry, and this failure would cause him grief. But the grief does not mean that he has after all done his duty. The grief does not give him a job or a wife.[22] Perhaps this is too harsh. After all, judges do sometimes recommend leniency to a jury on the grounds that the defendant has suffered enough already. His suffering *is*, in a weak sense, a kind of punishment. This is the merit we conceded to Kant's translation of the doctrine of the atonement in Chapter 2. But it is only within narrow limits that a judge has such discretion. If I borrow your car and damage it, I should certainly be sorry and apologize, but beyond that I should make good the damage and give you some additional token of my contrition. You can then forgive me. In the case of the exception within the ethical life, however, the offence is not against another individual but against what the ethical agent perceives as the fundamental principle of his life.[23] If the offence is against the principle, how is atonement supposed to work? Perhaps the best way to think of this is to see the offender as split, so that the victim is the offender himself to the extent he has succeeded in living the ethical life. In the case of an offence against another individual, what happens where the offender is unable to make reparation? Is it possible for the victim then to forgive? This is a difficult question, which I will take up in Chapter 9. Whichever answer is given, however, the auto-atonement within the ethical life can be seen to fail. Even if the victim can forgive the offender in two-person cases without the offender's reparation, it has to be the *victim* who does so; the offender is not in a legitimate position to excuse

[22] In the same way the aesthete, in *The Unhappiest One* in *EO* i, simply declares the unhappiest man the happiest, because he has reached the supreme point of aesthetic tension or pathos. But nothing has changed in the unhappiest man's situation; he is still in depression.

[23] The offence may also be against an individual, for example the fiancée who had to be rejected when the exception discovered he could not marry; but the offence against the principle can occur without any other individual victim than the ethical agent himself.

himself from these tasks on the victim's behalf. In the split-person case the exception would have to occupy the position of the victim in order to excuse the offender (namely himself) from having to make his own reparation before reconciliation could take place. But a victim who forgives the offender has to be innocent with respect to the offence. The exception, just by being an exception, fails to be in a legitimate position to forgive himself for being exceptional (in the less noble sense!). In Chapter 2 I quoted Kant's statement of Spener's problem, how we can become *other* men and not merely better men (as if we were already good but only negligent about the degree of our goodness). If the exception had only to become a better man, rather than another man, or if he could really reach a god inside himself to become a member of the kingdom of gods, then his auto-atonement might work.

This does not mean that self-forgiveness is *never* possible. Suppose I have reached some goal that embodies a central commitment of my life. Perhaps I have been awarded my doctorate, or have established my credentials as a careful scholar by publishing in reputable journals. I can then forgive myself for failures that fall within the scope of that commitment. Perhaps I have made an embarrassing error in an article published out of my dissertation. I can then draw attention to this error in the next piece I write, and do some extra research to show how a proper understanding of the matter helps with answering a wider question in the literature. But suppose what governs my life is the aspiration to be a great composer (like Salieri in Shaffer's play *Amadeus*), and all I seem to produce is mediocrity. Can I forgive myself for this? It is not just that I cannot make reparation, but that I am not in the right position to forgive *without* reparation. The problem here is like that with R. M. Hare's critical level of moral thinking, discussed in Chapter 1. It is incoherent to think of forgiving myself at the critical level for not being able to reach the critical level. I cannot be in the right position to carry this out. As Kierkegaard likes to say about Hegel, the problem is the first step.

The point about everyone else being an exception as well can be made more briefly. The exception is perhaps arguing as follows: 'I have been unable to do what is "universally human", if that means working for my living and taking a wife. But in fact *no one* completely instantiates the "universally human"; we are all exceptions. Therefore the universally human, since it is supposed to be shared by all humans, must itself accommodate exceptions; and it can therefore accommodate me.'[24]

The exception may be arguing in this way, but he is not entitled to do so within the ethical life as the judge has described it. For the universally human is not intended by the judge as a description of how human beings in fact are, but as a law or imperative requiring them to be a certain way. To put it this way is slightly misleading, for the judge *is* claiming that there is something divine in human beings, which is their eternal dignity.[25] But their eternal dignity lies not so much in what all of them do, such as working or marrying, but in what the judge calls 'the inner deed' which is 'the true life of freedom'; and this is not a life which all humans already live, but a life which is *incumbent* on them all. The judge is an exception even though he has married and found his calling. What the aesthete is supposed to discover, if he chooses his despair, is *respect* for the moral law; and his respect will not be diminished, even if he can find (as Kant would say) no examples of the moral law being lived. What follows, if indeed failure is general amongst human beings, is that humans are generally not ethical, not that they are ethical after all.

b. THE RELIGIOUS LIFE

The pastor's sermon at the end of *Either/Or*, volume 2, makes the point repeatedly that we have to acknowledge that we are in the wrong before God; only this is complete repentance, and only this allows the transition into the religious life and 'an infinitely free relationship with God.'[26] Then we are given the possibility of living in a way pleasing to God, but this possibility is established in the power of God, not in our own power.[27] In talking about the religious or Christian life, I will rely mostly on Kierkegaard's pseudonymous

---

[24] See *EO* ii. 345 and T. S. Eliot, *The Cocktail Party*, Act 2, where the psychologist makes the same argument: 'When you find, Mr. Chamberlayne, The best of a bad job is all any of us make of it—Except of course, the saints'. What characterizes the saints is 'the sense of sin' (ibid.) or 'failure towards someone, or something, outside of myself'. The play vividly represents Kierkegaard's three lives.

[25] *EO* ii 250.   [26] Ibid. 352.

[27] The judge talks of a third term (beyond the 'finite' and the 'infinite') in the transition to the ethical. In the transition to the religious, Kierkegaard talks of a 'third factor, which is outside and compels one' (*JP* i. 188). It is the third term which prevents mere auto-atonement.

author who claims to occupy this life, namely Anti-Climacus. I will, however, go beyond Kierkegaard in discussing Christian doctrine about God's assistance. Kierkegaard is himself cagey about some of this doctrine.[28]

Anxiety

To understand how the anxiety within the ethical life leads into the religious life, we need to see that Kierkegaard is writing within the Lutheran tradition that 'the law brings wrath. And where there is no law there is no transgression' (Rom. 4: 15 NIV). Luther interprets this by saying, 'For by the law comes, not righteousness, but knowledge of sin. This is the fruit, the work, the office of the law; it is a light to the ignorant and blind, but one that displays disease, sin, evil, death, hell and the wrath of God. It does not help nor set them free from these things; it is content merely to point them out.'[29] When we have been brought to see the demands of the ethical life, we see that we are all exceptions. The exception tried various manœuvres, intended to reach what the pastor in the sermon at the end of *Either/Or*, volume 2, describes as 'the cozy conclusion, "One does what one can." '[30] But this is not enough, he says, to calm the more earnest doubt: 'Was not the real reason for your unrest that you did not know for sure how much one can do, that it seems to you to be so infinitely much at one moment, and at the next moment so very little?'; there is still the anxiety 'that you might not have done what you could, or that you might actually have done what you could but no one came to your assistance.'[31]

The exception is said to acquire a sense, at first dimly, of a life that would not be split in the way his own is split, but which does not require either whittling down his ideal or puffing up his capacity. The initial response to this sense is one of anxiety. Another of Kierkegaard's pseudonymous authors, Vigilius Haufniensis in *The*

---

[28] See Price (1963) 198: 'Neither in the Journals nor elsewhere does Kierkegaard throw any clear light on what he means by atonement.' Kierkegaard describes himself as proceeding maieutically on this topic, like a Socratic midwife (*JP* v. 5991). It is interesting that *PC* was originally to have been written under the title *Radical Cure: Christian Healing. The Atonement.* But in the index to the work as published, 'atonement' appears once, in a passage which says only that the topic is ignored for the moment.   [29] Luther (1957) 287.   [30] *EO* ii. 345.
[31] The pastor has in mind divine assistance. See Phil. 4: 13: 'I can do all things through Christ which strengtheneth me.'

Concept of Anxiety, describes this as a kind of dizziness. 'Hence anxiety is the dizziness of freedom, which emerges when the spirit wants to posit the synthesis and freedom looks down into its own possibility, laying hold of finiteness to support itself. Freedom succumbs in this dizziness. Further than this, psychology cannot and will not go.'[32] Dizziness is an important analogy for understanding the transition to the religious life, since it gives us a way to think of how the merely discrepant life becomes 'sin'. Suppose my son is climbing down a tree, and needs to swing both legs off the branch he is on in order to get to a lower branch. He may suddenly lose his nerve, if he looks down and feels that he is unable to let go of his present support; if this happens he may be stuck until the fire brigade arrives with a ladder. His reliance on his present support, which was indeed necessary for him to get down, has now become the obstacle to this. Analogously, a person's commitments may become an obstacle to a morally good life. This failure may occur in two ways that are significant at this point. First, she may insist that she is the agent, so that she will not be satisfied with a result in which her end was achieved except that she was not the person who achieved it.[33] Second, she may insist that any end she pursues must contribute towards her own happiness as she currently understands it. The insistence is not merely that the end be consistent with her own happiness, but that a contribution towards her own happiness as she currently understands it is a condition for her adopting the end.[34]

In the position of freedom an agent is supposed to be detached from her aesthetic commitments, until these commitments can again be chosen ethically. We are supposed to imagine that the ethical choice is made on the basis of the new standard she has discovered by taking responsibility for her life as a whole. This is the standard of the moral law. But the moral law seems to provide both too much and too little. It provides too much, because it overloads us with demands. I will put this point in utilitarian form, as I did in Chapter 4, but other ethical systems encounter the same difficulty. A person

[32] *CA* 61. For dizziness in the aesthetic life see *EO* i. 291 and 396.

[33] e.g. suppose I am committed to getting you a job in the company I work for; but you get a job in this company without my lifting a finger. Will I be satisfied? Not if it was important that your job come *through me*.

[34] See the difficulties, discussed in Ch. 3 Sect. *b*, about the coherence of Kant's notion of the highest good.

has the obligation to do at any time what will do the most good, impartially considered. She should, therefore, when considering going to a film, consider what her money could do for a starving family, for example in Somalia. While there are ways to lessen the demand legitimately within utilitarianism, the demand is still for a significant sacrifice, for most middle-class people in the richer countries of the world, of their time, energy, and possessions. Adding particular moral obligations, as we did in Chapter 6, is not going to reduce the demand; it will make it, if anything, worse. There is no space for a 'moral holiday', for *any* holiday has to be justified by its contribution (by avoiding exhaustion, for example) to the greatest good. This is Aristotle's strenuous view of holidays: 'Rather, it seems correct to amuse ourselves so that we can do something serious . . . It is because we cannot toil continuously that we require relaxation. Relaxation is not the end, since we pursue it to prepare for activity.'[35] On the other hand, the moral law gives us too little. It does not fit our experience of what our abilities have enabled us to accomplish or of what has given us happiness in the past.[36] Such a demand leaves us without any notion of how we might concretely go about reaching it or how to fit it into a life that seems happy by our present standards. Here is a sense for the dizziness of freedom; 'dizziness' seems a good image for this combination of enormous demand and inadequate support.

Suppose I have been given, however, some sense of a kind of life in which a synthesis between what I ought to be and what I am is possible, and suppose it defies my understanding how I can accomplish the transition to such a life. But suppose I have also been given the sense that I can rely on some kind of divine assistance and that God will make this a happy life in the long run. The transition will, in that case, require a kind of trust which I may not have (like my son on the tree, except that all he has to trust is gravity and the lower branch staying put when he cannot see it). It will in fact require the two kinds of moral faith I distinguished in Chapters 2 and 3. In this situation I may insist on my existing commitments, thinking that at least *these* have to be satisfied. If I do this, I am

[35] *NE* 10. 6, 1176^{b}32 ff.
[36] See Nagel (1986) 135 f.: 'Thus in a sense I come to act on the world from outside my particular personal place in it—to control the behavior of TN [Thomas Nagel] from a standpoint that is not mine qua TN.'

giving them a kind of absolute veto power. In Kantian language, I am making them the condition of any movement I make. But the emphasis this puts upon these particular commitments makes it impossible for me to achieve the morally good life I want; the insistence on them is self-defeating. It is like my son's panic which prevents him getting down from the tree. If I am committed to achieving through my own agency any synthesis I achieve, I will not be able to trust the divine assistance which alone can make the synthesis possible. If I hold onto my current conception of myself, and hence of my happiness, I will not be able to discover the new self and hence the new happiness which would otherwise be possible for me. If I succumb to dizziness, and hold on for dear life to my previous commitments, these commitments become sin.[37] An example is the case of Ananias and Sapphira, discussed in Chapter 5, where the desire to retain their own possessions became sinful after they heard the call to give them away. Haufniensis thinks we all sin in this way, but we do not all recognize it as sin. The transition to the religious life can occur when we recognize this succumbing as sin, or as failure *before God*.

The Sin is Taken Over

In Christian doctrine, Christ is said to take on our sins. This is the root of Kant's difficulty with the traditional view of the atonement. He thinks that reason cannot make sense of transmissible liability for moral failures; they are not like financial debts. Each person is morally accountable only for his own fault. I think we can begin to see a solution to Kant's difficulty by reflecting about the union between Christ and the believer.

Anti-Climacus, the pseudonymous author who is a Christian, makes a double distinction between Christianity and Speculation (or modern philosophy). Speculation is both more lenient towards sin, in that it does not hold us utterly corrupt (because there is a god still in us, waiting for us to find it); and less generous, because it does not allow that the sin we have can be completely removed from us.

---

[37] Haufniensis is exploring the notion of original sin, according to which we all do succumb in this way. His account of original sin is more plausible than Kant's as a way of explaining how sin can be both (in Kant's terms) innate and attributable to us. Cf. *CA* 61 and 91. I cannot here go further into the details of his discussion. See Quinn (1984) 188 f. and (1990) 236 f.

Christianity on the other hand first 'establishes sin so securely as a position that now it seems to be utterly impossible to eliminate it again—and then it is this very Christianity that by means of the Atonement wants to eliminate sin as completely as if it were drowned in the sea'.[38] The way that sin is eliminated by the atonement is that Christ, 'the Saviour of the world, bears the infinite responsibility'.[39]

There are differences between the supposed transition to the ethical life and the transition to the religious, but the similarities are also striking. One large difference is that the new man in the first transition, who is supposed to take responsibility for the failures of the old man is still the person himself. It is still William. In the second transition the person who bears the responsibility is Christ. In Kant's translation of the doctrine within the pure religion of reason this difference is obscured by calling the new man 'Christ'. But even though in Judge William's description of the transition, it is still William after the revolution of the will, he can talk at length about the kind of unity there is between the new and the old as though he were talking about two people. Thus, the new William has the task of 'putting on himself', of 'interpenetrating himself', and most strikingly, 'Through the individual's intercourse with himself the individual is made pregnant by himself and gives birth to himself.'[40] On this picture the new self has the task of taking responsibility for himself. There are really two steps to this. The first is to take responsibility for all of the old self, and admit that none of his projects were sufficient, singly or together with others, to provide what the judge calls 'salvation'. Perhaps the aesthete goes straight to his big guns, let us say Mozart's *Don Giovanni*. But the perfect pleasure once obtained from a definitive production, the transparency of that experience, cannot any longer be repeated. Seducing another girl? But honesty compels the recognition, as he records one spectacular seduction, that the interest started to flag long before the project was completed. The second step is to sift the things which he will take on as a task from those things he will refuse to take on. Each of the aesthete's disparate commitments is submitted to the clear-eyed scrutiny of the new self, who wants to take responsibility for his whole life.

---

[38] *SUD* 100. See Mic. 7: 19.
[39] See *PC* 328. The deletion from the final version is significant. It is one example of the general deletion of explicit mention of the atonement in a work whose subtitle intially included it. [40] *EO* ii. 248, 256, 258–60.

More is going on in this scrutiny than merely judgement. The new self is sorting out what sort of person he is, what preferences and attachments he has; for it is into those preferences and attachments that he will be returning. He first chooses despair, because he chooses (to acknowledge) himself as failing by the standards of the aesthetic life. The revolution of the will is supposed to occur when he sees that his aesthetic attachments have, as a whole, failed him; but that he has the capacity to make this judgement from a perspective that he has not previously occupied, namely the perspective of freedom. The goal he is headed for is ethical transparency, where the moral law can shine through everything he is and everything he does.

The relation between Christ and the believer within the religious life is likewise expressed in the New Testament by a number of rich images of unity or identification. Paul says, 'I am crucified with Christ: nevertheless I live; yet not I, but Christ liveth in me' (Gal. 2: 20), and 'For to me to live is Christ' (Phil. 1: 21). We are instructed to clothe ourselves with the Lord Jesus Christ (Rom. 13: 14). Another passage talks of Christ coming into our lives, if we will open the door (Rev. 3: 20). Another talks of our being branches of the true vine, which is Christ (John 15: 1), another of the church as the bride of Christ (Rev. 21: 9), and another of our adoption into his family (Gal. 4: 5). We are said to be bought with a price, so as to belong to God (1 Cor. 6: 20). Our bodies are said to be the members of Christ (1 Cor. 6: 15).

There are many ways to explicate these ideas. One is that the believer is supposed to resemble Christ, so that Christ is like a pattern after whom we are supposed to model ourselves; we are supposed to live the kind of life that he led. But this is not yet to see Christ as redeemer.[41] Kierkegaard makes this distinction under his own name.[42] He is not an exemplarist in his view of the atonement;

---

[41] See *PC* 239.

[42] 'Help us all and everyone, thou who art both willing and able to help, thou who art both the Pattern and the Redeemer, and again both the Redeemer and the Pattern, so that when the striver sinks under the Pattern, then the Redeemer raises him up again, but at the same instant Thou art the Pattern, to keep him continually striving. Thou, our Redeemer, by Thy blessed suffering and death, hast made satisfaction for all and for everything; no eternal happiness can be or shall be earned by desert—it has been deserved' (*Judge for Yourselves*, in *FSE*, 161).

salvation is not accomplished, that is to say, merely by example.[43] Christ's life and death do indeed serve as our pattern, he thinks; but by that pattern we are judged, not saved.

Theologians have also explicated the passages about union between Christian and Christ by referring to the work of the Holy Spirit who comes to dwell inside us. Christ is not present in a believer's life, therefore, merely as an example or model, but in the Spirit as a person. We can then imagine an internal dialogue taking place between Christ and the believer. It will be somewhat like the dialogue Judge William envisages between the new person and the old as the new person seeks to take responsibility for her whole life. Again there will be two steps: first taking over the whole thing, and then sifting out what is to be retained and what is to be discarded. In Lutheran theology these two steps are justification and sanctification. We can imagine the exception submitting each of his previous choices to the scrutiny of Christ.[44] Suppose the exception goes straight to his big guns; let us say, his marriage. The judge loves to sit and watch his wife scurrying about the house; she is like a bird singing its aria, she has an absolute virtuosity for explaining the finite, she is in harmony with existence, and 'she is not supposed to know the anxiety of doubt or the agony of despair'.[45] Note, though, that despair and anxiety are required for transition to the ethical and religious lives; these are transitions, one concludes, that his wife is not supposed to make. To what degree, then, is the judge treating her as an end in herself, as the categorical imperative requires him to do?

Here is the judgement by which the exception stands condemned. In what sense, though, does Christ not only judge the exception but take over her failures as his own?[46] If we return to the images of

---

[43] See *Two Discourses at the Communion on Fridays*, 22: 'If justice were to become furious, what more could it want? There is after all full satisfaction; if in your repentance and brokenness you expect to get justice outside yourself as an aid in finding out what the guilt is, there is, after all, full satisfaction, one who makes full satisfaction and completely covers all your guilt, making sight of it impossible, impossible for justice, and therefore also for repentance in you or over yourself, for repentance also loses its eyesight when justice, to which it appeals, says: I can see nothing.' Printed in *FSE*; quoted in Malantschuk (1971) 356.

[44] 'Each individual is judged' (*CA* 123).

[45] *EO* ii. 305–11. Kierkegaard's own view of women may not be the judge's. See Walsh (1987) 123–4, who discusses *SUD* 50: 'her despair is: not to will to be oneself.'

[46] From this point, I am no longer providing an exegesis of Kierkegaard's texts, and I will not be constrained any longer by his use of male pronouns.

unity between Christ and the believer, we can start to make sense of it. Christians are the members of Christ's body. One thing this means is that Christians are Christ's vehicle for action in the world; they are in this sense his hands and his feet. He has, though, to make them into better vehicles than they already are, if they are to carry out his will. In another image, he is like a beautician, removing their spots and wrinkles and blemishes (Eph. 5: 26–7). Christ, in taking the believer into his body, is taking on initially someone who is and has been an impediment to his work. By this incorporation the impediment becomes Christ's own impediment. In this way Christ's body is changed by the people it acquires, and by acquiring them he takes over responsibility for their past failures and the deficit of their present failings. The analogy to Judge William's description of the transition into the ethical life can now be seen. Christ is choosing the exception, and choosing her as a failure, as a sinner; and in this choice, these failures become his own failures. As before, however, the standard by which the failure is judged has shifted. The aesthete not merely failed to sustain aesthetic interest, but he failed by the standard of freedom which he discovers. For the exception it is no longer merely the standard of the moral law which he has failed to meet, but the standard of Christ's own life.

Kant holds to the principle that liability cannot be transferred, like a financial indebtedness, from one person to another. He translates the atonement as an internal transaction between an old man and a new man. In the transition the judge describes into the ethical life, this feature is preserved; this is why this 'atonement' in the end fails. But seeing Christ as taking over our failures, when he takes us on as members of his own body, provides the beginning of a response to the objection to transmissible liability. The objector will reply that no sense can be made of this notion of Christ having believers as members of his body. So has any progress been made? Yes, to the extent that we have located the transmission of liability in a network of images for the unity of Christ and Christian. The objector cannot simply rely on the fact that humans cannot transfer liability to each other (though even humans can in fact do this to each other, in certain circumstances, and I shall return to this in Chapter 10). For the Christian claim is that believers are related to Christ in a complex way which is not the same as inter-human relations. It is this whole complex relation that needs to be considered in relation to the atonement, not transmissible liability alone.

I will give three further analogies from human life to show (inadequately) the kind of structure I am attributing to the atonement. All of them derive from analogies used in Scripture to describe the kind of unity between Christ and believers, as listed above. Suppose a family adopts a child, and thereby takes on responsibility for its failings (this is one context within human life where transmissible liability seems to occur, despite what Kant says). If the child steals, the parents pay.[47] It may be that the only way the child can be cured is through the sufferings it causes to its adoptive family; the sufferings may be great enough practically to destroy the family. We can imagine, though, that there is a kind of life which the family leads which eventually becomes also the kind of life the child leads. There is here a kind of transmission both ways: first from the child to the family and then from the family back to the child. Second, the picture of Christ taking us into his body suggests a comparison with the immune system. We can think of sin as a virus, to which a body becomes exposed by having the organ from another body transplanted into it. The question will then be whether the host body's immune system has the antibodies to resist the new virus. If it does, the virus is destroyed also in the transplanted organ, and ceases to be an impediment to its functioning in the new body. Again there is the two-way transmission. Or, third, the analogy of Christ buying us with a price can suggest the picture of 'corporate' responsibility. Suppose a large company buys a smaller one, and thereby adopts responsibility for its obligations (here again we seem to have something like transmissible liability). If the smaller company makes a component used throughout the product line of the larger company, a flaw in the component can threaten the survival of the whole new enterprise. But the large company may have the resources, which the smaller company did not, to identify the flaw in the component and correct it.

Not one of these analogies works by itself, and we should not expect to find any that do. For the relation of Christ and the believer is not going to be very like any relation between mere human beings. But some light is shed, I think, by the analogy between the transition

---

[47] They take not merely legal liability, but a sense of ownership of the failings. The family has been disgraced, and the parents themselves feel the disgrace needs to be cleared. This is an idealized picture, however, and adoptions may often not work this way at all.

into the religious life and the transition Judge William claims into the ethical life. The three analogies in the previous paragraph are supplementary. They are designed to illuminate the way in which Christ might take over a person's sins, and how his destruction of the power of sin might result in the ability of the believer to lead a new life.

Catharsis

To return, then, to Christ's atonement. Perhaps this too happens because of an incongruity. Here I am going beyond Kierkegaard, and perhaps I am being irresponsibly speculative. I am following some proposals of John McLeod Campbell.[48] Christ, I have suggested, takes our failures on himself. To put it this way is misleading, because it suggests that Christ takes only our failures and leaves the rest of us behind. It is better to say that he takes on the whole of us by incorporation, including our failures, and then defeats the parts that do not fit the kind of life he wants us to lead. He is both sinner and sinless, 'for he hath made him to be sin for us, him who knew no sin' (2 Cor. 5: 21). He is in the position that Judge William ascribes to the repentant aesthete: 'Repentance specifically expresses that evil essentially belongs to me and at the same time expresses that it does not essentially belong to me.' It belongs to me because I have accepted responsibility for it; but it does not belong to me in my new-found character. The ethical agent by choosing despair is supposed to break through to a realization of his nature as freedom. Perhaps when Christ takes on our failures, these separate him from his own sinless character. He will see them with clarity in a way that we cannot, because one result of sin is that we lose our ability to see it. This clarification of our sin corresponds to the judge's therapeutic curse, which causes the artificial stimulations of

---

[48] I am encouraged in my speculation by the suggestion of John McLeod Campbell (1886) 116–18: 'He who so responds to the divine wrath against sin, saying "Thou art righteous, O Lord, who judgest", is necessarily receiving the full apprehension and realisation of that wrath, as well as of that sin against which it comes forth into His soul and spirit, into the bosom of his divine humanity, and, so receiving it, He responds to it with a perfect response—a response from the depths of that divine humanity—and in that perfect response He absorbs it.' In this passage there is the same notion I am pressing of an internal struggle and victory in Christ, without turning his work on our behalf into mere example. But we do not have to understand punishment in the way Campbell rejects. See Van Dyk (1992) Ch. 4, who argues convincingly that his Calvinist critics seriously misunderstood him.

the theatre to lose their escape value for the aesthete. Perhaps Christ then works back to his basic character by something like catharsis, by defeating the parts of us which are incongruous with his nature. The model of catharsis is not quite appropriate because Christ does not forget who he is, unlike the Bacchic revelers on the hillside. But there is something analogous to catharsis or purification in the process by which Christ defeats the sin he has taken on from us. In the main term of this chapter, we can say that he repents of it or even confesses it. Campbell says that Christ 'makes a perfect confession of our sins. This confession, as to its own nature, must have been a perfect Amen in humanity to the judgement of God on the sins of man.'[49] Christ does not have to repent in the ordinary sense, because he is not guilty in the ordinary sense. On the judge's picture (and Kant's) the new man is not guilty in the ordinary sense either, but by union with the old man. But the function of repentance is retained in Christ's case. The sin that Christ took on himself is put out of gear; it no longer has the power to impede his work.

The battle and victory over sin will be, on this reading, internal to Christ; he is seen as recovering his unity with the Father after the separation caused by our sin which he has taken on himself by taking us on.[50] By saying the victory is internal, I do not mean that it is merely psychological. The Christian tradition, and especially Luther's version of it, is full of language about the battle with Satan; the descent into hell was to accomplish this. But the victory is still internal in the sense that it is Christ's recapture of his own unity with his Father, his 'coming to himself'. The resurrection is then the sign of his victory, and the new life he has won is the life he shares with us. The biblical language is more usually that God the Father raises his son from death. But this is one of many places in Christian theology where a Trinitarian account gives a role to more than one person of the Trinity at the same time. It is Christ who is said to have led captivity captive, and who says of his own life 'I have power to lay it down, and I have power to take it again.'[51]

---

[49] Campbell (1886) 135–6.

[50] Anti-Climacus says, 'As sinner, man is separated from God by the most chasmal qualitative abyss' (*SUD* 122). Christ's cry from the cross, 'My God, my God, why hast thou forsaken me?' (Mark 15: 34), is sometimes taken as an expression of his separation from his Father. Calvin says of the descent into hell that it is 'an expression of the spiritual torment that Christ underwent for us' (*Institutes*, II. xvi. 10).

[51] Eph. 4: 8, John 10: 18 and 2: 19: 'In three days I will raise it up.'

Second Ethics

What is restored to us as a result of Christ's work is the power to lead
a life pleasing to God. This is what Judge William was aiming at, but
could not achieve. Vigilius Haufniensis (the pseudonymous author
of Kierkegaard's *The Concept of Anxiety*) talks about a 'second
ethics', which is the ethical life lived after the recognition of sin and
the transition into the religious life.[52] This is Kierkegaard's notion of
repetition, just as the aesthetic life is supposed to be repeated within
the ethical. Judge William thinks that aesthetic pleasure is actually
more sustainable within the ethical life because the *emphasis* on
keeping life interesting is removed. This is a familiar point about
pleasure; if we make it the goal and focus of our activity, we will not
get it, at least not in the long run. Judge William adds that if we will
make the ethical life our goal, we can then sustain our interest in life
as a side-effect. Partly this is because we now have commitments,
like marriage, which can provide a long-lasting source of delight. It
is also possible now to be bored without despair, because boredom is
no longer the negation of what we care most about. The judge is
quite prepared to run the risk of boring the aesthete in the two huge
and repetitious letters that make up *Either/Or*, volume 2. The
emphasis placed on aesthetic interest was one thing that made it
impossible to sustain. If the fundamental commitment is to the
ethical life, it does not matter so much that one has heard a better

---

[52] *CA* 20. Perhaps another question needs answering first. Am I claiming that non-
religious people or non-Christians cannot be morally good? This is a question that
Kant also had to face, because of his view about the necessity in the moral life for the
postulates of God and the immortality of the soul. What about Spinoza, who led a life
of conspicuous virtue, but did not accept the postulates? Kant's reply was that
Spinoza had not fully thought it through. I want to say something similar. What I
called in Ch. 1 the three-part structure of morality is one that we have inherited in part
from our religious tradition. Kant recognized that this structure requires some
account of God's assistance in order to explain how we can live by the moral law. To
the extent that this recognition has disappeared, which it largely has within
professional philosophy, we are left with a muddle. This does not mean that it will be
impossible to live within this three-part structure; but the structure will seem
confusing and will tend to lose its force. It is therefore not surprising to find in the
philosophical literature increasing impatience with the structure, and the kind of life
it requires. But I was careful to say 'some account'. I have not ruled out the possibility
of other accounts of God's assistance than the Christian one. Evaluating such accounts
would be a different project.

performance of *Don Giovanni* before. The judge's point is that if we relax about keeping ourselves interested, because this is no longer what matters most in the world, it is much easier to sustain our enjoyment.

To apply the analogy, the transition to the religious life should mean that we can now relax about the ethical life, because it no longer has the emphasis it did before; and this should mean both that we can now sustain the ethical life and that it should not matter to us so desperately when we do not. This is not to say that the religious life replaces the ethical life, but that it allows the ethical life to be repeated. We should not usually expect to find people within the religious life breaking ethical principles.[53] But the ethical commitment will now be placed within the commitment to do Christ's work in the world. A shift is thus accomplished in both the demand and the support available, a shift away from the dizziness of the judge's ethical life. The support is the larger life of the body, in which we now belong as members. Our capacities have changed because of the transmission to us of this new life. If Christ does ask us to sacrifice something dear, which he may, it will be for our eventual good as well as the good of the body. This is an explicitly Christian version of the moral faith I discussed in Chapter 3. The demand is to do what Christ tells us to do from situation to situation. One way he may tell us is through ethical principles, but another way will be through the community of his body or through direct instruction by the Spirit. He will put us in situations in which we are to exercise our ethical concern, namely those situations where what we are and what we have can be best used. The parable of the Good Samaritan is a good

---

[53] I say 'usually' because of the case of Abraham, discussed by Kierkegaard in *Fear and Trembling*, in *R*. We may find ourselves asked to do something for which we can find no ethical justification. The aesthete similarly finds Judge William expecting him to take an interest in some things which completely exceed his capacity to justify by aesthetic standards. Kierkegaard changed his mind about what he calls the incognito, and hence about the relation between first and second ethics. In *Fear and Trembling* (*R* 82 f.), the knight of faith, who is hidden, might be hoeing potatoes; we would not recognize him because we cannot see inside him into his basic commitments. In *PC* 214 f., however, Anti-Climacus points out the danger of 'relegating being a Christian to inwardness'; this is a mark of what he calls 'Christendom', the established church, which finds inwardness a safe doctrine because it does not require conflict with the established order. In the Church Militant on the other hand, which Anti-Climacus holds up as the proper model, 'being a Christian was recognizable by the opposition one suffered.'

example.[54] Undoubtedly it is hard for us to limit the moral demand when there is so much information available to us about the suffering in the world. But the Good Samaritan will also have known of many people he could have helped by selling his own beast, and giving not just the two pence to the innkeeper but all his goods to the poor.[55] He was given *this* traveller to care for. One way Christ does this for us is by the community to which we belong extending itself outwards, as discussed at the end of Chapter 6. He asks a lot of us, but we can trust that he will not ask us to do more than he gives us the power to do. We can also trust that he will forgive us when we fail. In both these ways the new relationship is unlike the judge's situation with the moral law.

In second ethics the commitment to the ethical life becomes part of one's overriding commitment. To say this is to deny the claim that to hold something as an ethical obligation is to hold it to override any other kind of obligation.[56] We can say, instead, that ethical commitments are indeed overriding within the ethical life as the judge describes it, but that this ethical life is defective and unable to sustain itself. Second ethics will not normally, however, be the rejection of ethical obligations in favour of something else. E. M. Forster was not championing second ethics when he said that if he had to choose between his friends and his country, he hoped he would have the courage to choose his friends. He probably meant that his (non-ethical) relation to his friends overrode his ethical obligations to his country.[57] But Forster on this construal is like the aesthete defending himself against Judge William; that is, we have a rejection of the ethical life from within a stage before it

---

[54] Luke 10: 30 ff.: 'A certain man went down from Jerusalem to Jericho, and fell among thieves . . . But a certain Samaritan, as he journeyed, came where he was.' See O'Donovan (1986) 239 f.: 'When we render the love-command in terms of "respect for persons" or "equal regard", we strain out precisely the element of contingent proximity on which the parable most strongly insists.'

[55] As Christ required of the rich young man (Matt. 19: 21); but the requirement was characteristically personal.

[56] See R. M. Hare (1981) 50–61.

[57] Perhaps this is a substandard use of the phrase 'ethical obligations'. We could e.g. suppose that Forster is here prescribing that his obligations to his friends override what *people generally think* to be a person's ethical obligations, or, less likely, that his *ethical* obligations to his friends overrode his ethical obligations to his country. See R. M. Hare (1963) 83.

rather than a repetition of the ethical life from within a stage after it.

In second ethics the standard that is appealed to, namely the life of Christ, includes the ethically good but is not restricted to it, just as the ethically good includes but is not restricted to the aesthetically interesting. There may be two kinds of failure in the ethical life here, in relation to the religious life. The first is a failure of completeness. Christ's life included much ethical goodness, but its goodness (and its value as our pattern) is not exclusively or even primarily in its ethical goodness; it lies in its intimacy with God the Father. Jesus states two great commandments, to love God and to love the neighbour.[58] The second command is like the first; but if we take Christ to mean that the first can be reduced to the second, we impoverish his teaching and the life which expressed it. We have, in the religious life, the goal of communion with God, and this is not itself an *ethical* obligation in Judge William's sense.[59] The Christlike life includes more than the moral life, and sin includes more than moral failure.

The second kind of failure is that Judge William's life is not merely incomplete, by the standard of the religious life, but actually not a good life. To put this in Paul's terms, it is under law and not under grace (Gal. 3: 21 f.). Without the divine assistance that leads into the religious life, the ethical agent is forced to rely on her own strength; and because this strength is insufficient she is led either into pervasive subjective guilt or into all sorts of inadequate compensations. There is a rich field of research here in contemporary culture. But in neither case will she be living a good life by the standard of the religious life; she will be miserable or deceiving herself or (as Kant thought of Spinoza) she will need to think more carefully through the implications of her ethical commitment.

Judge William would think that denying the claim of ethical obligations to be overriding denies human autonomy. This is a topic

---

[58] Matt. 22: 36–9.
[59] It is possible to insist that the ethical is *whatever* is our highest duty, even in the religious life. But then the ethical will include much more than Judge William thinks it does. Thus Euthyphro got into trouble with Socrates when he tried to explain prayer and sacrifice as obligations of justice. In our terms, we could say that because God does not need our prayer or sacrifice, we are not meeting the most needs or satisfying the most preferences (i.e. doing the ethical in R. M. Hare's sense) when we spend our time praying or sacrificing. See Plato, *Euthyphro* 14c.

for another book, but I think there are resources in the Kierkegaardian framework for defeating the Kantian argument on this point.[60] Looking from the religious life, second ethics will be preferable ethically to Judge William's. This is because when the ethical life is contained (or repeated) within the religious life there is the possibility of it becoming transparent, in the sense that God's goodness can be seen through it.

This metaphor of transparency is one which various of Kierkegaard's pseudonymous authors use, though what they mean by the metaphor depends on what stage they are occupying. Transparency enables one to see without obstruction through a person's surface to something that lies underneath or beyond it. Thus there is an aesthetic transparency, which is the aesthete's highest state, his peak: 'All existence seemed to have fallen in love with me, and everything quivered in fateful rapport with my being.'[61] This is the lovely condition in which a person seems perfectly attuned to what she is experiencing, so that there is nothing in her response which jars or obstructs. What shattered this mood for the aesthete was that something suddenly began to irritate one of his eyes. In a concert, it might be the person in front who cannot resist commenting on the performance while it is going on (though sometimes the pleasure in the music is strong enough to reduce the distraction into insignificance).

For Judge William, transparency is the condition in which a person 'has totally interpenetrated himself so that every movement he makes is accompanied by a consciousness of responsibility for himself'.[62] Here the agent submits all of her preferences to the test of the moral law (Kant would say to the categorical imperative), and holds none of them back. The goal is one of complete accountability, where nothing in the agent's life is allowed to disguise or obscure its own relation to the ethical imperative. Transparency here is threatened by the fear that one's own well-being is in danger, or the fear that one is incapable of such a life, and this prevents the surrender of all one's preferences to the ethical criterion. Ethical transparency is where a person's inner life and actions are in conscious harmony with the moral law.

---

[60] See Quinn (1978) Chs. 1–3. Kant himself believed in a *form* of divine command theory, that we should think of our duties as divine commands. See *Rel.* 142 (153).

[61] *R* 173.

[62] *EO* ii. 248.

Anti-Climacus describes the religious life as follows: 'in relating itself to itself and in willing to be itself, the self rests transparently in the power that establishes it.'[63] We saw that the exception cannot by his own devices live the life which the moral law requires. But what, then, of the principle that 'ought implies can', a principle which we saw lay behind Kant's sense of the need for an account of the atonement. Augustine says, 'Sins are your own, but merits are God's.'[64] Leading a life pleasing to God *is*, in this tradition, possible for us but not attributable to us. To put this in terms of transparency, there is a new life constituted by God's assistance, and through the surface of this life what we see is the working of God.

[63] *SUD* 14, 29.
[64] *Psalms*, Ps. 70. 2. 5; see also Calvin, *Institutes*, II. v. 2.

9

FORGIVENESS

IN this chapter I will discuss what it means for one human being to forgive another.[1] The purpose of this is that we can then see the ways in which God's forgiveness of us is both like and unlike our forgiveness of each other. I will start by considering why the burden of past failures should matter to us, when we cannot repair them, even after we have done everything we can to make them good. I will then discuss the sense in which an offender and victim can together undo the past, and the connection between forgiveness and what I will call 'mutuality'. I will end by considering the cases where the offender tries to do what is necessary to restore the relationship but the victim does not forgive, and the reverse case, where the offender does not do what is necessary but the victim forgives anyway.

a. THE BURDEN OF THE PAST

Why do our own past failures matter to us so much? It is easy to think the concern irrational. Suppose I taught badly this morning, confusing my students about Socrates' argument in the *Euthyphro* against defining the holy as what is loved by all the gods.[2] It is now too late. I cannot afford the time to revisit the argument in the next session. What should be my attitude towards my failure? Certainly, I should resolve to do better next time I teach the argument. Perhaps I can work on some notes now, while I am still thinking about it, and put them in the file. Perhaps I can confess to my students that I was not clear, and perhaps I can allow myself more preparation time for the rest of the term. But once I have done all this, once I have done all that can be done by way of apology and reparation, is there any reason for me to continue to feel badly about my failure? There is nothing more, I am supposing, to be *done* about it, even though I

---

[1] I want to thank my commentator at the American Philosophical Association meetings, Nancy Snow, for her comments on a previous draft of this chapter.
[2] Plato, *Euthyphro* 10–11.

have not completely succeeded in making good the failure. Why should I not simply think of the failure as water over the dam, forget about it, and go on to something else?

Admittedly it can often be irrational and indeed pathological to dwell on past failure. The experience can be one of hearing condemnatory voices from the past which are traces of unassimilated childhood pain. The feeling of guilt can be excessive and psychologically damaging. It is a mistake, however, to conclude that the feeling of guilt is not usually part of a mature human response to moral failure. Not to feel guilty at all after a moral failure requires either not perceiving it as a moral failure (moral blindness) or acknowledging it as such but not caring about it (amoralism).[3] If it is granted that it is *sometimes* appropriate to feel guilty for an offence, the question arises of what it is appropriate to feel when no apology and reparation can make it good. There will be a residue in such cases that has not been dealt with, even after the offender has done everything she can do to make good the offence. I referred to this problem in Chapter 8 when talking about the difficulty of self-forgiveness. I claimed that one of the difficulties of the character I called the exception is that he cannot occupy the position from which to forgive himself for his continual failures to live up to the moral demand he recognizes. If he has never lived up to the moral standards he recognizes, he does not have the authority to let himself off.

But is it rational to continue to hold failure against oneself, once everything has been done that can be done about it? There is one way in which this is intelligible. I can, for example, take the failure as evidence of what a lousy person I was and still am. I am the sort of person who is capable of that sort of failure.[4] But this is not enough to explain the moral loss involved in forgetting it once I have done all I can do about it. I will indeed be losing evidence of what my character is like. But this is not the only moral significance of ceasing to hold the failure against myself. I will probably have lots of other

[3] There is also, separately, the *judgement* that something was a moral failure. See Roberts (1988) 195–201 on the place of what he calls construal in emotion.

[4] Kant supposed that there is an infinite gap between the moral demand and the initial human capacity to live by it, given the propensity to evil. See *Rel.* 66 (72). It is not that a person has committed infinite evil, but that a person has the disposition to actualize indefinitely often the subordination of the moral law to inclination.

evidence for the state of my character. If I can retain the self-knowledge while forgetting this particular evidence for it, I will still lose something of moral significance by letting my memory of the failure slide into oblivion. The moral significance of continuing to reproach myself cannot be merely that it leads to self-knowledge about my present dispositions. But what is this additional moral significance?

To return to the initial example, maybe the explanation is that I have harmed the students by my muddled presentation of Plato's argument, and I should continue to feel bad about this until I have made it up to them in some way. My sense of burden is, however, disproportionate to this harm. They will probably not care very much about the muddle, and in any case clarity about this argument is far less important to their lives than it is to mine. It is closer to the truth to say that I should continue to feel the burden because I have failed in my obligations to the material. But this is a mysterious notion. Do I have an obligation to Plato to present his ideas as clearly as I can? Or is my failure burdensome because I have been incompetent as a philosopher, and have thus been unfaithful to the standards of the discipline? Perhaps it is possible to think of the discipline as a collective entity, like a regiment, and to think of the possibility of one of its members letting this entity down. I may, for example, hear in my imagination the voice of my graduate supervisor rebuking me, or compare my performance with those of the great teachers who inspired me to go into philosophy in the first place. In this example, some such explanation is plausible. But it will only work for cases where the sense of failure is connected with an institution. It is not hard to think of cases where the continuing burden of failure does not depend upon membership of an institution of this kind. Suppose I run over a hedgehog on the road, and I was not paying close attention to my driving. I may do what I can, stopping the car to see if the animal is still alive; but there is no possibility here of apology or reparation to the victim, and there is no institution I am letting down.

A better explanation is that within human relationships we should care about the residue of failure because the offence is still an obstacle to reconciliation, if it has not been made good. There is an additional reason why it should matter to me that I taught badly this morning. I have a relationship with my students, which is based on each party carrying out certain responsibilities: I to teach clearly and they to pay attention and do the assigned work. We have a common end in view, namely their education. When I teach badly, I start to degrade this relationship. This can often be felt in the room. One day of failed communication is all right, if they do not understand what I am talking about because I have muddled it. Two days are dangerous. Three in a row, and I may have lost them for the rest of the term. This is not quite the same as the previous claim that I should mind about the past failure because I have harmed the students. The damage is now to the relationship between us, when I have not done my part. This will indeed result in harm to the students, if the course goes bad and I cannot communicate to them the important themes that I have planned. But this greater harm is caused by the damage to the relationship, not directly by the muddle about the argument in the *Euthyphro*.[5]

This is still not the whole story about why we should care about past failure. Sometimes there are no human relationships involved: when I run over the hedgehog, for example, or when the failure involves only myself. Even where there is a human relationship involved, the damage to the relationship does not seem the whole of the damage. Kant would say I have offended against the moral law, and it should be for me as if I have offended against the divine lawgiver. Suppose I can think of myself as having a relationship to God. In Chapter 8 I discussed the language Kierkegaard uses about resting transparently in God's power. The problem with past failure is that it blocks this relationship or makes it opaque. To commit an offence against another human being is also to commit an offence against God.[6] Any relationship is blocked when one party offends against the standards on which the relationship is based. The relationship with God, according to the traditional Christian idea, is based on a covenant; our part is to keep God's law. When we fail, we break the covenant. Atonement is the task of the offender, which has to be carried out if reconciliation is to take place. 'Atone', says the *Oxford English Dictionary*, is derived from 'At + One, = set at one, unite'. In this chapter I will look at how atonement and forgiveness

---

[5] There is also an inclusion relation between the small harm from the *Euthyphro* muddle and the larger harm from the failure to communicate the important themes of the course. If none of the material taught in the course significantly benefits the students, then the relationship with the lecturer does not benefit them either.

[6] See Matt. 25: 45. See also Swinburne (1989) 124. I am grateful to Swinburne for commenting on an earlier version of this chapter.

work between human beings. In Chapter 10 I will consider the ways in which divine atonement and forgiveness resemble and differ from the human kind. If we can understand the idea of a relationship between ourselves and God, then we can understand the burden of past failure as a sense of an abiding obstacle to this relationship. To put this differently, the possibility of such a relationship reveals why past failures should matter, even after the offender has done all he can to repair them.

b. UNDOING THE PAST

There is something mysterious about forgiveness, even between humans, and in this section I will try to reduce this mystery. It may seem odd to call forgiveness mysterious, when it is so mundane and pervasive an aspect of our everyday lives. Within a marriage, for example, the two partners may have to forgive each other many times each day. The husband will lose an important piece of paper, and they both have to search for it, making the wife late for an appointment; and she snaps at him that he has never learnt to file his papers properly, and he needs a nanny. Then the two of them have to forgive each other. I mean that they have to do so *if* they want their relationship not to be damaged. Sometimes we think of forgiveness as reserved for grave breaches; but it is better to think of it as required routinely by the small wrongs we do to each other all the time.

Forgiveness is, none the less, mysterious. If I have done you wrong, says Richard Swinburne, I must then repent, apologize, make reparation, and do something else as a token (like giving a box of chocolates), which Swinburne calls 'penance' (though he does not think all of these are necessary in every case).[7] All this is 'my contribution towards destroying the consequences (physical and not so physical) of my act of hurting you. You accept my disowning by forwarding the purpose I had in showing you this disowning—to make it the case, as far as logically can be done, that I was not the originator of an act by which I wronged you.' On this analysis there are four kinds of task for the person I will call the 'offender', and forgiveness is the response by the person I will call the 'victim' to the accomplishment of these tasks. According to Swinburne, repentance

[7] Swinburne (1989) 25.

is at least the internal admission of guilt by the offender.[8] Apology is the external admission of guilt by the offender, standardly to the victim. Reparation is the removal by the offender of the material harm caused by the offence; thus the thief returns my stolen wallet, and we add compensation for the inconvenience caused to me, for example, by credit card cancellation and the costs to society of apprehending and punishing such offenders. Finally, penance has several different functions. It can be a token of sincerity (though all tokens can be used insincerely, so that none of them guarantees good faith). It can be an expression of the thought, 'I know that no reparation is sufficient'. It can, especially in cases where there is no clearly appropriate form of material compensation, make the expression of apology more costly to the offender and thus more equal to the offence.[9]

Swinburne's analysis reveals the centrally mysterious ingredient of forgiveness, which is that it seems like an attempt to do the impossible, namely to bring it about that for both parties something which did happen did not happen. Some of the appearance of paradox here can be removed, and I will try to do this. Before getting to this, however, there is a problem about what we might call the 'grammar' of forgiveness. For Swinburne, forgiveness is a species of communication, though it can be accomplished non-verbally, by a smile for example. Thus there can be no such thing, in his view, as forgiving but failing to communicate one's forgiveness to the

---

[8] In the rest of this chapter I will use the term 'guilt' to refer not to the feeling of guilt (subjective guilt) but to what the feeling of guilt acknowledges (objective guilt). I say 'at least the internal admission', because repentance also includes the resolve to change, and more than this, as we saw in Ch. 8.

[9] It may not be that the same penance carries out these various functions equally well; a box of chocolates, for example, may serve the first two, but not be costly enough to serve the third. There are numerous problems with understanding all four tasks. All four of them, for example, can be carried out in ways that err on the side of excess or defect. Repentance, to take the first, involves not merely the admission of guilt, but the resolve to change. It comes in degrees of sincerity and degrees of intensity. It can also be momentary, or it can consume whole stretches of a life. It can be well thought out, so that the full extent of the offence is acknowledged, or it can be partial and superficial (though still completely sincere and deeply felt). Many of these dimensions of repentance will not be visible to the victim, since the offender's task is here interior. But the repentance will have its fruit in the quality of the apology, reparation, and penance, which the victim will sometimes be able to evaluate. The difficulties about how much reparation is enough are especially troublesome. For example, is the measure to be the cost to the victim of what he has lost, or the cost to the offender of replacing or repairing it?

offender. For Jeffrie Murphy, by contrast, forgiveness is the overcoming of anger towards the offender for moral reasons; it is a change of heart.[10] Here my linguistic intuitions side with Murphy. Forgiving somebody seems to me, like blaming somebody, something we often do in the presence of the person we are forgiving or blaming, but which we can also do in our hearts. It is in both cases an act directed towards someone, but the act may fail to be communicated. It is possible, for example, to forgive the dead.

To return, then, to the mystery. The first thing I want to point out is that the statement I quoted from Swinburne is ambiguous. He says that you forgive me if you undertake 'that in future you will not treat me as the originator of an act by which I wronged you'. But consider the following example. I am a contractor, and also a friend of yours, and I let you down badly on a building job because of my inexperience in this kind of work. I apologize sincerely and I make up the loss to you (perhaps by paying for a more experienced contractor to repair the job). Suppose you forgive me the wrong and we restore the friendship. Still, next time you are choosing a contractor for this kind of work, you will not choose me unless you see that I have changed in the relevant way and have acquired the relevant experience. This is not altered by the fact that you have forgiven me. The point is that you now know something about me, that I am not good at this sort of work. Forgiveness does not require you to forget this knowledge. You will still, therefore, in one sense treat me as the originator of an act by which I wronged you. That is, my being the originator of an act by which I wronged you will still inform your choices with respect to me.

So in what sense do you, when you forgive me, cease to treat me as the originator of the wrong? Perhaps in the future you treat that past

---

[10] Murphy and Hampton (1988) 21: 'Forgiveness is primarily a matter of how I *feel* about you (not how I treat you), and thus I may forgive you in my heart of hearts or even after you are dead.' This quotation shuld not be taken as meaning that forgiveness is, for Murphy, merely a matter of feeling. It is 'the foreswearing of resentment', where this is a '*resolute* overcoming' of anger and hatred (p. 15). Such a change of heart may, I think, not be decided upon but discovered. An interesting case is that of Molly in Joyce's *Ulysses*, who comes to realize at the end of her monologue that she has forgiven Bloom. Marilyn Adams distinguishes 'performative forgiveness', which must be publicly declared, and 'forgiveness from the heart'. But she also allows that forgiveness as an internal act can be 'performative' in the sense (not Swinburne's) that it can accomplish the release of the offender. See Adams (1991) 294 and 303 n. 85.

act of letting you down not as an act of wronging you, but simply as
evidence of the fact that I am not reliable. But this analysis is still not
quite right. You are not committed, in forgiving me, to forget that I
wronged you in the past, but rather to stop holding that against me.
We need to explore what this means.[11] There is a slipperiness in the
term 'forgive', which makes progress more difficult. The term is not
used in quite the same way in the two phrases 'forgiving a debt' and
'forgiving a person'. To forgive a debt is to relinquish it, or
deliberately not to exact it. To forgive a person may not be, however,
to forgive that person's debt in that sense. It may be, rather, to
accept the payment of the debt that the person has made. Failure to
note this distinction has harmed several treatments of forgiveness in
the literature. H. P. Owen, for example, says, 'If A has sinned
against his friend B then B can adopt one of two courses. He can
either forgive A freely or he can demand a recompense or penalty
from A; but he cannot do both simultaneously . . . Forgiveness is by
its nature unconditional.'[12] Eleanore Stump says that to forgive
means 'to fail to exact all that is in justice due', so that if Christ paid
the sinner's debt (on one account of the atonement), this merely
shows that God 'has arranged that the debt be paid in full, not that
he has agreed to overlook any part of the debt'.[13] The point here goes
back at least as far as Faustus Socinus, in *De Jesu Christo Servatore*,
to whom Calvin repeatedly addressed himself. Socinus argued
against the substitutionary atonement on the basis that giving
pardon does not square with taking satisfaction.[14] But this Socinian
point seems wrong about forgiveness in general, though right about
forgiving debts. If someone who has wronged me has, as Swinburne
says, made apology, reparation, and penance, my forgiveness of him
is my acceptance of these acts. This is my side of the restoration of
the relationship, when he has done his side of it. On the Socinian
view it is impossible to forgive when reparation has been made; for if
it is made, there is nothing to be forgiven and the mere acceptance of
the reparation does not count as forgiveness. But by distinguishing
the forgiveness of debts and persons, we can say both that our debt
was paid and that God forgives us as persons.

[11] God is said 'not to remember our sins' in certain circumstances, but the relevant
sense is that he does not remember them 'against us', see Ps. 79: 8. At least it is hard
to see how his forgetting that they occurred is consistent with omniscience. The
emphasis in Scripture is that the *offence* is removed, as far as the east is from the west
(Ps. 103: 12).   [12] Owen (1984) 100.

[13] Stump (1988) 62. See also Talbott (1990) 8.   [14] See Packer (1974).

Jean Hampton's recent account of forgiveness presents a paradox which follows Socinus in this respect. Agreeing with Aurel Kolnai, she starts by distinguishing forgiving an action from condoning it.[15] Condoning a morally wrong action is accepting it without protest, suppressing both the judgement that it is wrong and the feelings that go along with that judgement. But then there is what she calls a paradox of forgiveness. For it seems that either forgiveness is condoning the offence, if the victim accepts the offender back without the offender repenting; or, if the offender does repent (and, we could add, makes reparation and penance), we do not any longer have forgiveness but merely justice. Hampton imagines the case of a person who hates those who hate the good and loves those who love it. If such a person is a victim, she will accept back the offender when he repents; but this 'would not be forgiving him. She would merely be treating him fairly, justly, reasonably, in view of his change of heart.'[16] Note that the premiss of the paradox is that it is not any longer forgiveness if the victim renews the relationship after the offender has performed his tasks. But forgiveness can also be an acceptance that the offender's tasks have been completed. It can therefore be morally required within a committed relationship, whereas forgiveness as a release from these tasks is probably always beyond the call of duty. If we allow, as I think we should, that there can be forgiveness after the offender has repented and made apology, reparation, and penance, there can be a duty, which the victim has undertaken within a committed relationship, to seek reconciliation and thus to accept the offender's tasks as completed when they are.[17]

---

[15] See Kolnai (1973–4).

[16] Murphy and Hampton (1988) 41. Kolnai dissolves the paradox by suggesting that forgiveness involves distinguishing the immoral action, which is not condoned, from the agent's character, which is forgiven. Hampton asks, 'But why doesn't forgiveness of people with bad character traits amount to a condonation of their character?' (p. 83). Her own solution is to distinguish the agent's immoral character, which is not condoned, from his or her inherent decency, possessed by all human beings (p. 152). If, on this view, we think of a person as 'rotten' all the way down, as *thoroughly identified* with his immoral cause (like Goebbels, she says), we will be stuck with 'moral hatred', and will not be able to forgive. If, as Kant believed, radical evil is innate and imputable, then we are all (until the revolution of the will) thoroughly identified with the evil we commit. We cannot go back deep into ourselves and find our 'inherent decency', though we will find still a 'seed of goodness'.

[17] Swinburne (1989) 88 says, 'There is of course no obligation on the victim to forgive'; forgiveness is something it is good for the victim to do, not something the victim ought to do. But he allows that there may be an obligation to forgive in cases

The victim does not, I have suggested, *forget* that the offender has wronged him or her. This was the point of the example of the inexperienced contractor. In some sense, though, the offender and the victim can together restore their relation to the vitality or health it had before the offence. The offender can, I think, *make good* the offence. This is what Swinburne analyses in terms of repentance, apology, reparation, and penance. What, though, is the measure of success in these tasks? They can all be understood in terms of degree. Once reparation has been decided upon, for example, we can still ask 'how much is enough?' As a preliminary measure, I want to suggest that the offence has been made good, on the side of the offender, when the victim holds herself equally content with two states of the world: the first contains the offence together with the offender's repentance, apology, reparation, and penance; the second contains neither.[18] If the victim, because of the actions of the offender, is indifferent between these two states of the world, or has a preference for the first, then the offender's tasks have been accomplished on his side.

This suggestion needs to be qualified immediately. The victim can be unreasonable in his preferences. He may exaggerate the offence and unreasonably depreciate the value of the offender's responses.[19] Suppose I have lost your tennis-racket which I borrowed, and I am sincerely sorry. I apologize with anger at myself for my stupidity, I buy you a new racket better than the old one, and I accompany it with a ticket to the opera. Yet you remain unmoved, and refuse to forgive me. I think I would be right to think that I have done enough, and that you are simply being unreasonable. We should add, then, that the measure of sufficiency is the victim's preference between the two states of the world *if* the victim is being reasonable.

where such an obligation has been undertaken. He thinks Christians are in such a situation. He may be prepared to allow that forgiveness within committed personal relations is such a case. If not, then he would have to say that when the offender performs the offender's tasks within such a relation, the victim is not failing a duty if he fails to forgive. This seems wrong. Within such a relation there is a duty to actively seek reconciliation, not merely to avoid nursing a grudge (which is *actively* keeping resentment alive).

[18] I say '*holds* herself', because I do not want to suggest that forgiveness is merely passive. It involves a choice, although this may not be fully explicit.

[19] Alternatively, the victim's estimate of the offence may be unreasonably low, and she may unreasonably exaggerate the value of the offender's responses.

There may or may not be satisfactory general principles for telling what the reasonable person's preferences are in such a matter.

This account of what it means to make good an offence enables us to explain the relevant sense in which two parties can together bring it about that something which did happen did not happen. Sometimes it is said that the past, because it is past, can never be made good. Thus Emil Brunner says, 'Guilt means that our past—that which can never be made good—always constitutes one element in our present situation.'[20] It may be thought that unless I can change the past and undo what I have done (which obviously I cannot do), the wrong I have done is a moral debt that neither I nor anyone else can ever pay. But if the victim prefers the state of the world with my offence and my subsequent response to the state of the world with neither, then I have undone what I have done in the relevant sense. There are two senses in which the past is permanent, and only one of them matters for the discussion of the possibility of making good. If I drop your tennis-racket into the Niagara river just above the falls at 4.15 p.m. on 26 July 1991, then it is permanently the case that I dropped your racket into the river at that time. That is something I cannot (on most views of time) subsequently undo. But does this mean that I have permanently lost your racket? Suppose it emerges unscathed at the bottom of the falls by some miracle, and I retrieve it. I have then, in the relevant sense, undone the past.

It is tempting to object, here, that merely retrieving the racket is not sufficient to undo the negligence (or, if it was deliberate, the malice) of my initial action, since I have harmed you whether the racket is retrieved or not. But consider a case without interpersonal complications. Suppose I was crossing the bridge above the falls, carrying my own racket, there was a sudden freak gust of wind, and the racket fell into the river. If I subsequently retrieve the racket, and thoroughly enjoy retrieving it, I have undone the harm to myself. In this sense the past is not permanent, but can be changed. I am just as happy with the world the way it is as I would have been happy if I had not lost the racket in the first place.

c. FORGIVENESS AND MUTUALITY

If the tasks of the offender are complete, we can describe forgiveness as the victim's acceptance of what the offender has done to make

---

[20] Brunner (1934) 443.

good the offence. But this is an oversimplification. The tasks of both the offender and the victim often require work by both the offender and the victim. This becomes clear if we look at cases where the offender has accomplished his tasks to the extent he can, but the victim withholds forgiveness, and the reverse cases, where the victim forgives without the offender having accomplished his tasks. I will discuss both situations, and I will confine myself to cases where the offence and the forgiveness occur within a relationship. This is not always the case. I may be driving through the country and see a development going up which is destroying a lovely piece of farmland (after which the development is named). I may feel a surge of anger against the developer. Suppose I then read that she has seen the evil of this kind of destruction, and has donated all her profits to countryside preservation. I can then forgive her, without any relationship between us either before or afterwards. Often, however, forgiveness is within a relationship. I will confine my discussion to these cases because I am interested in God's forgiveness, which is within a relationship even if this is not acknowledged by one of the parties. Moreover, my analysis of forgiveness will fit many relationships of a superficial kind.[21] Suppose someone whom I have never seen before in my life steps on my foot in the bus. She says, 'Excuse me, I'm sorry,' I say, 'That's all right,' and she passes on down the bus and out of my life for ever. Surely I have forgiven her; but other than her stepping on my foot we have had and will have no kind of contact. The kind of forgiveness operating in this kind of example is highly attenuated, and so is the kind of relationship; the two of us are no more than fellow passengers on the same bus. Even here, however, the relation is significant. There are certain expectations of courtesy which she has violated, and my response is not forgiveness if I merely mouth the conventional words. There is, in fact, a rather elaborate code for what we could call 'bus fellows', different in different countries and even in different cities within the same country.[22]

Aristotle's treatment of friendship is useful in the context of this discussion, because it is for him a very elastic notion.[23] Fellow

---

[21] See Morris (1988) 15–19.

[22] In Grand Rapids, Mich., for example, if two people are sitting next to each other and an empty pair of seats opens up, one of them will often move so that both can have an empty seat beside them.

[23] *NE* 8. 1, 1155^{a}24 ff., and 8. 7, 1158^{b}11 ff.

citizens are, for him, friends in virtue merely of being citizens of the
same *polis*, and parents and children are friends merely because they
belong to the same family. There are, then, many degrees and kinds
of friendship in his view, and we can think of there being a spectrum
of friendship. The best kind, and friendship to the highest degree, is
where the friend is 'another self'.[24] A friend who is another self has
joy when I have joy, and grief when I have grief. There is a kind of
common affective life to the two friends, and there is also a shared
commitment to the same vision of the good. This is why Aristotle
thinks this kind of friendship lasts. The poet John Donne says,

> When love, with one another so
> Interinanimates two souls,
> That abler soul, which thence doth flow,
> Defects of loneliness controls.'[25]

What Donne calls 'interinanimation' is the insertion of a soul
('animation') into ('in') the place between ('inter') two people. This
is a typically metaphysical way of putting a point familiar in our
experience of friendship; it is as though the love between us gives
birth to a new life shared between us.

When an offence has been committed within such a friendship,
the common life is interrupted and the offender and the victim both
have a part to play in its restoration. One thing that can happen, for
example, is that until the offence is made good, the parties become
identified with, as it were solidified into, the roles of offender and
victim. Not only, if I am the victim, do I confine the other into 'the
person who did that to me', and progressively see less and less of him
outside that description; but I start to see myself as more and more
centrally 'the person to whom he did that'. The life (or soul) which
Donne describes as generated by interinanimation starts to die.[26]

The tasks of the offender and the victim are aimed at restoring the
relationship. This cannot take place without work on both sides,
because the offence has interrupted the common life, and this cannot

---

[24] *NE* 9. 4, 1166ª31.

[25] 'The Ecstasy', stanza 11. There is an older idea, e.g. in Cicero, *De Amicitia*
25. 92: 'The force (*vis*) of the friendship is that it is as though one spirit (*animus*)
comes to be out of more than one (*e pluribus*).' *E pluribus unum* is found on the US
dollar note. See also Aelrad of Rievaulx, *De Spiritali Amicitia* 1. 20.

[26] There is a useful account in Beatty (1970). He argues that the very process of
asking for and granting forgiveness itself 'objectifies' the parties.

be resumed unless both parties are actively willing. We can see the offence as imposing distance between the friends. When two friends at the high end of the spectrum of friendship have been separated for any length of time by physical distance, they cannot usually re-enter immediately into the full life of the friendship before the separation. We use the phrase that they have to 'catch up with each other' first. What they have to do is to go back over the life they have lived separately, so as to make it as if they had been together. They have to re-establish continuity. This is strikingly like what happens when there has been not physical distance, but the distance caused by an offence. There is the same appearance of paradox, for just as the offence cannot (in one sense) be undone, so the physical separation cannot (in a similar sense) be undone. One party was in fact in Prague for six months, and the other in Boston. But the damage of both kinds of distance can be undone, and both parties, in both kinds of case, have to do this work.

The work of restoration, such as the catching up I have described, requires the same quality of double reflection (as in two mirrors facing each other) that Aristotle notes about friendship in general, as opposed to mere good will.[27] She knows that he knows that she loves him, and vice versa. Moreover (this sounds more arcane than it is in experience) she delights in each reflected or repeating stage of this knowledge. In the same way with offence, each party knows and knows that the other party knows about the wrong each has done to the other, and is sad both about the wrong and that the other has to know about it. I will call this quality of double reflection 'mutuality'. All the tasks at the high end of the spectrum of friendship require mutuality. The victim has to help the offender understand what the offence means to him, and has to help work out what kind of reparation and penance will be enough. The offender has to accept that the victim's forgiveness removes the offence; and this is not always easy. There are people who know that they have been forgiven, even forgiven by God, but who still cannot forgive themselves. The offence then remains an obstacle to the relationship. Here is one of the hard things about offence: it blocks mutuality, but it requires mutuality for its repair. Once mutuality is restored, the formal tasks are relatively easy. There are thus all sorts of things for

---

[27] *NE* 8. 2, 1155^{b}34 ff. 'But perhaps we should add that friends are aware of the reciprocated goodwill.' See Nagel (1979).

both parties to do in restoring the relationship, which are not readily classified under the four tasks. The formal declaration of forgiveness by the victim is often the recognition that restoration has already essentially occurred.

I have been talking about the high end of the spectrum of friendship, and forgiveness belongs all the way down this spectrum (and below it). Following Aristotle's elastic usage, even the person who steps on my foot in the bus can be called a kind of friend. The forgiveness at the low end of the spectrum takes much less psychological space, just as the friendship does. But even here there is work for the victim to do beyond the sincere declaration, 'That's all right.' The offender may have to be helped to perform her tasks, if the relationship is to be restored. Suppose the person who stepped on my toe has stumbled, and dropped her packages. She may be covered in confusion. Am I entitled to leave her assistance up to the other passengers on the grounds that I have suffered enough from her already? Our relationship is merely that of bus fellows, but even so I may have to help her regain her composure before she can get around to apologizing. Until she has apologized, I have forgiven her, and she has accepted it, even this minimal kind of relationship has been disrupted.[28]

d. THE OFFENDER'S POSITION

I have been talking about forgiveness teleologically, as headed towards the restoration of a relationship. What happens when the tasks of the offender are accomplished but not the task of the victim? Swinburne suggests that the victim's right or moral permission to withhold forgiveness lapses after some length of time (it is not clear what length) if the offender has performed the tasks appropriate to the offender. This means that after this interval there is no more task for the victim to accomplish, and the guilt of the offender is removed whether the victim acknowledges this or not.[29] It is like the right of an author to withhold permission to publish her work. After a certain number of years (in this case, defined by law), there is no

---

[28] If the reader is sceptical about the existence of a bus fellow relationship, this case can be construed as forgiving just another human being, which may still require work for the victim beyond the declaration of forgiveness.

[29] Swinburne (1989) 87.

longer any permission required, and so there is no longer any right to withhold it.

This seems to me to be not quite the case with forgiveness. The offender's tasks, like the victim's task, are headed towards the restoration of the relationship. The offender may decide, 'I am willing for the relationship to be restored to its full vitality before the offence; I want there to be no obstacle to this on my side', and he may act on this decision by apology, reparation, and penance, as far as he can without mutuality; but this does not yet restore the relationship. Even after he has done all he can of these tasks, there is much work *for the offender* in the reconciliation still to be done which he cannot accomplish without the mutual co-operation of the victim. It is possible that in some cases this mutuality will never be achieved, and therefore the tasks of the offender will never completely be accomplished. For example there is the task of catching up, which is something the parties have to do *together*. This means that in such a case the offender may not be able fully to remove his guilt, because he does not have the co-operation of the victim. The clearest case of this is where the victim is dead, but it also happens where there is no longer enough life left in the relationship to allow the necessary communication. For example, the victim may not be willing to listen to the offender's detailed apology.

It might be thought that the offender does not have anything left to do because in this sort of case, at the high end of the spectrum of friendship, there has been a commitment by both parties to seek reconciliation; it seems, therefore, *wrong* for the victim to refuse to forgive. There is not merely the active wrong of nursing a grudge, but a wrong of omission in failing to forgive. The disposition to nurse a grudge is a vice, opposed to the virtue called magnanimity.[30] But even if the victim does not actively keep the grudge alive, the offender who has completed the offender's tasks as far as this can be done without mutuality is *wronged* if the victim then refuses forgiveness. This does not yet show, however, that if the victim is obdurate, the offender can rightly claim to have accomplished all his tasks.

One complication here is that we need to distinguish between intentional offence and offence taken; that is, between offence as

---

[30] See Aristotle, *NE* 4. 3, 1125ᵃ8 f. Kolnai says that 'a credible change of heart' on the offender's part can make forgiveness into a 'quasi-obligation' (1973–4: 105).

some wrong actually intended to the victim and offence as something held wrong by the person who suffers it. The verb 'offend' is often used in the latter sense, so that I offend you or cause you offence if you merely 'take offence' at what I have done. I can offend you, for example, by innocently calling you a name you take as an insult, as when English people call Americans from the South 'Yanks'. We need to uncouple (objective) guilt from offence taken. The offence taken by the victim is not sufficient in itself to prevent the completion of the offender's tasks.

With this distinction in mind, however, we can still say that there may be a residue of guilt in cases where, because the victim is obdurate or unavailable, the offender cannot accomplish his side of the process of restoring the relationship. When the relationship is unrestorable because the victim cannot or will not forgive, the offender may be left with the accurate and frustrating perception that he can never complete his share of the restoration process. There may be duties left undischarged; and the victim may not give him enough co-operation to allow him to get rid of them.

e. THE VICTIM'S POSITION

We can now ask whether forgiveness, the task of the victim, is possible without the tasks of the offender having been accomplished. This question needs to be distinguished from the question of whether the victim is ever *right* to forgive in these circumstances.[31] Swinburne thinks that the victim cannot (not merely should not) forgive without the offender's tasks being accomplished to some degree; 'he cannot forgive', for example, 'when the apology is totally casual'. The reason for thinking this is that the victim will be *condoning* the offence if the offender's tasks are not accomplished at least to this degree. Swinburne quotes from Gabriele Taylor, 'For in reaccepting the unrepentant agent he would seem to think little of the wrong done and so compromise his own values.'[32]

---

[31] The same two questions can be asked about the case where the task of the offender is accomplished but not the task of the victim. The relation between the two questions is that if the answer to the first is 'no', the answer to the second is also 'no'; but the answer to the first can be 'yes', and the answer to the second still 'no'.

[32] Swinburne (1989) 86. He admits, though, that ordinary usage is not very clear here, and his conclusion that forgiveness is impossible when no atonement at all has been made is 'a verbal decision'.

I think, on the contrary, that forgiveness *is* possible in these circumstances. If we take the high end of the spectrum of friendship, it is possible for the victim to decide, 'I am willing for the relationship to be restored to its condition before the offence; there is now no obstacle to this on my side.' It is true that this decision will not of itself accomplish the restoration of the relationship, which is the goal of forgiveness. Much of the actual work of restoration, at this high end of the spectrum, cannot be accomplished without mutuality. For example, the two parties will not be able to work together through the time they have been separated by the offence. None the less, it seems appropriate to call what the victim does in this case forgiveness, even though there is more work for the *victim* (as well as the offender) to do in restoring the relationship.

Forgiveness is possible without the tasks of the offender having been accomplished. But is it ever *right* to forgive in this way? I mention the following example in fear and trembling: is it a good thing for a woman who has been abused by her husband to forgive the offender if he is unrepentant? Is not such forgiveness part of the pattern of wrongful submission which, on a social scale, leads to the tolerance of wife abuse in the first place? Or suppose he says he is sorry, and means it, and buys a bunch of roses—but the victim knows that in a few weeks the same thing is going to happen all over again. To forgive in this way can be, as Gabriele Taylor says, to condone. But does it have to be? There are some Christian patterns of thought which would deny this. For God requires us to bless those who persecute us, and this requirement is not conditional on the enemies' repentance.[33] 'Father, forgive them,' said Jesus on the cross, 'for they know not what they do.'[34] It is not that Jesus is here condoning the actions of those who are putting him to death. Some Christians have held that ordinary believers are not to be held under

[33] Rom. 12: 14.

[34] Luke 23: 34. See also the death by stoning of Stephen, who cries out 'Lord, lay not this sin to their charge,' and then dies (Acts 7: 60). It is true that in both these cases forgiveness is not performed, but God the Father is asked to forgive. Perhaps Jesus and Stephen were *ready* to forgive, but actual forgiveness would wait for repentance. See Luke 17: 3. Because of the ignorance of Jesus's persecutors, Murphy says, that 'Father forgive them for they know not what they do' goes better as 'Father *excuse* them for they know not what they do (1988: 20). Perhaps Jesus means that for the offence of knowingly killing the Son of God, which cannot be forgiven, they are to be excused because of ignorance; for the offence of killing an innocent man, he is asking God to forgive them (not excuse them). See Haber (1991) 109.

the so-called evangelical counsels, which are reserved for those with special vocations.[35] Forgiveness of the unrepentant might, on such a view, not be required of the ordinary believer but only of saints. If we reject this view of the evangelical counsels, however, we are left with the obligation to forgive those who are persecuting us. Perhaps God requires this of us for our own good. Maybe it is for the woman's own good to abandon her anger at some point, and get on with her life, even though her husband has no right that she do so. Even if it is not always right, it is surely *sometimes* right for a victim to forgive, even where the offender has not performed the offender's tasks. Even outside a Christian framework, a victim can surely sometimes be justified in letting the value of the relationship, for example with a child, override the value against which the offender has offended. It is in general thinking little of an offence or condoning it (when it is forgiven for the sake of a greater good) only if the greater good is in fact considered a little good.

Sometimes the forgiveness may be right, but it may be wrong to *communicate* it to the offender. Here I am assuming, against Swinburne, that it is possible to forgive without communicating the forgiveness. In the case of wife abuse, expressing the forgiveness makes it too easy for the offender. In particular it makes it too easy for him to continue, so that grace may abound (Rom. 6: 1). If the offender is already repentant, expressing forgiveness may have the effect of heaping coals of fire on his head (Rom. 12: 20). But it is hard to see how this can happen if the offender is *not* already repentant, at least in germ. In the case of wife abuse, forgiveness may be compatible with not only failing to communicate the forgiveness, but leaving the offender altogether.

There is one final question I want to address. What happens in the situation where it is not possible for the offender to accomplish his tasks in a way that a reasonable person would accept? There is nothing an offender can do to make up for rape, for example. Not all offences are like this, because the mere fact that an offence happened in the past does *not* mean that it cannot be undone in the relevant sense. But there are many offences which cannot be made good by the offender. If the victim is to forgive the offender for such offences, it seems that she has, as it were, to take the loss. This is

---

[35] See Calvin's objections to this proposal, *Institutes*, II. viii. 56. See also Adams (1991) 298.

again language from commerce, as with talk of debt and making good. Forgiveness by the victim in these circumstances is apparently vicarious, in the sense that the victim is taking a penalty that properly belongs to the offender. It is sometimes said that forgiveness is always vicarious, but this seems to me an overstatement depending on the mistaken view that the past can never be undone.[36] What is true is that forgiveness is vicarious when the offender has not made good or cannot make good the offence. It is as though the victim says to the offender, 'You ought to be bearing this suffering, but I am going to bear it instead; and because I am bearing it, you and I can be reconciled.' This kind of forgiveness seems especially dangerous in the case of wife abuse I mentioned earlier. But is it ever possible, or ever right to forgive in this way?

What it requires is for the victim to go through the suffering, as it were, twice. The commercial analogy of taking the loss suggests that the victim first loses the money by loan, and then loses it again by default. It is the same money both times, but there is a double loss of it. When applied to vicarious forgiveness, what the analogy suggests is that the victim not merely suffers the offence, but has to accept the offence, and this in two senses. First he has to accept the *fact* that the suffering will never be made good, that it is not a temporary condition for which the offender will eventually make compensation. Second, he has to accept this permanent harm, in the different sense that compensation is no longer even *sought*.[37] Here the paradigm of private or civil law is helpful, rather than that of criminal law.[38] The victim is like a plaintiff in a civil court waiving a right over a defendant, and thus releasing the defendant from obligation. This is a *sacrifice* on the plaintiff's part (though it may result for him in a greater good). The sacrifice is vicarious in the sense that the plaintiff is undertaking the cost which the defendant should be paying.

Suppose two people are joined in a friendship with a high degree of mutuality, and suppose one of them does something that hurts the other so seriously that there is nothing the offender can do to make it good. One thing that can happen is that the friendship is exposed to the victim as illusory. But there is another possibility. The victim may value the friendship so highly that she is willing to forgive vicariously in the way I have tried to describe. What can happen, for

---

[36] See Buswell (1962) 76.   [37] See J. E. Hare (1983), esp. 14–15.
[38] See Twambley (1976).

example, is that the victim comes to feel a kind of incongruity between the distance caused by the offence and the life of the relationship which she still lives in memory, and in present trace and habit. Where this happens I think vicarious forgiveness is both sometimes possible and sometimes good.

This forgiveness may not change the offender's mind in any way; she may persist in refusing the offender's tasks. In some cases, however, especially where the offender has repented and apologized but is unable to do anything that would count as sufficient reparation, vicarious forgiveness can accomplish the release of the offender as well as of the victim. This picture is admittedly influenced by the analogy of God's forgiveness of us, as understood within Christianity; but I think it has merit independently. We can think of the victim as insisting, despite the offence, on the common life he shares with the offender, and bringing her to suffer with him the damage done to this common life (to suffer it by the association between them). Then if the victim can get through the hurt and loss, he can release both himself and the offender. The offender can share in the victim's defeat of the forces of resentment and alienation which the offence put in play between them. On this picture there is a struggle internal to the victim about how to see himself and his relation to the offender. Part of the process of taking the loss is his coming not to desire any further restitution. This is a further sacrifice on his part. If the offender can be associated with him in this internal struggle and victory, the offender can come to a sense that enough has been done to render further restitution unnecessary; reconciliation has then been achieved.

GOD'S ASSISTANCE

I N this final chapter, I will look more closely at the central Christian doctrines about the assistance God offers us in bridging the moral gap. I will not be able to maintain the ecumenical goal here of speaking only in terms that are common to all the main lines of the Christian tradition, because it is in the details of these doctrines that the main lines diverge. Still, I am interested in giving my own account rather than in denying the accounts of other Christians. There is a wide variety of language and interpretation, both in Scripture and in the main lines of theology and practice that come out of Scripture. It is not my project to refute the claims of alternatives to my own account. I am aware of enormous literatures about sacrifice, baptism, and Holy Communion, with which I will not try to engage given the limited purposes of my book. The chapter will have three main sections: on atonement, justification, and sanctification. I want to defend an understanding of the atonement in terms of penal substitution, and I will do this by making central the notion of our incorporation into Christ. With regard to justification and sanctification I will try to steer a course between the doctrines of negative justification and essential right-eousness, and I will emphasize the corporate nature of the new life in Christ. I will end by returning to Kant and what I called in Chapter 2 the third experiment, to see if there are parts of our moral belief and practice which require support from the outer of Kant's two concentric circles, namely from historical faith.

a. ATONEMENT

Penal Substitution

I will start with Swinburne, as in Chapter 9, because his account of the relation of human forgiveness to divine forgiveness is so elegant. This paragraph is a summary of his account. Because God is our creator, when we wrong each other and the natural world we also wrong God.[1] He cannot forgive us without requiring repentance and apology, because to do this would be to *condone* our wrongdoing. God has, on Swinburne's account, no duty to require reparation and penance from us.[2] It is none the less good that he do so, because it takes seriously the wrong that we do. But we do not have the means to make reparation and penance. We could only offer to God things we did not owe him already, and we do not have such things. God therefore, like a good parent, gives us the means by which we can make amends.

If the child has broken the parent's window and does not have the money to pay for a replacement, the parent may give him the money wherewith to pay a glazier to put in a new window, or he may give him a cheque made payable to the glazier which he can then use to pay the glazier to put in the window, and thereby make due reparation.[3]

To apply the analogy, the life and death of Christ are like the cheque. God sends his son to live and die on earth, as a sacrifice, and we can then offer this sacrifice to God as our reparation and penance for the wrongdoing we have done to God. There is no need, Swinburne says, to assume that Christ's life and death are *equivalent* to what we owe to God; they are simply a costly penance and reparation which pay off part of the debt and are sufficient for a merciful God to let us off the rest. Swinburne does not hold that only Christ's life and death could have been sufficient; but he holds that there is something peculiarly appropriate in the means chosen. 'Since what needs atonement to God is human sin, men living second-rate lives when they have been given such great opportunities by their creator, appropriate reparation and penance would be made by a perfect human life, given away through being lived perfectly.'[4]

---

[1] Here is one disanalogy between human and divine forgiveness. We wrong God, but he is not the victim of our wrongdoing. It is artificial, however, even in human relations to think that the recipient of an offence is always properly called a 'victim'. It is often possible for a subordinate to commit an offence against a superior without 'victimizing' her.

[2] Swinburne quotes Aquinas, *Summa Theologiae* IIIa q. 46 a. 2 ad. 3. It is possible to derive the claim that God is not (morally) required to demand reparation from the premiss that God is under no (moral) requirements at all. This is not the place to discuss this premiss. Or it can be argued that one person by wronging a second cannot give the second an additional duty (in this case that of punishing the first person). But it does not seem true, in general, that I cannot create obligations for my victims by wronging them. If I drive unsafely, for example, I can create an obligation for those driving in front of me and behind me to take extra caution.

[3] Swinburne (1989) 149.   [4] Ibid. 157.

I want to comment on two features of this account, on one thing Swinburne puts in and on one thing he leaves out. First, it is central to his account that it is we sinners who offer to God as reparation and penance Christ's life and death. In human forgiveness, the offender's tasks are repentance, apology, reparation, and penance; and when the offender has performed these tasks, the victim can respond with forgiveness, releasing the offender from objective guilt. With divine forgiveness, Swinburne says, the offender's tasks are the same, though the means to make reparation are a gift from God, and God can forgive us when we have performed them. Christian doctrine has another, more familiar way to describe Christ's sacrifice: not that *we* offer Christ's sacrifice, but that *he* offers it. He is both sacrificial victim and *priest*.[5] This becomes a continuing motif in the fathers. Thus Augustine writes,

Since there are four things to be considered in any sacrifice: to whom it is offered, by whom it is offered, what it is that is offered, and for whom it is offered, so the One True Mediator, who reconciles us to God by the sacrifice of peace, remained one with him to whom he offered; made one in himself those for whom he offered; and was himself both the offerer and the thing which was offered.[6]

Swinburne does not give us any predecessor references, except a hint by Aquinas that whereas it is the sinner who must repent and confess, he or she can make satisfaction by using the 'instruments' provided by others. Aquinas does not apply this hint to the case of us sinners providing satisfaction by using the instrument of Christ's sacrifice.[7]

More significant, I think, is the second feature of Swinburne's account of the atonement which I want to mention. Christ's death is, in his account, something we sinners use as reparation and penance.

---

[5] Heb. is full of refs. to Christ as our high priest, who appeared 'to put away sin by the sacrifice of himself' (9: 26; see also 2: 17, 3: 1, 4: 14–15, 5: 5, 6: 20, 7: 26–7, 8: 1–3, 10: 21). Swinburne does not want to deny this. He talks of Christ 'giving the most valuable thing he has as a present to God' (1989: 152).

[6] *De Trinitate* 4. 14. 19.

[7] *Summa Theologiae* IIIa q. 48 a. 2 ad. 1; q. 48 a. 3. It is Christ here who offers the sacrifice to the Father. There is however, a long tradition of thinking of the church as offering up Christ. This is expressed in the hymn by Jervois: 'Wherefore, O Father, we thy humble servants, Here bring before thee Christ, thy well-beloved, All-perfect offering, sacrifice immortal, spotless oblation' (*New English Hymnal*, no. 313).

But Christ is not, as Swinburne sees it, dying a death in which we share. I want to defend a qualified version of the 'penal substitution' theory of the atonement, in terms of our incorporation into Christ and into his death. I will start by saying in what sense I think we should talk about *penal* substitution, and then in what sense we should talk about *substitution*.

Swinburne does not like penal substitution as an account of the atonement because he thinks of punishment as the *forcible* taking of reparation from the offender, either by the victim or by the state acting on the victim's behalf.[8] Since Christ undertook voluntarily his sacrificial death, it might seem that 'punishment' and hence 'penal' are the wrong terms. But whereas it is true that punishment is usually forcible, this does not seem to be part of the meaning of the word. It is usually true that the punisher does not wait upon the offender's consent; but it is not necessary that the offender *not* give his consent. The offender can give consent where the giving or withholding of consent makes no difference to the outcome. There can also be cases where the offender has the power to prevent his own punishment, but chooses not to do so. Finally, there can be cases where the offender eagerly seeks punishment, for whatever reason. There does not seem to be anything in the meaning of the term 'punishment' to prevent us talking of one person voluntarily taking the punishment on behalf of another. Moses, for example, offered to take the punishment that was due to the Israelites because of their sin in making the golden calf. He offered to God that God should 'blot him out of his book';[9] but this time God insisted on visiting the punishment on the offenders, and the people of Israel were struck with a plague. What is true, I think, is not that punishment has to be forcible, but that it has to be *exacted*. I will take this to mean that once punishment has been properly decided upon, its execution should take place, other things being equal, regardless of whether the particular person who will receive it agrees to it or not.

Sometimes (though not in Swinburne's case) the objection to penal substitution is based on an objection to the retributive theory of punishment.[10] But penal substitution can be understood in terms

---

[8] Swinburne (1989) 93 f.   [9] Exod. 32: 30–5.
[10] This lies behind R. M. Hare's objection to the idea of Christ taking our punishment (1989: 211–16).

of what we can call an 'expressive' theory of punishment.[11] This is like other retributive theories, in that it does not derive the value of punishment from its functions of deterring wrongdoers and removing them from circulation. But it does not take retribution as foundational, as though the harm inflicted back by the victim or the victim's agent is self-evidently justified by the fact that it is a response to harm inflicted in the first place by the offender. Rather, it sees retributive punishment as a means to a good end, namely the vindication of the victim's value. The suffering inflicted on the offender can be seen as the victim's value 'striking back'. The basic idea here is that the offender's wrongdoing demeans the victim by giving expression to the view that the offender's value is high enough to make this treatment of the victim legitimate or permissible. For a vivid example, take the case of the bully in the school playground. The demand for retributive punishment is then the demand that this false elevation of the offender's value be corrected visibly. This is not merely vengeance (though retribution can be that); it is the insistence on the recognition of a moral value, the correct relative value of wrongdoer and victim. The punishment is in this way a defeat for the offender at the hands of the victim, either directly or indirectly through the state (or school) as agent. This is one reason why punishment has to be seen as *exacted*. As formulated before, this means that once punishment has been properly decided upon, it should be executed, other things being equal, whether the particular person who will receive it agrees to it or not. The punishment expresses the 'diminution' of the offender if it is seen as exacted in this sense.

In the light of this account of punishment, we can make sense of the claim that God's demanding reparation for our wrongdoing is a good thing because it takes seriously not only the offender, but the offender's victim. If we can make sense of the idea of our incorporation into Christ, then we we can understand that he might take us on initially as sinners. The bully still has to be punished by the temporal authorities, but suppose he is now a Christian, joined to Christ, and, in terms of the distinction made in Chapter 5, Christ *acknowledges* this impediment as belonging to himself. That is, he does not endorse it and he is not neutral about whether it should be

[11] See Murphy and Hampton (1988), esp. 122–43. But I do not think the point of the retribution is to overcome *evidence* that the victim's value is reduced (p. 128), but to represent a denial of the *expression* by the offender of the reduction of this value.

changed, but he has accepted (as an elder brother might) that this is a part of what his adopted brother is like, and he has determined to take on himself his Father's punishment for the bullying.[12] The good that is done by God's requiring reparation means, on the expressive theory, that the reparation has to be exacted; that is, that it be punishment. It is hard to see how *this* good can be achieved, if the reparation involved in Christ's sacrifice is not viewed in this sense as punishment.[13] Taking seriously the wrong that offenders do means taking seriously the value of the people that the offenders wrong. On the expressive theory, this in turn means exacting the offenders' defeat.[14]

Incorporation

If this is what punishment means in the context of the atonement, what about *substitution*?[15] There is one kind of substitution which fits. We can find it in 2 Corinthians 5: 14:, 'For the love of Christ constraineth us; because we thus judge, that if one died for all, then were all dead.' The 'then' is puzzling. It looks as though Paul is saying that Christ died instead of us, and therefore we died as well.[16]

---

[12] It might be argued that the effect on the original offender will be less, and vicarious punishment will therefore be less effective as moral education. But Bach's Passions, for example, are full of expressions of remorse at the thought that Christ died in our stead, and Lutheran pietism is full of such expressions before Bach. In any case, the effect on the offender is not the main point, on the expressive theory of punishment. The main point is the demonstration of the value of the victim.

[13] Suppose we do not take Christ's sufferings as punishment, but we think of them as the consequences (foreseen but not directly intended) of a godly life lived in defiance of the established authorities. Then we can ask, would it have been enough if Christ had persuaded the Jewish leaders, and thus avoided the crucifixion? Would that have been enough for our salvation? (I owe this question to Bill Hasker.) If all we need to offer as reparation is someone's godly life, there was no need for the crucifixion. This does not seem to capture the scriptural emphasis on Christ's death.

[14] Retributive punishment is often seen in quantitative terms (an eye for an eye), and therefore one objection to penal substitution is that Christ's death is not enough to pay for the millions of murders and other offences whose punishment he takes on from us. The reply by the defenders of penal substitution has been that the Son of God undertakes infinite loss in the separation from his Father. On the expressive theory of punishment this move is unnecessary. Punishment as expression does not have to be quantitatively exact. We can still say that Christ's death is a fitting penalty, given that for each offender it is Christ who dies for him.

[15] See Hooker (1990) 48. For other reasons for hesitation about the term 'substitution' see Dunn (1975) 51 f.

[16] The preposition translated as 'for' is *huper*, not *anti*, and there is much debate about the use of both of them. There is a good discussion of the NT texts and secular literature of the period in Grotius (1889) 180–6.

While this may not be the meaning, there is one familiar context in which such an inference makes sense. This is the context in which a representative is a substitute. Thus Peter is told to give a piece of money *for* himself and Christ, because, as Grotius says, 'in that act he being one sustained the part of two'.[17] In the same passage from 2 Corinthians the Apostles are described as ambassadors *for* Christ, and the relationship of an ambassador to the country she represents has both of the required characteristics. She makes a commitment instead of her fellow citizens having to fly out to make it; and when she makes a commitment it follows that they all make it. The relation of a sacrificial victim to those for whom it dies also has these two characteristics, as I shall suggest later. We can already see that different interpretations of atonement and different interpretations of sacrifice will be interdependent. On the account of substitution I want to defend, it is true both that Christ had to suffer what we do not have to suffer, and that we share in his death and resurrection. In order to see how both these things might be true together, it will be helpful to look again at what might be meant by saying, as the New Testament often does, that Christians are 'in Christ'.

It is obscure, initially, how one person could be in another. But there are in fact various occasions in human life of this sort of inclusion by one person of another, which I shall call a 'partial merging of identity'. What is important in each case is an expansion of the normal boundaries of what one can wish for oneself, praise and blame in oneself, apologize for and take credit for in oneself. That is, the evaluative boundaries of a person are expanded beyond that person's skin. These cases not only occur, but account for much of what makes a good life. I will start with the relation between a mother and her infant child. We could also take the mothering role, rather than the relation of the biological mother and child. Virginia Held says, repeating Donne's thought about 'interinanimation' though in different language, 'The emotional satisfaction of a person engaged in mothering arises . . . from the health of the relation between the two persons, not the gain that results from an egoistic bargain.'[18] There is a context for thinking about this relation in the work on feminist ethics which I discussed in Chapter 6. Some

---

[17] Matt. 17: 27. See Grotius (1889) 181.
[18] Held (1993) 205. Mothering persons and their children typically do not think of their relation as one governed by contract.

writers in feminist ethics have suggested that we need an approach to personal identity that does not define the self *against* the other, but as understood *through* the other.[19]

It is striking how much of the mother's and child's lives is held in common between them during pregnancy and the child's infancy. There is a life *between* them, in Donne's language. During pregnancy there is a literal inclusion of one human being in another; at birth, the infant is semi-detached. The health of the one, for example, is intimately tied to the health of the other. During pregnancy, the foetus takes in through the placenta much of the same physical substance as the mother. After birth, there is some of the same dependency through nursing. When the mother says, in the first few months after birth, that she will be somewhere, she often means that she and the baby will be there together. The baby will not be like an inanimate appendage, but the two of them will be paying close attention to each other, sometimes to the point of absorption. She is proud of her baby. Or is she proud of herself and her baby? The point is that this is not a good question. The two of them are bonded into a single unit in this evaluation. Suppose I offer to hold the baby, and he is sick all over my shirt. The mother will behave as if she had been sick on my shirt herself. She will go through the offender's tasks of repentance, apology, reparation, and penance. Here there is substitution in the qualified sense: she does it for both of them.

The same two characteristics of representation I mentioned before in connection with ambassador and country apply to mother and child in a more natural and less contractual way. The first truth is that the child experiences along with the mother, and the second is that the child does not have to experience what the mother experiences. The first of these truths can be seen by the remarkable degree to which a child lives through his mother, by an imitation that is not so much play-acting as sympathetic identification. Thus a

---

[19] See Whitbeck (1989) and Ruddick (1989). This is a point Carol Gilligan (1987) makes forcefully. We assume that moral development takes us from independence to mutuality. But after listening to women talk about their own experience, she suggests that it may be typical to develop from the web of relationships that characterize childhood *into* a secure sense of the self as distinct from others. Gilligan refers to the work of Chodorow (1978) 140 f., who claims that in families where the primary care-giver is female, female children develop differently from male children because their initial bond is with a person of the same gender. For the dangers of mothering as a moral paradigm, see Meyers (1987).

child who has done something he knows his mother dislikes may hit himself on the hand, if that is how his mother usually punishes him. The second truth is that the mother faces the dangers and demands of the world for the child. She has to face them because the child cannot face them for himself.

The partial merging of identity is possible within a family beyond the relation of mother to infant. Aristotle first introduces the phrase 'another self' to describe the father's relation to his children. 'A parent loves his children as [he loves] himself. For what has come from him is a sort of other himself; [it is other because] it is separate. Children love a parent because they regard themselves as having come from him.'[20] The father sees in his child another himself, and the child reciprocates (though Aristotle does not say this explicitly). Suppose my wife and I have invited a guest to dinner at our home, and during dinner one of our children does something horrible to the guest. I will feel guilt. This is not merely subjective guilt, but a response to an objective wrong. In part, this is because I am responsible for having put my guest in the situation in which the offence occurred. I have also been responsible for failing to bring up my child to be polite to guests. Is this now the whole of my guilt? No, because there is also my being part of a unit (the family) which is together discredited by the actions of one member. My guilt is not merely retrospective, an acknowledgement of my own past failures in moral education. If I am a sibling of the offender, especially if I am a twin, I will feel the sense of guilt even though I did not have the responsibility for bringing him up. I will still be part of a unit which has together violated the duties of host to guest. If I have the opportunity, I will want to apologize. Moreover, if I do apologize, I can do so on behalf of my family. This is substitution in the qualified sense; I do it for them, and they do it with me. R. M. Hare suggests that 'I' is not wholly a descriptive word but in part prescriptive, and personal identity is accordingly a question of degree. 'I can identify', he says, 'to a greater or lesser extent with the prescriptions of the future inhabitant of my body (if I may be allowed that seriously misleading metaphor), and I can identify with the prescriptions of other people (*my children for example*).'[21] I can apply to myself, even

---

[20] *NE* 8. 12, 1161ᵇ28.

[21] R. M. Hare (1981) 97, emphasis added. There is an interesting literature on moral taint, or moral pollution. We could talk about moral lustre as the positive counterpart. See Appiah (1991).

if I am not the primary agent, what Gibbard calls 'norms which prescribe guilt on the part of the agent and resentment (or anger) on the part of others.'[22]

Aristotle goes on to say that if a child matures into a person of virtue, he can then have this 'other self' relation with his virtuous friends. Thus Cicero tells how the tyrant Dionysius was impressed with the story of Damon and Phintias, two close friends who were disciples of Pythagoras.[23]

One of these youths had been condemned to death, and the other was allowed to stand surety for his appearance. But the first young man turned up punctually at the hour fixed for his own execution and released his friend from his pledge. Dionysius's comment was this: 'I should give a great deal to be enrolled as the third partner in your friendship.'

But Dionysius knew that it was impossible for him to have friends like this. Cicero does not put it this way, but the tyrant's life could no longer be identified with anyone else's life to any great degree. This is an illustration of Aristotle's argument that a decent person is related to himself in various distinctive ways, and has this same kind of relation to his virtuous friends. 'The decent person, then, has each of these features in relation to himself, and is related to his friend as he is to himself, since the friend is another himself.'[24] One of Aristotle's points here is that the two friends have a common affective life, so that they grieve and rejoice together, and a common intellectual life, so that they share a vision of the good. He makes the point that tyrants do not have this kind of friendship.

Another kind of union where incorporation occurs is sexual union, where the two become one flesh. One of the characteristics of sexual union is the sense of being caught up together in a single life between the two. Two people who are fond of each other and have lived together for a long time become, we can say, part of each other; so that when one dies the other is left with the sense that part of herself has died with him.

It is not just in families and close friendships that partial merging of identity occurs. One can be ashamed and proud of things one's colleagues do. There can be partial merging of identity with entertainment and sports figures and with national figures, like the

[22] See Ch. 7 Sect. c.   [23] *Tusculan Disputations* 5 22. 63.
[24] *NE* 9. 4, 1166ᵃ30.

members of a royal family. It is also possible for individuals to merge
themselves to various degrees into groups of smaller and larger size:
clubs and colleges and countries. Socrates thought of the laws and
institutions of Athens as like his parents in making him who he was.
Beyond the nation, there may be wider and wider groupings. In all
these relations from mothering outwards, a partial merging of
identity can be dysfunctional. For example, parents need to
disassociate from their children, and vice versa. I discussed in
Chapter 8 Judge William's warnings about getting trapped by
identification with characters on the stage. Patriotism can be the
source of enormous evil. There are different phenomena here, and I
do not want to suggest they are all examples of a single kind. They all
have in common, however, that they expand the normal evaluative
boundaries of the self beyond a person's skin. Kant's chief difficulty
with the traditional doctrine of the atonement was that he did not see
how guilt could be transmitted from one person to another. But if
the evaluative boundaries can be expanded to different degrees, then
guilt can be shared to different degrees. How much of the guilt will
be distributed between the parties will depend on the nature of the
union between them.

The Bible uses many of the relations that provide a partial
merging of identity as images of our relation to Christ. Thus Christ
compares the relation of mothering; he talks of wanting to take the
children of Jerusalem into his own protection as a mother hen
gathers her brood under her wing.[25] Those who think Christianity is
a religion which reduces followers to infants will take comfort from
this language, but Christ ends the passage by lamenting that the
children of Jerusalem have refused him. Incorporation does not
ignore the decision of the person who is incorporated, though there
are many views within the Christian tradition about how the will of
the believer and God's initiative relate. Christ also uses the language
that we are his friends. The New Testamant uses the image of sexual
union in marriage for the relation between Christ and the church.[26]

There are also several differences between the believer's relation to
Christ and the relation of even the closest of friends; but the
differences do not, I think, destroy the analogy. One difference is
that Christ is no longer present to our senses on this earth. This will
not be an insuperable obstacle to the believer, for she can continue to

[25] Luke 13: 34.   [26] Eph. 5: 32.

think of herself as experiencing the presence of Christ. This experience of Christ being alive and with his disciples, even after his ascension, lies behind some uses of the phrase 'in Christ' in the New Testament.[27] The believers who knew Christ during his ministry on earth seem to have experienced his presence with them after he had gone back to his father.

A second difference between the relationship of close friends and the relationship of Christ to the believer is that the latter is not what Aristotle would call a 'relation of equals'. Christ's relation to the believer may be mutual, in that Christ can be said to be 'in' the believer and the believer can be said to be 'in' Christ.[28] But the relation is not symmetrical. Christ initiates and sustains the relation, and he does so as Lord of it.[29] When Christ dies, he leaves us as our champion; when he rises from the dead, he returns to defend us.

A third difference is the temporal gap of two thousand years. How can incorporation into a life shared with Christ involve sharing in a death which happened two thousand years ago? According to the picture of the atonement I have been presenting, Christ (who is now alive) takes us back through his own death by being our substitute in the sense I have given to this term. Are we supposed to think of some kind of time travel, so that he takes us back with him to the first century AD? Perhaps a better analogy is the kind of incorporation into a community which happens when someone from a different tradition enters an institution with a vivid history. Compare what happens in a close relationship between two people. In talking about forgiveness, I said that after an offence the two parties have to catch up with each other, just as they do after separation by physical distance. They have to go back together over the life they have lived while separated by the offence, so as to make it as if they had been together. Something similar happens when a newcomer joins an institution with a well-established identity. If he wants to belong to

[27] See Dunn (1975) 324. He cites, among many refs., Phil. 4: 13: 'I can do all things through Christ which strengtheneth me.' See also Phil. 2: 19 and 24 and Eph. 3: 12.

[28] Among the biblical authors there is a difference between John, who talks of the believer being in Christ and also Christ being in the believer, and Paul, who talks more readily of the believer being in Christ than the other way round. See Moule (1977) 56–8 and 64 for a list of the Johannine texts. But see also Gal. 2: 20, and the Pauline notion of the infusion of the Holy Spirit.

[29] See John 20: 21: 'As the Father hath sent me, even so send I you.'

this new community, he will have to go back over the history and, as far as possible, feel the high points and low points himself. He will want to make it as if he had belonged from the beginning. He may be asked, in extreme cases, to sign a form of subscription to historical documents which arose out of these high points or low points and which have had a formative influence on the life of the community. Incorporation thus has a retroactive component. He is being incorporated into the past of the institution as well as into its present and future. If the incorporation works, he will start to feel proud of some parts of this history and ashamed of other parts. In the same way when I marry into a family, I am taking on myself a history of relations, especially with my new parents-in-law. If my wife has been hurt by them, then I will have been too in my partially merged identity and I will come to experience this more as merging proceeds. Marriage has a retroactive component, just as other forms of incorporation do. What makes the relation with Christ different is that he is different. According to Christian doctrine he died, rose, and lives with us two thousand years later.[30] This two-thousand-year gap is not recapitulated in our relation with anyone else who lives with us. The retroactive component in our incorporation, therefore, takes us to a past more remote than any we can envisage in purely human relationships. But the retroactivity itself is not, I think, unintelligible.

I have drawn my examples from everyday experience in order to understand better the sense in which one person can take on the offender's tasks from another, if the two of them have a partially merged identity. In such cases there will be substitution in the qualified sense I have tried to define. One person will perform the tasks for the other; but this will be consistent with also saying that the other shares in the performance of the tasks. Substitution of this kind can happen throughout the continuum of relationship, from mothering outwards. Thus one side's champion in an ancient or medieval battle carries his side with him in his victory or defeat. If he wins, they win; and if he loses, they lose. But he is still fighting instead of them. We can say that Christ is the primary sufferer in his

[30] Another way of thinking about this question is to stress the texts that suggest Christ is still suffering or offering his sacrifice on our behalf, so that the temporal gap disappears. See Rev. 13: 8 and Heb. 8: 2. The hard thing is to say in what sense Christ's sacrifice at Golgotha is then complete.

death; in this sense he died for us. But because he incorporates us into him, we become the secondary sufferers, sharing in his death. If one died for all, then all were all dead.

Being incorporated into this new life does not mean that the believer ceases to experience the pull of the old one. There is likely to be a tension within her experience; for 'if we say we have no sin, we deceive ourselves'.[31] There is therefore a combination, hard to understand, of the conviction that she is a new creature, no longer a slave to sin, with the recognition that her life continues to manifest the old patterns of repeated failure. In fact, it can be observed in the lives of the saints that their sense of their own sin gets stronger as they seem, to the outward observer, to be progressing in godliness. The oddness of this is that, as Paul says, 'All of us who were baptized into Christ Jesus were baptized into his death.'[32] Our old self 'was crucified with him, so that the body of sin might be rendered powerless, that we should no longer be slaves to sin'. We saw this tension already recognized in Kant, who distinguished between the revolution of the will (as seen by God) and the gradual reform experienced by us. Reform is compatible with the continued experience of temptation and defeat. It is important to stress this because otherwise the doctrine of our incorporation sounds self-congratulatory. What has changed after incorporation is the availability of the new life; there may still be a gap between what we ought to do and what we do.

Sacrifice

Paul often uses the language of sacrifice to illuminate the sense in which Christ associates us with himself in his dying.[33] In some sense the ritual killing of the sacrificial animal in Hebrew practice was supposed to remove the sin from the unclean offender. It is very hard for us to give any sense to the claim that a goat can become guilty of anything, let alone guilty of the sin of its owner, or of a

---

[31] 1 John 1: 8.

[32] Rom. 6: 3–6 (NIV). Paul does not talk about the coexistence of the new man and the old man, although he does talk about the persistence of sin. See Hoekema (1989) 210.

[33] See Dunn (1975) and (1991), esp. 40–8. There is a useful treatment in Gunton (1989) ch. 5. He makes the important point that we do not need to be limited to a single account of the atonement, and that the Bible contains a rich variety of images to explain it.

whole people.[34] The notion of identification seems, however, to be central to the ritual. In one part of the ritual the offerer laid his hand on the beast's head, thereby identifying himself with the beast, or at least indicating that the beast in some way belonged to him. This same action has significance in other ritual contexts.[35] In the Day of Atonement ceremony the priest lays the sins of the people on the head of a second goat, who is driven into the desert.[36] Only a perfect goat can be used, because it is then clear that when it is driven out it is not suffering for its own defect but for the sin which has been laid onto it. This is the context for understanding the language of sacrifice in the New Testament. When Paul describes Christ's death as a sacrifice, he probably means us to think of a sharing of sin from us to Christ; this time, though, the agent of the sharing is not the sinner but God. Thus Paul says, 'For he hath made him [Jesus] to be sin for us, him who knew no sin.'[37] When Peter talks about Christ's death, he refers to Isaiah. He says, 'He himself bore our sins in his body on the cross, so that we might die to sins and live for righteousness. By his wounds you have been healed.' He is referring to Isaiah's prophecy, 'The chastisement of our peace was upon him; and with his stripes we are healed.'[38]

If we understand sacrifice this way, we already have a doctrine of penal substitution. Both parts of this qualified notion of substitution are present: the animal suffers instead of the sinner, and the sinner is

[34] Strictly, what the goat becomes is unclean. 'Uncleanness' is a term of the holiness code. Cleanness is a state intermediate between holiness and uncleanness; sanctification elevates the clean into the holy, and pollution degrades the clean into the unclean. Now it is possible for the uncleanness of a man to extend to his whole household, including his animals. In the sacrifice, however, the sinner lays his hand on a goat which is *not* already unclean, but is set aside as holy. It is nevertheless because the goat is already seen as identified with the household that its punishment can be taken for the punishment of its owner.

[35] Lev. 4: 4–33. For the significance of the hand, see also Wenham (1979) 93–6. But there is a large anthropological literature on sacrifice, of which I have read only a small part, and I cannot comment on it. In Num. 27: 18, 23 and Deut. 34: 9, Moses lays his hands on Joshua, so that Joshua becomes, as it were, a second Moses. In Num. 8: 10, the people lay their hands on the Levites, so that the Levites can take the place of the first-born who are owed to the Lord. In Lev. 24: 14, those who have witnessed a blasphemer put their hands on his head before he is executed, seemingly because they have been contaminated by his sin by witnessing it.

[36] For the Day of Atonement ceremony, see Lev. 16.

[37] 2 Cor. 5: 21. See also Rom. 3: 25; 5: 9; 8: 3; 1 Cor. 5: 7; Eph. 1: 7; 2: 13; Col. 1: 20.   [38] 1 Pet. 2: 24 (NIV); Isa. 53: 5–6, 12.

identified with the animal who suffers. Penal substitution is not an alternative view of the atonement to one that emphasizes sacrifice; it is rather one understanding of what Christ's sacrifice means in the context of Hebrew sacrificial cult.[39] Sacrifice, on this understanding, is not merely giving something valuable to God, but giving to death an animal as the primary victim instead of oneself. 'One may regard the animal either as dying in the worshipper's place as his substitute, or as receiving the death penalty because of the sin transferred to it by the laying on of hands.'[40] Psalm 51: 14–17 may have been recited during sacrifices, and it perhaps expresses the other side of substitution. The animal's death is not pleasing to God unless it carries with it the worshipper's own internal brokenness of spirit.

Another place where we can see the suggestion that we share Christ's death is the sacraments of baptism and Eucharist. We are said to be baptized into Christ's death and to be united with his death in the breaking of the bread. One way to think of baptism is to compare what Paul says about being baptized into Moses.[41] The parallel is a rich one, but also shows up a difference. The Israelites who went down into the Red Sea were separated decisively from their life in Egypt and were liberated into becoming a new community with a new mission. The subsequent generations of Israel became a continuation of God's elect community by retroactive incorporation into what God did through Moses. The baptism into Christ's death is similar in that it is a baptism into the life of a new community, the church. It is different, however, in that the people of Israel did not go on living a life together with Moses. There was not a continuing life 'between' them. But the baptism into Christ's death is also into a life in which he is still participating and which he is directing. To put the matter this way is not to say that we become divine (though that is an alternative which some traditions within Christianity have taken, and I will mention it in the next section). It is to say that the life of the church is a life between us and Christ, which we enter at baptism. He is divine and we are not, but he has

---

[39] See e.g. Erickson (1983), esp. 812 f. Apart from Paul's letter to the Romans, relevant passages include 2 Cor. 5: 21 and Gal. 3: 13.

[40] Wenham (1979) 62.

[41] 1 Cor. 10: 1–2 (NIV): 'Our forefathers were all under the cloud, and all passed through the sea. They were all baptized into Moses in the cloud and in the sea.' See Smedes (1970) 143: 'They died and rose again with Moses.'

incorporated us into a life together with him; and this life (and so our life) is one which is taken with him through his sacrifice and resurrection.

One way to think of the Eucharist is that the elements which are to be consecrated, the bread and the wine, are brought out from the congregation in order to represent the congregation itself. In some churches this is shown physically, when the elements are located where the congregation comes in at the beginning of the service, and they are not taken up to the altar until the time of consecration. With this symbolism, it is possible to think of the consecration as taking the congregation into the body and blood of Christ, so that when for example the bread is broken, the congregation is 'broken' with it. There is a long tradition of taking the symbolism this way. Thus Augustine says that 'the whole redeemed community, that is to say the congregation and fellowship of the saints, is offered to God as a universal sacrifice, through the great Priest who offered himself in his suffering for us'.[42] In the Eucharist Christ is thought of as the priest offering his body, and this body is in turn thought of in three ways: the human body which suffered on Calvary, the bread and wine on the altar, and the faithful themselves. The Eucharist thus expresses our union with Christ in his death, and it can be understood as expressing both that Christ died for us and that we die in him.

b. JUSTIFICATION

In justification God sees us to be or declares us to be just, or in the right, before him.[43] We leave the condition of being in the wrong before God, as the pastor expresses the condition of the exception at the end of *Either/Or*, volume 2. God thus forgives us; he decides to accept what has been done by the offender's substitute. I am going to proceed by contrasting three views of justification, which derive

---

[42] *De Civitate Dei* 10. 6: Corpus Christianorum, Series Latina, XLVII. 279. See Bonner (1991) 109–11. I do not want here to discuss the vexed question of what the sense is, if any, in which the sacrifice is repeated. Before Augustine, Cyprian had used the idea of all the church being made into the bread which is broken. See Cyprian, letter 63, 13.

[43] The Greek term translated as 'justification' and its cognates do not always mean this in the NT. For a discussion of some passages, see Murray (1977) 204 f. See also Hooker (1990) 27–33.

from a particular context of discussion. I want to deny one interpretation of what I have been saying about 'a partial merging of identity', and I want to fasten this interpretation onto Kant.

There is a tradition in the understanding of justification which emerges in the following quotation: 'The effect of justification is primarily negative: the cancellation of the judgment against us.'[44] Justification is here distinguished from the giving of new life, which is the positive work of the Holy Spirit. Christ's righteousness is said to be imputed to us in justification, but not imparted to us. Justification is here forensic, a matter of declaring the person righteous, as a judge does in acquitting the accused. It is said not to be a matter of making people righteous or altering their actual spiritual condition. Christ's righteousness is, on this account, imputed to us externally, like a robe draped over us, and God then sees us as just even though there has been no internal change in us.

There are several difficulties with this view. The first is that in its unqualified form it attributes to God a species of self-deception. Suppose I am thinking of buying a house whose structure I can see to be fundamentally unsound. If I tell the owner to put new cladding on it, I may disguise the cracks; but I will be deceiving myself if I then buy the house. How can God see us as righteous if we are still just as rotten inside, but wearing Christ's robe of righteousness? A second difficulty is that if justification is negative in this sense, this devalues the human response and makes problematic the necessity of faith for salvation. Taken to its extreme, the doctrine of negative justification becomes the doctrine of eternal justification, that faith is merely the registering of what has already occurred before the foundation of the world.[45]

A second view of justification can be found in the position ascribed by Calvin to Osiander, a Lutheran who spent the crown of his career in Königsberg. This is the doctrine of 'essential righteousness'. Osiander's position (as Calvin describes it) is close to the doctrine as translated within the pure religion of reason by Kant.[46] Calvin says of Osiander that 'he has clearly expressed himself as not content with that righteousness which has been

---

[44] Erickson (1983) 961.   [45] See Berkouwer (1954) 143–51.
[46] It is tempting to suppose that Kant knew of Osiander's position, since they were both conspicuous residents of Königsberg. I do not know, however, of any evidence that Kant was deliberately following Osiander.

acquired for us by Christ's obedience and sacrificial death, but pretends that we are substantially righteous in God by the infusion both of his essence and of his quality'.[47] One objection here is that Osiander makes the infused righteousness a merit of ours on the basis of which God can then declare us righteous; this threatens to undermine the doctrine 'by grace alone', according to which there is nothing in us which merits God's declaration of our righteousness, even his previous gift to us.[48] The second objection is more important for present purposes. The doctrine of essential righteousness holds to a 'gross mingling' of the divine and the human in us. Calvin says that Osiander 'throws in a mixture of substances by which God—transfusing himself into us, as it were—makes us part of himself'.[49]

It is possible to interpret what I have said about 'a partial merging of identity' as a statement of the doctrine of essential righteousness. The question can be put this way: when Christ incorporates us into himself, do we become part of God? An alternative way to think of the merging is to use Donne's language of 'interinanimation'. Incorporation on this picture involves not our becoming part of God, but Christ and ourselves becoming involved in a common life between us. Kant's translation of atonement and justification within

---

[47] *Institutes*, III. xi. 5.

[48] Calvin is concerned to deny that there is a causal connection between what we become through grace and God's acceptance of us. The contrary view is expressed by the Council of Trent, which starts by affirming that justification 'is not only the forgiving of sins, but also sanctification and renewal of the inward man through the free acceptance of grace and of the gifts through which man becomes righteous in place of unrighteous' (Trent, session 6, ch. 7). It goes on: 'If any say that the sinner is justified through faith alone, in the sense that nothing else is necessary that cooperates to obtain the grace of justification and that it is not necessary for the sinner to prepare himself by means of his own will, *anathema sit*' (ibid. ch. 11). Osiander would deny that he is saying something inconsistent with 'by grace alone'. He would point to his claim that essential righteousness is infused by God.

[49] *Institutes*, III. xi. 5. Part of Calvin's *animus* against Osiander is that Calvin wants to deny that divine nature is infused into us, as though we cease being merely human. This is true also of Calvin's doctrine of the creation of human beings, 'which is not inpouring, but the beginning of essence out of nothing' (*Institutes*, I. xv. 5). The Spirit's work in regeneration does not, he says, infuse into us a bit of God (ibid. II. i. 9). Calvin would reject the doctrine of Aristotle, who advises us about happiness: 'Such a life would be superior to the human level. For someone will live it not in so far as he is a human being, but in so far as he has some divine element in him' (*NE* 10. 7, 1177^b27). For a more recent account like Osiander's see Mascall (1946) 109, who says that we are lifted out of the status of mere creatures and given a share in the life of God.

the pure religion of reason puts him, I think, on the side of Osiander. Kant pictures the moral disposition as the spirit of God within us, and he thinks we can become conscious of this in ourselves through practical faith. 'In other words', Kant says, 'he, and he alone, is entitled to look upon himself as an object not unworthy of divine approval who is conscious of such a moral disposition as enables him to have a well-grounded confidence in himself.'[50] This is the picture of the moral life that Kierkegaard gives in the life of Judge William.

Calvin's own position is different from both of the two just given. I will quote from his exegesis of Romans 4: 25, 'He was put to death for our sins, and raised for our justification.' Calvin interprets as follows:

This is as if he had said: 'Sin was taken away by his death; righteousness was revived and restored by his resurrection.' . . . So then, let us remember that whenever mention is made of his death alone, we are to understand at the same time what belongs to his resurrection. Also, the same *synecdoche* applies to the word 'resurrection': whenever it is mentioned separately from death, we are to understand it as including what has to do especially with his death.

Finally, Calvin quotes Romans 6: 4, 'We are engrafted in the likeness of his death, so that sharing in his resurrection we might walk in newness of life', and he says, of this text and also of Colossians 3: 1–5, 'By these words we are not only invited through the example of the risen Christ to strive after newness of life; but we are taught that we are reborn into righteousness through his power.'[51]

---

[50] *Rel.* 55 (62). Kant's account of justification is that God acts graciously towards us 'so far as man does endeavor with all his strength to do the will of God', (*Rel.* 110 (120)).

[51] *Institutes*, II. xvi. 13. Calvin's separate commentary on Rom. is not entirely consistent, for he there refuses 'to refer this second clause [of *Rom.* 4: 25] to newness of life.' Cf the commentary on Rom. 4: 25 of a more recent Calvinist, Buswell (1962) 190: 'The thought here is not that our justification is brought about by his resurrection, but that, having accomplished our justification, He was, on account of that accomplishment, raised from the dead. The resurrection is not a part of Christ's justifying work as such, but it is the demonstrative indication of the victory of that work upon the cross.' Buswell's reading is motivated by the desire to be faithful to the notion of negative justification. But Calvin in the *Institutes* is much closer to the natural reading of the text. He might say to Buswell, 'God's declaration of us as righteous and the new life in us are both the effect of both Christ's work on the cross and his resurrection; you can, if you like, mention the cross alone, but you do so by synecdoche.'

When Calvin talks about our being 'reborn into righteousness', he is identifying justification with the new life. It is through the resurrection that righteousness is said to be restored and (our) life raised up, and this is a manifestation of the power and efficacy of Christ's death. Whenever, he is telling us, Christ's death alone is mentioned in the context of justification, we are to understand also what belongs to his resurrection. This is invaluable advice for understanding Calvin's own treatment of justification. I have described the relationship between the believer and Christ in terms of incorporation into a common life. Calvin describes it as a mystical union.[52] The emphasis is not on Christ's righteousness being external to us, but on the unity he establishes between himself and us. 'We do not, therefore, contemplate him outside ourselves from afar in order that his righteousness may be imputed to us but because we put on Christ and are engrafted into his body—in short, because he deigns to make us one with him.' Calvin, in other words, has a doctrine of positive justification as well as a doctrine of negative justification.[53] In this respect the view he presents is like Kant's *untranslated* doctrine, which holds that God judges us 'through a purely intellectual intutition'; that is, he creates us a certain way in seeing us that way.[54]

In this way Calvin differs from the view that justification is purely external.[55] He also differs from the doctrine of essential righteousness. What becomes part of us, on his view, is not divinity but humanity as it was supposed to be, the new man. There are, however, many branches of the Christian tradition which would disagree.

c. SANCTIFICATION

I will end this chapter by talking about the new life and the process by which a person becomes a new creation. 'Sanctification' and

---

[52] 'That joining together of head and members, that indwelling of Christ in our hearts—in short, that mystical union' (*Institutes*, III. xi. 10).

[53] See Murray (1977) 207: '[Soteric justification is the action in which God] actually causes to be the relation which in justification is declared to be.' The idea is that God *constitutes* the righteousness which he declares. See Hoekema (1989) 181: 'Justification includes more than the forgiveness of sins; it also embraces, on its positive side, our adoption as children of God.' See also O'Donovan (1986) 253–6.

[54] *Rel.* 60 (67): see Ch. 2 Sec. *b* above.

[55] *Institutes*, III. xi. 11. But Calvin does allow that God's receiving us into grace and his bestowing the spirit of adoption can in principle be distinguished, though they happen at the same time.

'regeneration' are both terms for this process, though they are used differently in different traditions.[56] I will start by talking about the corporate nature of the new life into which we are incorporated. I will then return to Kant and see what difference it makes to our belief in the possibility of goodness if we return back from the pure religion of reason into what Kant calls historical faith. This is what I called in Chapter 2 the third experiment.

The Life of the Body

Theologians sometimes distinguish Christ's active from his passive obedience. We can think of Christ as taking on humanity in the incarnation, and by his life and death and resurrection transforming it. His *active* obedience is his conforming his human life to the standard of God's law; his *passive* obedience is his taking on our sins and their punishment.[57] Through his active obedience he is transforming the life into which believers will be incorporated.[58] Those in Christ are, accordingly, able to live this new kind of life. To return to the image of mother and child, when the mother starts to live a certain quality of life herself she changes the character of the life which she and the child share. In Christian terms this new life, which is gradually realized in our own lives, is corporate, the life of a body. Here again Kant is useful. He too wants to say that the victory of the good over the evil principle requires a visible representation of an invisible kingdom of God on earth, and that we can reverence Christ as the founder of the first true *church*.[59] In this true church, we become instruments of good to each other rather than instruments of evil. As things now are, because of radical evil, people have only to be around other people 'for them mutually to corrupt each other's predispositions and make one another evil'.[60] By Christian doctrine the life into which we are incorporated is stronger, in Donne's term 'abler', than our lives on their own. This is one reason for not despairing about the moral demand; we now have greater resources

---

[56] Calvin's use of 'regeneration' makes it describe a process. Characteristically, he wants both to distinguish between justification and regeneration (which happens over time), and to maintain 'a mutual and indivisible connection'. See *Institutes*, III. xiii. 5: 'the gift of regeneration, which as it is always imperfect in this flesh, so contains in itself manifold grounds of doubt.' For a different Calvinist usage, see Buswell (1962) 171.   [57] See Berkhof (1936) 132–6.

[58] Thus Calvin says that 'Christ's shed blood served, not only as a satisfaction, but also as a laver to wash away our corruption' (*Institutes*, II. xvi. 6–7).

[59] *Rel.* 146–7 (159).   [60] *Rel.* 85 (94).

to draw upon. This is true not only because of our individual incorporation, the union between the individual and Christ, but also because the life into which we are incorporated is a communal life. It is not quite true to say that each believer is married to Christ individually. It is the church that is the bride of Christ. We cannot on our own live the kind of life God wants us to lead, because that kind of life requires the assistance of the other people he has incorporated with us. The leg cannot live the new life by itself, and neither can the hand. What God intends is for us to be vessels of his grace to each other; and this grace of his coming through each other helps us live in a way that pleases him.[61] The new life is something we live *together*.

Kant gives us in the *Groundwork* a model for this kind of life, even though he does not help us see how we can live it. His model thus serves the function of the law, as Luther describes it, the function of accusation. In Kant's examples of the application of the categorical imperative he says that we have to develop our talents and help those in need. His argument is that we will have ends that require the help of others if we are going to reach them; and the relevant others will not be able to do so unless they develop their talents. We are linked together by our needs and abilities into a single unit, or kingdom, which we must be prepared to will into existence as a whole. It contains our needs (for even in the true church we will be creatures of need), and it contains other people with the developed abilities to meet our needs; but it also contains the needs of others, and our developed abilities to meet their needs. As I said in Chapter 1, we have to will what is consistent with the operation of this kingdom as a whole, since the categorical imperative does not allow us to make reference to our particular positions within it.

This is one way to state the moral demand, namely that we have to live as members of this kingdom. But, as we saw with Kierkegaard's second ethics, the moral demand and our capacities are both changed by our incorporation into Christ. Christian doctrine tells us that we are incorporated into the kind of life displayed in Christ's active obedience, which is itself a life of incorporating others. The author of the first letter of John says (in the New International Version), 'We have seen and heard him, and we proclaim him to you

---

[61] In the language I used in Ch. 8, there is a shift in the second ethics in the demand and the support available.

so that you can have fellowship with us just as we have fellowship with the Father and his Son . . . But if anyone obeys his word, God's love is truly made complete in him. . . . This is how we know we are in him.' He continues, 'This is how we know what love is: Jesus Christ laid down his life for us. And we ought to lay down our lives for our brothers. If anyone has material possessions and sees his brother in need but has no pity on him, how can the love of God be in him?'[62] There is here the idea of a widening circle of fellowship. It starts between the Father and the Son; and the Son then comes to be with us and gives himself for us, so that he establishes fellowship between himself and us and thus between the Father and us; then we proclaim the Son to others, and establish fellowship with them, and they come to be included in a relation to the Son and the Father. This relationship between the Son and us and between us and others is characterized by laying down one's life. It is not merely that we imitate him, but that this kind of life is present in us because of our union with him.

This is love: not that we loved God, but that he loved us and sent his Son as an atoning sacrifice for our sins. Dear friends [in Greek, *agapetoi*, 'beloved'], since God so loved us, we also ought to love one another. No one has ever seen God; but if we love one another, God lives in us and his love is made complete in us.[63]

The view of incorporation into Christ I have been proposing is that we are incorporated into a common life which we share with him, and the character of this life is itself one of incorporating others.[64] The kind of love we have received from him moves us to give the same kind of love to others. Thus Paul speaks of 'always carrying around in our body the death of Jesus, so that the life of Jesus may also be revealed in our body. . . . So death is at work in us, but life is at work in you.'[65] He says that he becomes 'poor, yet making many rich', the same language he is going to use to describe what Christ does for us.[66] He says that 'we can comfort those in any

---

[62] I John 1: 3; 2: 5; 3: 16–17.

[63] I John 4: 10–12. John does not say, however, that the disciples are 'in' each other.

[64] Paul says that he 'fills up that which is behind of the afflictions of Christ' (Col. I: 24); and see Hooker (1990) 24, 64. [65] 2 Cor. 4: 10–12 (NIV).

[66] 2 Cor. 6: 10. See also 1: 4–5. Similarly, he is weak so that the Corinthians can be strong (2 Cor. 13: 9, and see 13: 4).

trouble with the comfort we ourselves have received from God', and he goes on to explain that this works because 'just as you share in our sufferings, so also you share in our comfort'. Paul's view in these passages seems to be that we recapitulate Christ's identification with us (his including us in his dying and rising again) by identifying with others. It is not that we *save* others, in the way that he saves us. But we can try to *love* others in the way he loves us.

I will return to three examples of the way in which Christians are called to share in Christ's work of incorporating others. The first is that we are called (as in John's letter) to make a sacrifice of material goods to meet other people's needs, and also to give of our time and abilities. I mentioned in Chapter 6 that generosity of this kind is easier if it comes out of a sense of being ourselves the recipients of God's generosity, a spirit of repentance rather than self-righteousness, and a recognition of being under covenant to give as God has given to us. It is also easier if we can feel part of a community which is meeting the needs of others, so that we can identify which helping projects are ours. This way we are not so overwhelmed with the scale and anonymity of the need. It is by being included in such a community that we are given the impulse to extend its reach.

A second example is that it is possible to identify with another person's suffering in such a way as to reduce it. This can seem puzzling; as when Sheldon Vanauken describes taking on his wife's fear of death, as though she had given him that burden.[67] Part of this is intelligible as the comfort in communication and the relief from the isolation involved in some kinds of distress. But it is worth asking *why* we are comforted to have someone else, for example, grieve with us. After all, the other's grief merely adds to the sum of grief in the world. We are comforted, presumably, because when we share the grief or fear, our own is reduced. But how is this accomplished? I think we can understand this by analogy with our incorporation into Christ. The grief or fear can become part of the common life between us; and if one party is for the time being stronger, he or she can bear the greater share of it. This role may

---

[67] Vanauken (1977) 165: 'Davy's burden was not death but the fear of death. I asked her to give me that burden, a real handing over, like surrendering a trunk to a porter. An act of handing over. And I *took* it—also act. I then entered into the fear, *her* fear, with all my heart and mind and imagination, felt it, carried it along with my own fear, which was also real but other. And her burden grew lighter.'

alternate in human relationships. If one is fearful, the other may be calm; and then if the second gets fearful, the first may become calm. But the relation may not be symmetrical in this way. People who have suffered a great deal themselves may have a greater ability to help others who are suffering.[68] The survivor can invite the sufferer into her own life by the kind of partial merging of identity I have been talking about. This invitation can have a retroactive dimension into the survivor's past as well as her present. This kind of incorporation can be exhausting. I am thinking of victims of abuse who have survived and have been able then to help other victims. A person may be giving up huge amounts of time and energy, to the sacrifice of her other concerns. Less straightforwardly, by incorporating a new person into her own past she has to experience that past over again; but the fruit can be that both of them come out at the other end with the healing shared between them as well. It is easier for someone who has experienced being incorporated (by God or by other people) to do this for someone else.

Another example of this kind of incorporating others is what I called in Chapter 9 'vicarious forgiveness'. This occurs when one person in a relationship does something that hurts the other so seriously that there is nothing the offender can do to make it good. If the victim forgives anyway, the offender can be brought to share the victim's defeat of the forces of alienation caused by the offence. If we have experienced this sort of forgiveness ourselves (from God and from other people), we can then more easily forgive others in this way.

These are three examples of ways in which the new life is lived together. The account has admittedly been influenced by Christian doctrine; but this is not an objection, for I am trying to describe what the life of the church can be like. It is the presence among Christ's people of the life in union with him, which we live by trying to love others in the way he has loved us.

Moral Faith Revisited

I will, for the close of this chapter, return to Kant and the third experiment that we can make with the idea of the two concentric circles of reason and historical faith.[69] The experiment is to see if

---

[68] The reverse can also happen. Suffering can lead to a low tolerance for helping with other people's troubles. See Neill (1955) 111.   [69] *Rel.* II (12).

there are parts of our moral belief and practice (the inner circle) which require support from beliefs and practices which belong to the outer circle. We can start with the question of what morality is aiming at. Kant said that the moral good has, as its two components, the agent's own virtue and the happiness of others. It does not contain the agent's own happiness directly, since this is not directly a moral good; and it does not contain the virtue of others, since 'it is self-contradictory to require that I do (make it my duty to do) something that only the other himself can do'.[70] Nevertheless, Kant argued that the virtue of others is a constraint on my ability to will their happiness morally. In the fragment of a moral catechism at the end of the *Metaphysics of Morals*, the pupil ventures that he would share happiness with others and make them happy and satisfied too. The teacher then replies, 'Now that proves that you have a good enough *heart*; but let us see whether you have a good *head* to go along with it. Would you really give a lazy fellow soft cushions so that he could pass his life away in sweet idleness?' More such questions follow, and the pupil is led to see that 'even if you had all happiness in your hands and, along with it, the best will, you still would not give it without consideration to anyone who put out his hand for it; instead you would first try to find out to what extent each was worthy of happiness'.[71] What the moral agent is required to do is to make the ends of others (that is, their happiness) her own ends as far as she can; and the moral law itself constrains *which* ends of others she can share. On this picture she is aiming at being a morally good person herself and at getting other people what they want as long as this is morally permitted. In Chapter 6 I gave some reasons for doubting Kant's universalism. But the picture I have just given of what the moral agent is aiming at does not yet specify what the phrases 'morally good' and 'morally permitted' mean, and I do not see any objection to it.

But how can we live like this? Here we are back with Spener's problem about the possibility of goodness. How can we give the ends of others and our own obedience to the moral law this kind of priority? The moral agent has to believe, Kant said, that the revolution of the will is possible, and that it has actually taken place inside her. He held that humans start their lives with the propensity to evil, even though they have an initial predisposition to the good,

---

[70] *MM* 191 (386).   [71] *MM* 269 (481).

and he thought that we had to believe in divine assistance in accomplishing the revolution of the will and in sustaining the moral life. I think he is right that it is hard to believe in our own and others' goodness, given how entrenched we experience evil to be both in ourselves and in the world outside ourselves. Kant hoped to shed light on the possibility of the revolution of the will (by which the bondage to evil is removed) by appealing to the mysteries of divine call, atonement, and election. But I argued that his treatment of these mysteries was not able to accomplish this result, because of his initial premiss that the Son of God should be understood as mankind in its moral perfection. This is a symptom, we can now see, of a larger mistake in Kant. He is too restrictive about what moral thinking is like, and this then makes him too restrictive in his moral theology. If I was right in Chapter 6, we should allow that moral thinking can include ineliminable singular reference. It can include, we can now say, singular reference to God. There is nothing that practical reason forbids in such reference, unless we define 'Reason' as requiring the elimination of particulars. Particular moral judgements can give reasons for action. Even if we wanted to include only general revelation in saving faith, this would not require restricting general revelation to statements or commands in purely universal terms. For there could be general revelation about a particular divine being, and in fact the belief in a supreme God above all other gods is strikingly pervasive across the cultures of the world. If we assume that there is a God who is not merely human moral perfection, but a divine person intervening in human history, we can think of him as enabling us to accomplish a change of heart. What I have suggested is that he does so by incorporating us into a new kind of life, which we did not have the capacity to live before his intervention. This was the function of God's assistance in the three-part structure of morality discussed in Chapter 1; the being who can live a holy life intervenes to make possible the improvement of our capacities so that we can live the kind of life he wants us to live. Suppose there is a God like this, who not only makes these demands of us, but helps us reach them. Should we not ask him for this? In Christian doctrine God has given us a sense of the demand and also a sense of the possibility of his assistance, just so that we *will* ask him. I have not given an argument, however, that living a morally good life requires belief in God, only that it requires belief in extra-human assistance. The Christian doctrines of atonement, justification, and sanctification provide a version of such assistance, and I have looked at a few rivals. I have also tried to counter some objections, that the doctrine is unintelligible or that belief in the doctrine is inconsistent with the nature of practical reason. To try to show that Christian doctrine is required would be far more ambitious.

One major difficulty with sustaining the moral life is that our own experience is one of continuing moral failure. It would be hard to take our own lives as evidence of moral progress, even if it were in fact correct for us to take them as such evidence. The failures are too vivid. One work of the Holy Spirit, as Kant translated it, is to give us the assurance that the revolution of the will has in fact taken place. In Kant's translation this is not very helpful, because the Spirit is just the moral disposition itself, and the assurance comes just from the actions we perform in accordance with it. If there is a God active on our behalf, he may give us through his Spirit the assurance that he has accomplished this work in us, and that he will not abandon those he has once adopted as his own. Again, as with the doctrines of salvation, I have not given an argument that morality requires the belief that God has done or will do these things. But we do commit ourselves to long-term undertakings like marriage and raising children when the empirical evidence, from our experience of our own lives and the lives of others, is against the chances of success. If we are going to do this and persevere in these undertakings we need some assurance beyond the merely human that we are not just self-deluded.

The moral agent has to believe, I have argued, that the world is the kind of place in which a person does not have to do what is morally wrong in order to be happy. She should believe in what I called the highest good in the less ambitious sense, in the existence of a system whereby virtue is made consistent with happiness in her life as a whole. Given our experience of moral evil in the world, and the great unlikelihood of our own happiness, this is a hard belief to hold. Since so much of our misery is caused by other people, it is not much help to be told (in Kant's translated version) that humanity in its moral perfection is running the world, as king of the kingdom of ends. I argued that we need to believe in someone or something not merely human to sustain the moral order of the world.

Finally, Kant has a reading of traditional Christian eschatology. 'As regards its guidance by Providence, the kingdom of heaven is represented in this historical account not only as being brought ever nearer, in an approach delayed at certain times yet never wholly interrupted, but also as arriving.'[72] Kant, in other words, suggests for us not merely moral faith but also moral *hope*.[73] The relation between the two is that if we can hope that the highest good in the more ambitious sense of Chapter 3 will be actual, then we can have the faith that it is possible; though hoping that it will be actual is not required by believing that it is possible. Moral hope is the belief in the eventual triumph of the good, and the belief that we are, by incorporation, part of that good. It is hard to have this hope, given how often we experience the victory of evil in history and in ourselves.

There is a large exegetical question about whether Kant supposed we had to hope for a fully realized triumph of the good on earth. I suggested in Chapter 3 that he did not suppose this. On the other hand, he did not think that the triumph of the good was confined to heaven. Rather, he thought that we should have the faith that it has started already, though imperfectly, and we should have the hope that it will be approximated on earth and perfectly realized in heaven. In any case, his translated account of eschatology is in trouble. If we start from the premiss of his translated version that the Son of God is humanity in its complete moral perfection, we cannot generate the kind of moral hope Kant wanted. For by his own premiss mankind is under the evil maxim, and we mutually corrupt one another's moral dispositions. How are we supposed to *get ourselves* into 'a system of well-disposed men, in which and through whose unity alone the highest moral good can come to pass'?[74] Kant recognized that the highest good in the more ambitious sense 'requires the presupposition of another idea, namely, that of a higher moral Being through whose universal dispensation the forces of separate individuals, insufficient in themselves, are united for a common end'. But if this higher moral Being is humanity in its moral perfection, it is not clear that it can help humanity in the required way. As Kant himself said, 'To found a moral people of

---

[72] *Rel.* 124 (134).

[73] The difference between faith and hope can be drawn differently: see O'Donovan (1986) 253. What I have in mind is that moral faith is the belief that the world is so ordered that my continued well-being is consistent with my trying to live a life that seems to me morally good. Moral hope is the belief that the world will at some point attain what Kant calls 'a (divine) ethical state' (*Rel.* 113 (122)).

[74] *Rel.* 89 (98).

God is therefore a task whose consummation can be looked for *not from men* but only from God himself.'[75] If we assume that there is a God active in human history, providing us with the means to accomplish the kind of unity he intends us to have, then we are free to hope that he will eventually prevail.

Again, I have not produced an argument that morality requires moral hope in the eventual triumph of the kingdom of God. But the vision of a world in which everyone is happy and everyone is good draws out both our engagement and our disappointment with the world as we experience it. It is a standard against which we see ourselves as partly succeeding and partly failing. Given our experience of the world, hope for an eventual reaching of this ideal requires belief in either God's assistance or some substitute. I am not claiming, however, that belief in the eventual victory of good over evil *on earth* is part of our morality. I think this belief waxes and wanes. It was strong at the end of the nineteenth century, and it is strong in some movements at the end of the twentieth. The belief in an eventual victory *in time*, as with a final judgement at the end of history, is more pervasive but still not a large-scale consensus. What seems to me definitely part of the common morality is the belief in the priority of good over evil in the basic order of things. This is not necessarily the same as victory in time. In Aristotle, for example, there is not a last judgement in time, but God moves all things by being loved. I am not a sociologist and I do not claim to have researched the data. But I draw my opinion from my own moral formation and from having observed the country in which I have lived for twenty years, from Gallup polls about moral and religious beliefs, from what politicians say in order to get elected, and from what films people choose to watch and what books they choose to read. In all of this I detect a fundamental agreement that there is a moral order to the world despite the overwhelming evidence of evil. Much of this evil comes from people choosing to do what suits themselves rather than what suits others. If this is what is most natural to us, if it is a disposition which is radical in us as Kant says, then we cannot look to our natural capacities to overcome it.

I have talked about our incorporation into Christ in a way that Kant would dislike. He talked dismissively of the 'supposed favorite of heaven [who] mounts to the point where he fanatically imagines

[75] *Rel.* 92 (100), emphasis added.

that he feels special works of grace within himself (or even actually presumes to be confident of a fancied occult *intercourse* with God)'.[76] But does Kant have adequate philosophical grounds for supposing that a person cannot truthfully claim to experience special works of grace or to have been given union with Christ? It might be true that in Kant's account of knowledge, a person cannot *know* that she has such experience or has been given such union. This would be a different point, however, and much less ambitious. I have not discussed in this book Kant's epistemology or his metaphysics. His account of knowledge requires that we can claim to know only what we could in principle experience with the senses. He is certainly at liberty to confine the word 'knowledge' in this way. But it will not follow that the Christian cannot responsibly claim to have experience of God or to be united with Christ. Kant's own view was that morality *requires* us to believe in things which we cannot know in his sense; and one of these things is God's grace to us. *This* belief, before translation within the pure religion of reason, can help us with the moral gap.

If the philosopher can show that the limits of possible sense experience are the limits not only, as Kant thought, of knowledge, but also of any meaningful assertion at all, then Kierkegaard's account and my account in this chapter fail. I have tried to show, however, that the notion of incorporation into the life of Christ is intelligible. I have tried to show this not by engaging in theoretical discussion of the limits of understanding, but by detailing some analogies between this claim of Christian faith and other parts of human experience. Kant himself suggests the possibility of a 'schematism of analogy, with which (as a means of explanation) we cannot dispense'. He warns that to transform this into a 'schematism of objective determination (for the extension of our *knowledge*) is anthropomorphism'.[77] Given his requirements for knowledge, his warning is quite correct, for he requires that we can know only what we could sense, and the divine side of the analogy is forever beyond the reach of the senses. Kant does not, however, extend the prohibition on claims about knowledge to claims about meaningfulness; he does not, that is, deny the possibility of meaningful language about God's work on our behalf. In my book I have used this language to describe a way of both acknowledging our natural

---

[76] *Rel.* 189 (201).   [77] *Rel.* 58 (65), emphasis added.

limitations and continuing to believe in the possibility of our goodness. I have claimed that we can do this without either puffing up our capacities or reducing the moral demand. I have not claimed that Christian doctrine gives us the only way to bridge the gap. There may be some substitute for God's assistance, as understood within Christian doctrine. Perhaps there is a substitute in science or in philosophy or in some other religion (or in none of these). All I have done is to look at a few proposed substitutes within philosophy. The Christian doctrine is, however, an essential background for understanding how the moral gap is seen in those parts of the world which have been heavily influenced by Christianity. The great texts of the Western philosophical tradition make sense only against this background. This book has been an attempt to bring back this doctrine into the discussion. This should be helpful not only for those who believe in the doctrine but for those who want to find a substitute for it and for those who want to change our understanding of the moral gap so that we do not need a substitute. My own belief is that there is a God who loves us enough both to demand a high standard from us and to help us meet it.

BIBLIOGRAPHY

ADAMS, MARILYN (1991), 'Forgiveness: A Christian Model', *Faith and Philosophy*, 8 (3): 277–304.

ADLER, JONATHAN E. (1989), 'Particularity, Gilligan, and the Two-Levels View: A Reply', *Ethics*, 100 (1): 149–156.

ANDERSON-GOLD, SHARON (1991), 'God and Community: An Inquiry into the Religious Implications of the Highest Good', in Rossi and Wreen (1991) (eds.) 113–31.

APPIAH, ANTHONY (1991), 'Racism and Moral Pollution', in Larry May and Stacey Hoffman (eds.), *Collective Responsibility* (Savage, Md.: Rowman and Littlefield).

ARENDT, HANNAH (1965), *Eichmann in Jerusalem: A Report on the Banality of Evil* (New York: Viking).

AUSTIN, JOHN (1970), 'A Plea for Excuses', in J. O. Urmson and G. J. Warnock (eds.), *Philosophical Papers*. (Oxford: Oxford University Press), 175–204.

AUXTER, THOMAS (1979), 'The Unimportance of Kant's Highest Good', *Journal of the History of Philosophy*, 17: 121–34.

—— (1982), *Kant's Moral Teleology* (Macon, Ga.: Mercer University Press).

BEATTY, JOSEPH (1970), 'Forgiveness', *American Philosophical Quarterly*, 7 (3): 246–52.

BECK, LEWIS WHITE (1960), *A Commentary on Kant's Critique of Practical Reason* (Chicago: University of Chicago Press).

BERKHOF, LOUIS (1936), *Vicarious Atonement through Christ* (Grand Rapids, Mich.: Eerdmans).

BERKOUWER, G. C. (1954), *Faith and Justification* (Grand Rapids, Mich.: Eerdmans).

BITTNER, RUDIGER (1989), *What Reason Demands* (Cambridge: Cambridge University Press).

BLUM, LAWRENCE (1980), *Friendship, Altruism and Morality* (London: Routledge & Kegan Paul).

—— (1986), 'Iris Murdoch and the Domain of the Moral', *Philosophical Studies*, 50: 344–65.

—— (1988), 'Gilligan and Kohlberg: Implications for Moral Theory', *Ethics*, 98 (3): 472–91.

—— (1991), 'Moral Perception and Particularity', *Ethics*, 101(4): 701–25.

BONHOEFFER, DIETRICH (1963), *The Cost of Discipleship* (New York: Macmillan).

BONNER, GERALD (1991), 'The Doctrine of Sacrifice: Augustine', in S. W. Sykes (ed.), *Sacrifice and Redemption* (Cambridge: Cambridge University Press), 101–17.

BRAITHWAITE, R. B. (1964), 'An Empiricist's View of the Nature of Religious Belief', in John Hick (ed.), *The Existence of God* (New York: Macmillan), 228–52.

BRANDT, RICHARD B. (1959), *Ethical Theory* (Englewood Cliffs, NJ: Prentice Hall).

—— (1979), *A Theory of the Good and the Right* (Oxford: Clarendon Press).

BRILL, H. SKOTT (1992), 'The Supererogation Objection to Hare's Utilitarianism', *Michigan Academician*, 24: 541–50.

BRINK, DAVID O. (1989), *Moral Realism and the Foundations of Ethics* (Cambridge: Cambridge University Press).

BROWN, DALE (1962), 'The Problem of Subjectivism in Pietism: A Redefinition with Special Reference to the Theology of Philipp Jakob Spener and August Hermann Francke', Ph.D. thesis, Northwestern University.

BRUNNER, EMIL (1934), *The Mediator*, trans. O. Wyon (London: Lutterworth Press).

BULLOUGH, EDWARD (1912), ' "Psychical Distance" as a Factor in Art and as an Aesthetic Principle', rep. in Frank A. Tillman and Steven M. Cahn (eds.), *Philosophy of Art and Aesthetics* (New York: Harper and Row, 1969), 397–414.

BUSWELL, JAMES OLIVER (1962), *A Systematic Theology of the Christian Religion* (Grand Rapids, Mich.: Zondervan).

CAMPBELL, DONALD T. (1975), 'On the Conflicts between Biological and Social Evolution and between Psychology and Moral Tradition', *American Psychologist*, 30: 1103–26.

—— (1978), 'Response to Dyer', *American Psychologist*, 33: 770–2.

—— (1979), 'Comments on the Sociobiology of Ethics and Moralizing', *Behavioural Science*, 24: 37–45.

—— (1982), 'Legal and Primary Group Social Controls', *Journal of Social and Biological Structures*, 5: 431–8.

—— (1984), 'Cultural Evolution and Religious Truth', in David Schenck (ed.), *Science, Philosophy and Religion* (Lehigh University Science, Technology and Society Program, Working Paper Series, 1; Bethlehem, Pa.: Lehigh University).

—— (1985), (with Judith C. Specht), 'Altruism: Biology, Culture, and Religion', *Journal of Social and Clinical Psychology*, 3 (1): 33–42.

CAMPBELL, JOHN MCLEOD (1886), *The Nature of the Atonement and its Relation to Remission of Sins and Eternal Life*, 6th edn. (London: Macmillan & Co).

CHODOROW, N. (1978), *The Reproduction of Mothering: Psychoanalysis and the Sociology of Gender*, (Berkeley: University of California Press).

COTTINGHAM, JOHN (1986), 'Ethics and Impartiality', *Philosophical Studies*, 83: 439–48.

DARWALL, STEPHEN (1983), *Impartial Reason* (Ithaca, NY: Cornell University Press).

DESPLAND, MICHEL (1973), *Kant on History and Religion* (Montreal: McGill–Queen's University Press).

DUMONT, MICHELE (1988), 'Carol Gilligan: The Two Moral Voices—Justice and Care', paper presented to conference 'Explorations of Feminist Ethics: Theory and Practice', University of Minnesota, Duluth, 8 Oct.

DUNN, J. D. G. (1975), *Jesus and the Spirit* (London: SCM Press).

—— (1991), 'Paul's Understanding of the Death of Jesus', in S. W. Sykes (ed.), *Sacrifice and Redemption* (Cambridge: Cambridge University Press), 35–56.

ERB, PETER C. (1983), *Pietists: Selected Writings* (New York: Paulist Press).

ERICKSON, MILLARD J. (1983), *Christian Theology* (Grand Rapids, Mich.: Baker Book House).

EVANS, C. STEPHEN (1983), *Kierkegaard's 'Fragments' and 'Postscript'* (Atlantic Highlands, NJ: Humanities Press International).

FARRER, AUSTIN (1961), *Love Almighty and Ills Unlimited* (New York: Doubleday).

FELDMAN, FRED (1986), *Doing the Best we Can* (Dordrecht: Reidel).

FRANKFURT, HARRY (1971), 'Freedom of the Will and the Concept of a Person', *Journal of Philosophy*, 68 (1): 5–20.

—— (1988a), 'Alternate Possibilities and Responsibility', in *The Importance of what we Care about* (Cambridge: Cambridge University Press), 1–10.

—— (1988b), 'Identification and Wholeheartedness', in *The Importance of what we Care about* (Cambridge: Cambridge University Press), 159–76.

FRIEDMAN, MARILYN (1991a), 'The Social Self and the Partiality of Debates', in Claudia Card (ed.), *Feminist Ethics*, (Lawrence, Kan.: University Press of Kansas), 161–79.

—— (1991b), 'The Practice of Partiality', *Ethics*, 101 (4): 818–35.

FRIEDMAN, R. Z. (1984), 'The Importance and Function of Kant's Highest Good', *Journal of the History of Philosophy*, 22: 325–42.

GAUTHIER, DAVID (1986), *Morals by Agreement* (Oxford: Oxford University Press.)

—— (1990), 'The Politics of Redemption', in *Moral Dealing: Contract, Ethics and Reason* (Ithaca, NY: Cornell University Press), 77–109.

GEWIRTH, ALAN (1988), 'Ethical Universalism and Particularism', *Journal of Philosophy*, 85: 295–8.

GIBBARD, ALAN (1990), *Wise Choices, Apt Feelings* (Cambridge, Mass.: Harvard University Press).

GILLIGAN, CAROL (1980), 'In a Different Voice: Women's Conceptions of Self and Morality', in Hester Eisenstein and Alice Jardine (eds.), *The Future of Difference* (Boston: G. K. Hall and Co.), 274–317.

—— (1987), 'Moral Orientation and Moral Development', in Eva Feder Kittay and Diana T. Myers (eds.), *Women and Moral Theory* (Totowa, NJ: Rowman & Littlefield), 19–33.

GLENDINNING, VICTORIA (1992), *Trollope* (London: Hutchinson).

GREEN, RONALD M. (1978), *Religious Reason* (Oxford: Oxford University Press).

—— (1992), *Kierkegaard and Kant: The Hidden Debt* (Ithaca, NY: State University Press of New York).

GREGOR, MARY (1963), *Laws of Freedom* (Oxford: Basil Blackwell).

GRIFFIN, JAMES (1986), *Well-Being* (Oxford: Clarendon Press).

GROEN-COLYN, SARAH (1982), 'The Effects of Morality Salience in a Religious Population: A Failure to Replicate', *Analyst* (spring): 9–13.

GUNTON, COLIN E. (1989), *The Actuality of Atonement* (Edinburgh: T. & T. Clark).

HABER, JORAM G. (1991), *Forgiveness* (Savage, Md.: Rowman & Littlefield).

HANNAY, ALASDAIR (1982), *Kierkegaard* (London: Routledge & Kegan Paul).

HARE, JOHN E. (1983), 'The Hospice Movement and the Acceptance of Death', in Austin H. Kutscher (ed.), *Hospice USA* (New York: Columbia University Press), 9–17.

—— (1988), '*Eleutheriotes* in Aristotle's Ethics', *Ancient Philosophy*, 8: 19–32.

—— (1991), 'The Problem of Evil', in John W. Montgomery (ed.), *Evidence for Faith* (Dallas: Probe Books), 231–52.

—— (1994a), 'Puffing up the Capacity', *Journal of Philosophical Research*, 19: 75–88.

—— (1994b), Review of Rossi and Wreen (1991) (eds.), *Faith and Philosophy*, 11 (1): 138–44.

—— (1995a), 'Kantian Ethics, International Politics and the Enlargement of the *Foedus Pacificum*', in *Sovereignty at the Crossroads? International Morality and the Search for a New World Order* (Grand Rapids, Mich.: Conference paper, Calvin College).

—— (1995b), Review of Rudd (1993), *Studies in Christian Ethics*, 8 (1): 138–43.

—— (1995c), 'The Unhappiest One and the Structure of Kierkegaard's *Either/Or*', in Robert L. Perkins (ed), *International Kierkegaard Commentary: Either/Or* (Macon, Ga.: Mercer University Press).

—— and JOYNT, CAREY B. (1982), *Ethics and International Affairs* (London: Macmillan).

HARE, R. M. (1952), *Language of Morals* (Oxford: Clarendon Press).

—— (1955), 'Reply to Flew', in Anthony Flew and Alasdair MacIntyre (eds.), *New Essays in Philosophical Theology* (New York: Macmillan), 99–103.

—— (1963), *Freedom and Reason* (Oxford: Clarendon Press).

—— (1972-3), 'Principles', *Aristotelian Society*, 72: 1-18.

—— (1973), 'The Simple Believer', in Gene Outka and John P. Reeder, Jr. (eds.), *Religion and Morality* (Garden City NY: Anchor Books), 393-427.

—— (1981), *Moral Thinking* (Oxford: Clarendon Press).

—— (1989), 'Punishment and Retributive Justice', in *Essays in Political Morality* (Oxford: Clarendon Press), 203-16.

—— (1992), 'Are there Moral Authorities?', in *Essays on Religion and Education* (Oxford: Clarendon Press), 56-71.

—— (1993), 'Could Kant have been a Utilitarian?', *Utilitas*, 5 (1): 1-16.

HAUERWAS, STANLEY, and WILLIMON, WILLIAM H. (1989), *Resident Aliens* (Nashville: Abingdon Press).

HEINE, HEINRICH (1959), *History of Philosophy and Religion in Germany*, trans. John Snodgrass (Boston: Beacon Press).

HELD, VIRGINIA (1993), *Feminist Morality: Transforming Culture, Society, and Politics* (Chicago: Chicago University Press).

HERMAN, BARBARA (1992), 'Agency, Attachment, and Difference', in John Deigh (ed.), *Ethics and Personality* (Chicago: University of Chicago Press), 41-63.

HILL, THOMAS E., JR. (1987), 'The Importance of Autonomy', in Eva Feder Kittay and Diana T. Myers (eds.), *Women and Moral Theory* (Totowa, NJ: Rowman & Littlefield), 131-2.

HOEKEMA, ANTHONY A. (1989), *Saved by Grace* (Grand Rapids, Mich.: Eerdmans).

HOOKER, MORNA (1990), *From Adam to Christ* (Cambridge: Cambridge University Press).

KAGAN, SHELLY (1989), *The Limits of Morality* (Oxford: Oxford University Press).

KOLNAI, AUREL (1973-4), 'Forgiveness', *Proceedings of the Aristotelian Society*, 74: 91-106.

KORSGAARD, CHRISTINE (1985), 'Kant's Formula of Universal Law', *Pacific Philosophical Quarterly*, 66 (1-2): 24-47.

—— (1989), 'Kant', in Robert J. Cavalier, James Govinlock, and James P. Sterba (eds.), *Ethics in the History of Western Philosophy* (New York: St Martin's Press), 201-43.

KRAUS, JODY S. and COLEMAN, JULES L. (1987), 'Morality and the Theory of Rational Choice', *Ethics*, 97 (4): 715-49.

LEWIS, C. S. (1963), *A Grief Observed* (Greenwich, Conn.: Seabury Press).

LO, P. C. (1981), 'A Critical Reevaluation of the Alleged "Empty Formalism" of Kantian Ethics', *Ethics*, 91 (2): 181-201.

—— (1987), *Treating Persons as Ends: An Essay on Kant's Moral Philosophy* (Lanham, Md.: University Press of America).

LUCAS, JOHN (1976), 'Reasons for Loving and Being Loved', in *Freedom and Grace: Essays by J. R. Lucas* (London: SPCK), 64-8.

MacIntyre, Alasdair (1981), *After Virtue* (Notre Dame, Ind.: University of Notre Dame Press).

—— (1988), *Whose Justice? Which Rationality?* (London: Duckworth).

Mackie, J. L. (1977), *Ethics: Inventing Right and Wrong* (London: Penguin.)

Malcolm, Norman (1965), 'The Ontological Argument', in Alvin Plantinga (ed.), *The Ontological Argument* (New York: Anchor Books), 136–59.

Malantschuk, Gregor (1971), *Kierkegaard's Thought* (Princeton: Princeton University Press).

Mascall, E. L. (1946), *Christ, the Christian, and the Church* (London: Longmans, Green).

McFall, Lynne (1987), 'Integrity', *Ethics*, 98 (1): 5–20.

Meyers, Diana (1987), 'Personal Autonomy and the Paradox of Feminine Socialization', *Journal of Philosophy*, 84 (11): 619–28.

Michalson, Gordon E., Jr. (1987), 'The Inscrutability of Moral Evil in Kant', *Thomist*, 51 (2): 246–69.

—— (1990), *Fallen Freedom* (Cambridge: Cambridge University Press).

Morris, Herbert (1988), 'Murphy on Forgiveness', *Criminal Justice in Ethics*, 7 (2): 15–19.

Moore, Michael S. (1987), 'The Moral Worth of Retribution', in Ferdinand Scoeman (ed.), *Responsibiity, Character and the Emotions: New Essays in Moral Psychology* (Cambridge: Cambridge University Press), 179–219.

Moule, C. F. D. (1977), *The Origin of Christology* (Cambridge: Cambridge University Press).

Mulholland, Leslie (1991), 'Freedom and Providence in Kant's Account of Religion: The Problem of Expiation', in Rossi and Wreen (1991) (eds.) 77–102.

Murdoch, Iris (1977), *The Fire and the Sun: Why Plato Banished the Artists* (Oxford: Oxford University Press).

Murphy, Jeffrie, and Hampton, Jean (1988), *Forgiveness and Mercy* (Cambridge: Cambridge University Press).

Murray, John (1977), *Collected Writings of John Murray*, ii (Edinburgh: The Banner of Truth Trust).

Nagel, Thomas (1979), 'Sexual Perversion', in *Mortal Questions* (Cambridge: Cambridge University Press), 39–52.

—— (1986), *The View from Nowhere* (Oxford: Oxford University Press).

Neill, Steven (1955), *Christian Faith Today* (London: Penguin).

Niebuhr, Reinhold (1932), *Moral Man and Immoral Society* (New York: Scribner).

—— (1941), *The Nature and Destiny of Man*, i (New York: Scribner).

Noddings, Nell (1984), *Caring: A Feminine Approach to Ethics and Moral Education* (Berkeley: University of California Press).

Nussbaum, Martha (1986), *The Fragility of Goodness* (Cambridge: Cambridge University Press).

O'DONOVAN, OLIVER (1986), *Resurrection and Moral Order* (Grand Rapids, Mich.: Eerdmans).

O'NEILL, ONORA (1989), *Constructions of Reason* (Cambridge: Cambridge University Press).

OWEN, H. P. (1984), *Christian Theism: A Study in its Basic Principles* (Edinburgh: T. & T. Clark).

PACKER, J. I. (1973), 'What did the Cross Achieve? The Logic of Penal Substitution', Tyndale Biblical Theology Lecture in *Tyndale Bulletin*, 25.

PARFIT, DEREK (1984), *Reasons and Persons* (Oxford: Clarendon Press).

PEARS, DAVID (1980), 'Courage as a Mean', in Amelie O. Rorty (ed.), *Essays on Aristotle's Ethics* (Berkeley: University of California Press), 171–87.

PEROVICH, ANTHONY N. (1991), ' "For Reason . . . also has its Mysteries": Immortality, *Religion*, and "The End of All Things" ', in Rossi and Wreen (1991) (eds.) 165–80.

PIETY, MARILYN (1993), 'Kierkegaard on Rationality', *Faith and Philosophy*, 10 (3): 365–79.

PINSON, K. S. (1934), *Pietism as a Factor in the Rise of German Nationalism* (New York: Columbia University Press).

PIPER, ADRIAN M. S. (1991), 'Impartiality, Compassion and Modal Imagination', *Ethics*, 101: 726–57.

PRICE, A. W. (1989), *Love and Friendship in Plato and Aristotle* (Oxford: Clarendon Press).

PRICE, GEORGE (1963), *The Narrow Pass: A Study of Kierkegaard's Concept of Man* (New York: McGraw-Hill).

QUINN, PHILIP L. (1978), *Divine Commands and Moral Requirements* (Oxford: Clarendon Press).

—— (1984), 'Original Sin, Radical Evil and Moral Identity', *Faith and Philosophy*, 1 (2): 188–202.

—— (1990), 'Does Anxiety Explain Original Sin?', *Nous*, 24: 227–44.

RAILTON, PETER (1984), 'Alienation, Consequentialism and the Demands of Morality', *Philosophy and Public Affairs*, 13: 134–71.

RAWLS, JOHN (1971), *A Theory of Justice* (Cambridge, Mass.: Harvard University Press).

—— (1985), 'Justice as Fairness: Political not Metaphysical', *Philosophy and Public Affairs*, 14: 223–51.

REATH, ANDREW (1988), 'Two Conceptions of the Highest Good in Kant', *Journal of the History of Philosophy*, 26: 593–619.

ROBERTS, ROBERT C. (1988), 'What an Emotion is: A Sketch', *Philosophical Review*, 97 (2): 183–209.

—— (1993), *Taking the Word to Heart: Self and Others in an Age of Therapies* (Grand Rapids, Mich.: Eerdmans).

ROSSI, PHILIP J. (1991), 'The Final End of All Things: The Highest Good as the Unity of Nature and Freedom', in Rossi and Wreen (1991) (eds.) 132–64.

—— and WREEN, MICHAEL (eds.) (1991), *Kant's Philosophy of Religion Reconsidered* (Bloomington, Ind.: Indiana University Press).

RUDD, ANTHONY (1993), *Kierkegaard and the Limits of the Ethical* (Oxford: Clarendon Press).

RUDDICK, SARA (1989), *Maternal Thinking: Towards a Politics of Peace* (Boston: Beacon Press).

SANDBACH, F. H. (1975), *The Stoics* (London: Chatto & Windus).

SCHEFFLER, SAMUEL, (1992), *Human Morality* (Oxford: Oxford University Press).

SILBER, JOHN (1962–3), 'The Importance of the Highest Good in Kant's Ethics', *Ethics*, 73: 179–97.

SINGER, PETER (1981), *The Expanding Circle: Ethics and Sociobiology* (New York: Farrar, Strauss & Giroux).

—— (1988), 'Reasoning towards Utilitarianism', in Douglas Seanor and N. Fotion (eds.), *Hare and Critics: Essays on Moral Thinking* (Oxford: Clarendon Press), 147–60.

—— (1993), *Practical Ethics*, 2nd edn. (Cambridge: Cambridge University Press).

SMEDES, LEWIS B. (1970), *All Things Made New* (Grand Rapids, Mich.: Eerdmans).

SMITH, STEVEN (1984), 'Worthiness to be Happy and Kant's Concept of the Highest Good', *Kant-Studien*, 75 (2): 168–90.

SPOERL, JOSEPH (1994), 'Impartiality and the Great Commandment: A Reply to John Cottingham (and Others)', *American Catholic Philosophical Quarterly*, 67 (2): 203–10.

STOEFFLER, F. ERNEST (1973), *German Pietism during the Eighteenth Century* (Leiden: E. J. Brill).

STUMP, ELEANORE (1988), 'Atonement According to Aquinas', in T. V. Morris (ed.), *Philosophy and the Christian Faith* (Notre Dame, Ind.: Notre Dame University Press).

SWINBURNE, RICHARD (1989), *Responsibility and Atonement* (Oxford: Clarendon Press).

TADA, JONI EARECKSON, and ESTES, STEVE (1978), *A Step Further* (Grand Rapids, Mich.: Zondervan).

TALBOTT, THOMAS (1990), 'What Jesus Did for Us', *Reformed Journal*, 40 (Mar.).

TAYLOR, CHARLES (1989), *Sources of the Self* (Cambridge, Mass.: Harvard University Press).

THOMPSON, JOSIAH (1967), *The Lonely Labyrinth: Kierkegaard's Pseudonymous Works* (Carbondale, Ill.: Southern Illinois University Press).

TWAMBLEY, P. (1976), 'Mercy and Forgiveness', *Analysis*, 36: 84–90.

VANAUKEN, SHELDON (1977), *A Severe Mercy* (San Francisco: Harper & Row).

VAN DYK, LEANNE (1992), 'John McLeod Campbell's Doctrine of the

Atonement: A Revision and Expansion of the Reformed Tradition', Ph.D diss., Princeton Theological Seminary.

VAN HOUTEN, CHRISTIANA (1991), *The Alien in Israelite Law* (Sheffield: Sheffield Academic Press).

VAN LEEUWEN, MARY (ed.) (1993), *After Eden: Facing the Challenge of Gender Reconciliation* (Grand Rapids, Mich.: Eerdmans).

VLASTOS, GREGORY (1981), 'The Individual as Object of Love in Plato', in *Platonic Studies*, 2nd edn. (Princeton: Princeton University Press), 3–42.

VYGOTSKY, L. (1978), *Mind in Society* (Cambridge: Harvard University Press).

WALKER, MARGARET URBAN (1987), 'Moral Particularity', *Metaphilosophy*, 18: 171–85.

WALSH, SYLVIA (1987), 'On "Feminine" and "Masculine" Forms of Despair', in Robert L. Perkins (ed.), *International Kierkegaard Commentary: The Sickness unto Death* (Macon, Ga.: Mercer University Press), 121–34.

WATSON, GARY (1975), 'Free Agency', *Journal of Philosophy*, 72 (8): 205–20.

WEBER, M. (1952), *Ancient Judaism*, trans. and ed. H. H. Gerth and D. Martindale (Glencoe: Free Press).

WENHAM, G. J. (1979), *The Book of Leviticus* (Grand Rapids, Mich.: Eerdmans).

WESTPHAL, MEROLD (1987), *God, Guilt and Death* (Bloomington, Ind.: Indiana University Press).

WHITBECK, CAROLINE (1989), 'A Different Reality: Feminist Ontology', in Ann Garry and Marilyn Pearsall (eds.), *Women, Knowledge, and Reality: Explorations in Feminist Philosophy* (Boston: Unwin Hyman), 51–76.

WIKE, VICTORIA (1994), *Kant on Happiness in Ethics* (Albany, NY: State University of New York Press).

WILLIAMS, BERNARD (1981), 'Persons, Character and Morality', in *Moral Luck* (Cambridge: Cambridge University Press), 1–19.

—— (1994), *Shame and Necessity* (Berkeley, University of California Press).

WOLF, SUSAN (1990), *Freedom within Reason* (Oxford: Oxford University Press).

WOLLHEIM, RICHARD (1984), *The Thread of Life* (Cambridge, Mass.: Harvard University Press).

WOLTERSTORFF, NICHOLAS (1987), *Lament for a Son* (Grand Rapids, Mich.: Eerdmans).

—— (1991), 'Conundrums in Kant's Rational Religion', in Rossi and Wreen (1991) (eds.) 40–53.

WOOD, ALLEN (1970), *Kant's Moral Religion* (Ithaca, NY: Cornell University Press).

—— (1978), *Kant's Rational Theology* (Ithaca, NY: Cornell University Press).

—— (1991), 'Kant's Deism', in Rossi and Wreen (1991) (eds.) 1–21.

—— (1992), 'Rational Theology, Moral Faith, and Religion', in Paul Guyer (ed.), *The Cambridge Companion to Kant* (Cambridge, Mass.: Cambridge University Press), 394–416.

YOVEL, YIRMIAHU (1980), *Kant and the Philosophy of History* (Princeton: Princeton University Press).

INDEX OF BIBLICAL PASSAGES

GENERAL INDEX